LANA

The Memories, the Myths, the Movies

by Cheryl Crane
with Cindy De La Hoz

Photographs from the Lou Valentino Collection

Running Press
PHILADELPHIA · LONDON

Dedication

From Cheryl: To JLR, my cavalry officer and my Hollywood ending.

From Cindy: To my RP friends. Even those who think

they had nothing to do with this book,

you make me look forward to going to work every day.

© 2008 by Cheryl Crane and Cindy De La Hoz

All rights reserved under the Pan-American and International Copyright Conventions

Printed in China

9 8 7 6 5 4 3 2 1

Digit on the right indicates the number of this printing

Library of Congress Control Number: 2008924252

ISBN 978-0-7624-3316-2

Designed by Corinda Cook

Edited by Jennifer Kasius

Front cover art by Tom Maroudas

Photographs on page 177 © Getty Images

All other photographs used with permission from the collection of Lou Valentino and the Crane-LeRoy Collection

Author photos: Cheryl Crane by Mark Davidson; Cindy De La Hoz by Derek Rand

Running Press Book Publishers

2300 Chestnut Street

Philadelphia, PA 19103-4371

Visit us on the web!

www.runningpress.com

Contents

Part One: Memories and Myths

Part Two: The Movies

Introduction

No Hollywood story launched more dreams than the fable about how my mother, a small-town girl from Wallace, Idaho, got into the movies. Sitting by a soda fountain sipping a Coke, a certain influential gentleman approached her with a question: "Would you like to be in the movies?" and a star was born. Julia Jean Turner, soon to be immortalized as Lana, was all of fifteen years old and had only arrived in Hollywood with her mother three months earlier.

This true story turned into a fable under the auspices of Sidney Skolsky, a well-known entertainment reporter who wrote his syndicated column from a booth at Schwab's Drugstore, which once stood proudly on the south side of Sunset Boulevard and Crescent Heights. His version of Lana Turner's discovery later sent innumerable would-be starlets to Schwab's counter stools waiting to be spotted, probably getting stomachaches while ordering chocolate malteds or strawberry sodas or whatever they had heard she drank. If Schwab's was the right place, perhaps at the right time, stardust would fall on them, too. The story bankrolled Schwab's for years. Mother always felt she should have been made a stockholder.

The facts are that Julia Jean ("Judy") was a new student at Hollywood High School in January 1937. Never quite a scholar, she cut the class of one of her least favorite subjects,

A publicity shot for *Ziegfeld Girl*, 1941.

Sipping her signature soda, a plain Coke, with no chocolate ice cream frills.

typing, opting instead to go to the Top Hat, a little café catty-corner from the school. There she ordered a soda. Mother insisted it was a plain Coke, because it only cost a nickel. Seated down the counter from her, finishing up his lunch, was Billy Wilkerson, the publisher of the *Hollywood Reporter*. Struck by the "breathtakingly beautiful" teenager, he refrained from approaching her at once and respectfully had the manager ask the girl if she would allow him to speak with her. "You can imagine what I thought," Mother later said, but the manager told her who he was and assured her Mr. Wilkerson was okay. It was then Wilkerson famously asked Judy Turner if she would like to be in movies and the schoolgirl's response was, "I don't know. I'd have to ask my mother."

Greeting fans in Washington D.C., 1941.

Soon this simple story took on mythic proportions, as endless variations began appearing in newspapers and fan magazines. Seeds of the truth were sewn into the version of the story that became famous, typifying the Hollywood fantasy world in which she moved. The mingling of fact and fiction was a constant throughout her life as one of the most widely publicized personalities of the twentieth century.

Unfortunately, very little of what has been published about her has been honest and so much has been blatantly fabricated. At face value, Mother was the glamorous and exciting star of movies like *The Postman Always Rings Twice*, *The Bad and the Beautiful*, and *Imitation of Life*, the buxom "Sweater Girl" in her youth, and the siren who brought men to their knees and had numerous affairs between seven marriages that couldn't last. All of this is true, but it's superficial.

A star emerging from her dressing room.

Miss Lana Turner

Careful publicity on stars of the silent era kept them in a mysterious dream bubble called Hollywood. In the 1930s and '40s, the media grew better at humanizing the stars without being unflatteringly revealing, as went the tone of celebrity reporting decades later. Typical of the fan magazines of Mother's day is the following quote: "Whatever her antics in private life, they are only the results of her impulsiveness, her amazing beauty, and her joy of living—nothing more."

Whatever can be said of my mother, she was never boring. She was always terrified of creating a stir in the press, yet the way she lived she couldn't avoid it. And for the first time in the world of movie stars, it didn't harm her career but only fueled her fame. Mother had a connection with her fans such that it didn't matter what she did. They flocked to her movies, and in her heyday I watched the militia keep crowds at bay outside of hotels when we traveled.

In her element at an Elsa Maxwell party.

A star of the classic era, she could be grand at times, but she was also human and incredibly fun. My mother possessed an extraordinary sense of humor which, I believe, is what saved her from becoming a Hollywood tragedy. She was, above all, a survivor, and she loved to laugh more than anything in the world. On screen she was a rare mix of cuteness and tempting sensuality and had a riveting gaze that the camera loved. She was a quintessential movie star

During a trip to South America in 1946.

"I do things people think about doing but haven't the courage."

who adored being dressed in the most expensive gowns, dripping in gems, and demanding the best hotels. On the flipside, she was basically shy, and retained an earthy side that made her love hole-in-the-wall Mexican restaurants, dancing until dawn, insist on driving her own car, and perhaps most surprisingly, given her famous predilection for jewelry, appreciate sentimental trinkets as much as diamonds. That was my mother, Lana Turner.

I don't feel that anything heretofore published has captured the woman that I knew, including her own autobiography. She comes to life in all her facets in these pages. I wanted a way of presenting her that would be honest, visually interesting, and also fun, so there is an unusual structure to this book. In focusing on different aspects of her life and work, rather than following a linear path, every section adds layers to who she was—as an actress, mother, daughter, lover, friend, and idol to legions of movie fans.

Mommy and Me, 1950.

The Nomads

The Dream Factory was the perfect place for Mother because she was a dreamer and a romantic to the core. This aspect of her being comes directly from her mother and father, the ultimate dreamers, Mildred Frances Cowan and John Virgil Turner. They moved around and reinvented themselves throughout my mother's childhood, sometimes on a whim, sometimes to keep ahead of the authorities, because one of Virgil's professions in desperate times was bootlegging. He had a habit of storing his cash in his left sock. The Turners were poor most of the time, but when there was enough collected in that sock to impair his walking, they would blow it all on a few days of fancy living and then move back into smaller quarters.

Mildred, my "Gran," was born in 1904 in the town of Lamar, Arkansas. Gran's mother died during childbirth due to the "Rh factor," an issue that would plague my own mother throughout her adult life. Gran's father later remarried. His second wife was a nurse practitioner and the couple had four children. My mother and her grandfather were very close. He lived with Mother and Gran in their first home in Los Angeles and it was there that he passed away in 1939.

Gran met the man she would marry, Virgil Turner, at a dance in Lamar. "Mr. Turner," as she called him from that day forward, was there on a short visit from his birthplace of Alabama. They married in 1920. Gran was going on sixteen at the time. Virgil had been a soldier during World War I. His primary work was as a miner, but he also dabbled in the dry-cleaning business, selling insurance, and even did a bit of vaudeville. MGM's later claims in studio biographies that he was a mining engineer were greatly exaggerated. What Gran and Mother remembered most vividly about Virgil was that he had a great sense of humor, loved partying and gambling, and was a very good dancer. All of these traits passed to Mother.

Mother's looks also came entirely from Virgil. He was not tall, about equal with Gran's willowy five-foot-seven stature. He was stocky, had wide shoulders and narrow hips. Mother inherited his small nose, red hair, and the majestic Turner hairline and dimples. But perhaps most important of all was the passion for music and dancing that passed from Virgil to Mother and remained with her all of her life.

Mother had a penetrating gaze down at age one.

Mrs. Mildred Turner and daughter Julia Jean, 1924.

My grandparents shared a wanderlust that kept them moving throughout the Midwest. Wallace, Idaho was the town they called home when Julia Jean Mildred Frances Turner entered their world on February 8, 1921. Their movements were prompted more often by Gran. She would save up her pennies, bundle up their only child in her best outfit, and hop aboard a train whose path they would follow as far as their tickets would take them. Oftentimes Mr.

Three-year-old Julia Jean with her father and mother. Even though money was in short supply, Gran insisted that her family be well dressed.

Turner knew nothing about their unscheduled excursions until he would get a phone call asking him to come and meet them in whatever town they ended up. Their comings and goings throughout Mother's childhood are impossible to document. Gran's oft-repeated answer to the whys and hows of what took them from point A to point B was, "with many stops along the way." "Can I hear about those 'stops'?" I would ask, but she would skirt the question.

Gran was a fascinating woman. She was master at blocking out episodes in her life that were too difficult to dwell upon, so the fact that she dropped only tantalizing hints regarding this period signaled to me that it was a time she did not want to discuss because it was rough. There were good times, to be sure. My mother had happy memories of her parents together. Her strongest were of a lot of laughter and whirling around the room, carried away by her father's dancing feet. But there were problems in the marriage that led to their separation. The fact that Gran kept running, not necessarily away from Virgil, but toward new horizons nonetheless, says something about their relationship. My grandparents separated and reunited again a few times. The three of them reached the West Coast together in 1927.

At first they lived in what was then called an auto court, where people on long drives would stop for the night. It was the Depression era and Virgil was the sole support of Mother and Gran. When they separated, Gran was at a loss as to what she would do to earn a living, until a friend got

"We were a laughing family."

her a job in a beauty shop. Before Gran established herself, Mother was boarded with a family in Modesto. For years Mother told me very little about this time except to say that the people were very cruel to her. After two years, when Gran found evidence of physical abuse on her daughter's back, she brought her back to San Francisco.

Little Judy had thought it was an enchanted city, welcoming newcomers with a "golden gate." When she discovered its famous gate wasn't solid gold, she took it as a bad omen. Here, the tragedy of Virgil's murder took place. Virgil, who had taken the name of Tex Johnson as part of his routine of reinvention in a new job, spent the night of December 14, 1930 gambling with men from the docks. It was ten days before Christmas Eve. He was the big winner and told his fellow crap shooters he planned to spend his modest jackpot on a bicycle as a gift for his daughter. Virgil never kept secret the place he kept his money, in his left shoe. When his murdered body was discovered the next morning behind the *Chronicle* building, both his shoe and the money were missing, his head beaten by a blackjack. The case was never solved. Mother downplayed the effect of her father's death on her, but once asked if she thought it was a factor in the troubles she had over the years she said, "Since my life had been wayward and impulsive, always a search for something that is not there and then disillusionment, I believe I need all the excuses I can make."

After Virgil's death, Gran and Mother's unsettled life continued, with Gran working long hours at the beauty parlor. Mother became a latchkey child, coming home alone from school, finding the key to the apartment under the mat, and letting herself in. It was lonely and she hated being an only child. For this reason, Mother fully intended to have a number of kids herself, though as it turned out, she could have only one. I think because she was an only child and had to entertain herself, she developed a great imagination, which helped shape the woman she became.

Virgil Turner passed on many traits to his daughter.

Gran made friends with the beauticians, including Gladys "Gladdy" Heath, a real character who was a lifelong pal of Gran's. When they would have parties, my mother would be put to bed on a cot in the closet. With the noise of the parties, she never slept a wink. I found this out in the 1980s, quite late in Mother's life, when I bought a dog that I intended to name Millie. "You cannot name that dog Millie," Mother said in her grandest manner. "That's your own mother's name." I said, "Why shouldn't I call her Millie?" That's when she first told me about being put in a closet. From inside, Mother would lie awake, unable to sleep with the sounds of the parties, the laughter, the music, and Gran's friends calling, "Millie, Millie." She associated the name with being stuck in a closet, so I ended up naming the dog Molly instead.

Shots of little Julia Jean from the mid-1920s, with her first dog, and standing by one of the trains with which she became so familiar during her childhood travels.

Life was not a round of parties for Gran, however. She was in poor health, with recurring respiratory problems brought on by an infection in her lungs called San Joaquin River Valley Fungus. Her doctor told her that the fog of San Francisco was only making her health worse. Gladdy, who had moved south, advised her to join her in Los Angeles, where she could help get her a job. They never said so, but because of their love of movies, the idea of going to Hollywood must have been very appealing. Just to feel they were in that rarified atmosphere was a thrill, though they had no intention of storming the gates of the studios themselves.

One day in San Francisco late in 1936, they strapped their scanty luggage to a friend's car and drove to Los Angeles, where they moved in with Gladdy. Mother entered Hollywood High. Within the first three months (Mother would say three weeks) she made the decision to cut typing class that changed her life. Once Billy Wilkerson discovered Julia in the Top Hat Café, Mother and Gran's lives changed pretty quickly. When Mother received her first paycheck in the amount of fifty dollars for a week's work, she presented it to Gran, telling her to quit her job because she would never have to work again.

School Days

Mother's fondest memory of her days as a schoolgirl was when she received her first Valentine. It was a story I was familiar with because Mother told it with pride many times, but here is the story in the words of one of her former classmates:

"The year was 1935 and I was in the eighth grade at Presidio Junior High School in the Richmond District of San Francisco. One day in Room 221, our homeroom door opened and either the principal, or your Gran, walked in with the most beautiful little girl any of us had ever seen or have ever seen again. Julia Jean Turner joined our eighth grade homeroom class. In those days, everybody was a good friend, and Judy soon became ours.

"A boy named Bill Gerst fell so much in love with Judy that on her first Valentine's Day in our school, he gave her a box of candy, which was unheard of in those days. The rest of us just had handmade cards for each other. I can still see the expressions on our schoolmates' faces some seventy years later." Mother, meanwhile, could still feel the red satin, heart-shaped box in which this gift came decades later.

At thirteen, Mother was sent to Presentation, an all-girl Catholic school, where the angelic-looking nuns in their habits made her want to enter the sisterhood. A parochial day school wasn't terribly expensive in those days, but still Gran could only afford it for so long. Mom met up with some of her friends from Presidio again when she entered Washington High. She became a cheerleader and left a great impression on her fellow students, one of whom remembered, "She was gorgeous in her white skirt and sweater, with our colors scarlet and gray in a form of a megaphone on the front of the sweater. . . . In all the years ahead we never missed going downtown to immediately see a Lana Turner movie. To this day, one of my friends says, 'Lana still owes me a nickel I lent her for a tamale at the stand.'"

A school photo. "I've never seen anyone who looked so beautiful when she was only twelve or thirteen years old," remembered a junior high classmate.

Early publicity on Mother talked about her having been a student at Hollywood High when she was discovered, so they took her back for a photo shoot on the school grounds, 1937.

In her short time at Hollywood High after the move south, Mother again made an impact on a number of her classmates, including future actresses Alexis Smith and Nanette Fabray. Fabray remembered her as so beautiful "even the teachers stared at her." Though she attended Hollywood High for only three months, her face adorns a mural on the side of the school.

Once Mother was at MGM she was part of the studio's Little Red Schoolhouse system. She summed it up pretty well in a few words, "Well, I would show up maybe. I graduated. They handed me a piece of paper." Mother never had proper education beyond the tenth grade. Once she started her career and active social life, she never had much time for education. She always had an inquisitive nature, however, and an eclectic taste in books. I think her favorite of all was the dictionary, which she studied to expand her vocabulary. When she heard a word she didn't know, she would reach for her dictionary, find out what it meant, use it in a sentence, and then never forget it. This was her way of compensating for the fact that her formal education was cut short.

Mom loved books, especially the dictionary.

Gran

There was pain in Mother's early years that she never talked about with me until I was an adult. When she did open up, it helped me to understand a great deal more about her and Gran. They were both complex women, carrying around a lot of baggage. Looking back years later, having survived a lot myself, I began to understand what made these two women who they were and live their lives as they did.

Gran made it very difficult to get our history. I think the angriest Gran ever got at Mother was in 1951, when

Julia Jean with her mother, 1924.

Mother revealed a lot about their lives in a magazine article that was ghostwritten for her. Gran was the most private person I ever knew and anything unpleasant was locked away in her mind. My mother and I would ask her why they went from one location to the next. "Oh, I just felt like it," she would say in her most off-hand way. She could weave a tale and make me believe every word, only to find out years later that it was just a story.

Her sensibilities were very much that of an antebellum-era southern belle. They were actually plain peasant stock, but both she and Mother cultivated manners and proper etiquette for all occasions, mostly gleaned from Emily Post. Even in the early years, Gran tried to present herself and her daughter as English aristocrats. She was always style conscious and insisted that her young daughter be well dressed. Gran didn't sew very well so she was not making the outfits herself. She was willing to spend what little they had on presentable clothes.

After Virgil was killed, Gran never married again or even dated much, even though she was only twenty-six at the time of his death. Instead, she focused her entire life on her only child. When I was born Gran made room for me, but we were her whole life until the day she passed away. This unerring devotion caused problems when my mother reached an age when she wanted to feel like and be treated as an adult.

Once she began working, Mother was Gran's sole support and though Mother was thrilled to be able to do this, it became a source of friction between them because the lines between mother and daughter were blurred. They

When Mother was the Nightclub Queen, Gran was young enough to enjoy accompanying her out now and then. This shot of them was a family favorite— very '40s.

were not terribly far apart in age. Gran was still only sixteen when she became a mother. Then Mother began taking care of Gran when she was sixteen and a role reversal took place that was particularly difficult for Gran. She could try to exert parental control, but it was undermined by the fact that Mother was paying the bills and had a strong will of her own. It was interesting to watch the dynamics between the two of them as I grew up. They seemed to me more like friends than mother and daughter.

In spite of this, Gran and Mother had the same kind of problems experienced by most mothers and daughters, but fought on a more glamorous plane. When Mother was in her mid-twenties, Gran was still waiting up for her to come home. If my mother invited a date in for a drink, they'd turn on the lights and there Gran would be, greeting them from a chair, "Well, good morning." That was a decidedly difficult time in their relationship that Mother resolved in typical elaborate manner. She bought a new house with room enough for only herself and for me, set Gran up in an apartment, and they were fine again. There were rifts, but overall Mother and Gran were very close until Gran's death in 1982.

In January 1941, Mother and Gran traveled to Washington, where they were on hand to celebrate President Franklin D. Roosevelt's fifty-ninth birthday.

Gran was never a stage mother. I think if my mother had wanted to quit show business, Gran would have said, "Fine, Darling, whatever makes you happy." She visited the studio very rarely, saying she didn't want to interfere. She was supportive in her own way—beginning with her first film, Gran kept a gold chain-link bracelet for Lana customized with round charms bearing the name of every movie and the year. When one bracelet filled up, a new one was started, so there were a few of them.

A celebration of Mother's twenty-third birthday brought a rare visit by Gran to MGM.

Pennies from Heaven

After Julia Jean told Billy Wilkerson that she would have to ask her mother if she could indeed be in the movies, he asked her to have her mother give him a call. She went home that day and told Gran what had happened. Unsure of what to do, they took the advice of Gladdy, who knew Wilkerson was the publisher of the *Hollywood Reporter*. She told them, "Go for it!" and they did.

Wilkerson first took Mother to Zeppo Marx, youngest of the Marx Brothers and an agent, who passed her off on his associate, Solly Biano. She was turned down by a couple of casting directors before Biano took her to producer-director Mervyn LeRoy, who was casting a role in his next film, *They Won't Forget*. Her nervousness at their meeting showed in her trembling hands, but after being asked to demonstrate her manner of walking, LeRoy said she'd be perfect. He signed her to a personal contract rather than to Warner Bros., the studio producing *They Won't Forget*. That meant her budding career would be in his hands rather than the studio's.

Mother had many names in her early years, not the least of which were the four that appeared on her birth certificate—Julia Jean Mildred Frances. Friends called her Judy. Her father tagged her "Jujean." To Gran she was Julia Jean, or Julia (alternated with "Darling," "Dear," or "Sweetheart"). But Mother's new mentor, Mervyn LeRoy, wanted Mother to change her name. He thought "Turner" was a good marquee name—short enough and easy to remember—but "Judy" was deemed too common. They considered first names going through the alphabet. LeRoy liked the name Donna. Mother didn't. Then, Mother later said, divine intervention occurred. In her mind she heard the name Lana (pronounced Lah nah). The others in the room liked it. "How do you spell it?" "L-A-N-A—easy," she said. It was perfect. Short, musical, memorable. Mother was funny about what people called her. Her name was Lana, "as in La-di-dah," she would say while correcting people. It offended her ears to

In her mid-teens, on the brink of fame. Gran began keeping scrapbooks. Mother kept magazine covers because they were usually in color. She had a habit of adding rose shading to her cheeks and lips in black and white photos.

An early color portrait session. A lot of changes were in store for Judy Turner.

hear it pronounced any other way and it's still jarring for me to hear it pronounced with a flat A, as in "land".

It's fitting that this reinvention took place because it was all far removed from what Judy Turner thought she would be when she grew up. It should be noted that prior to her invitation to movies my mother had no show business experience outside of getting a part as an angel in a Christmas play at the age of six, and then losing it because she developed a boil on her leg on the night of the show. That boil stopped any acting aspirations cold.

Her dream, in fact, was to enter the field of costume design. In childhood, that was where her artistic energies were focused. This is not to say that both Mother and Gran were not starstruck. They went to the movies all the time, read the fan magazines, and tried to emulate their favorite stars. They loved the elegant actresses who fed Mother with ideas for new fashions. Gran adored Frances Dee. Young Judy idolized Norma Shearer. After viewing her first movie, *They Won't Forget*, Mother wished she'd stuck to her sketches.

"Mama, you will never have to work again."

The Sweater Girl

The first time Mother saw herself in a movie was at a preview of *They Won't Forget*. Seated beside Gran in the theater, "this *thing* came across the screen." As she watched herself bounce down that street larger than life, she was absolutely mortified. She wanted to crawl under the seat. Instead, she slumped down lower and lower. Mother hadn't seen the daily footage during shooting or even know what "dailies" were yet. This vision of a girl, shown from back to front and back again, whose body bounced as she walked, eliciting whistles from male members of the audience, was quite a shock to her.

Her bra size was a 36B, which is not very big by Hollywood standards, but her bra was unpadded and didn't offer any support. That's why she bounced. She was just being her natural self, an uninhibited sixteen-year-old girl with a rakish beret on her head, walking down the street unaware of her body. When the scene was filmed she had been told to walk from one part of the set to the other and she did. From that onscreen moment, people knew her name, but she was initially so upset I don't know how she continued, except for the paycheck.

The "Sweater Girl" publicity added insult to injury. I know it's a label Mother and Gran were not happy about. But it became such a phenomenon, popularizing form-fitting wool across the nation. As Mother said, "I believe it is no exaggeration to say that I have done more for the sweater than the sheep, the silkworm, or the Yale football team." Walter Winchell, the journalist credited with inventing the gossip column, dubbed her "America's Sweater Sweetheart," as all the glamour girls then had to have a nickname. There was an element of shame in that name that stayed with her. At the tender age of sixteen, she began to hear the term "sex symbol" apply to her. She never understood this, as she was a woman who never considered herself sexy. Sensuous, sensual, yes, but not overtly sexy.

Mixing drama and "Sweater Girl" cheesecake for *They Won't Forget* was a lot for an inexperienced sixteen-year-old.

"From the moment I walked down the street in that first picture, *They Won't Forget*, I evidently was a so-called sex symbol—to everyone except myself."

"For quite a while I was ashamed to face people—I also found it embarrassing to turn my back on them."

Mervyn LeRoy

Mervyn LeRoy was one of the top directors and producers of his day. Before Mother, he had already been responsible

One of the first photos of Mother with Mervyn LeRoy, after she came under personal contract to him in 1937.

for the hard-hitting pre-code entertainment of *I Am a Fugitive from a Chain Gang*, *Little Caesar*, and *Three on a Match*, and occasional lighter fare that still reflected the Depression-era seen in *Gold Diggers of 1933*. Mother respected him tremendously and gave him all due credit for starting her career. When he moved from Warner Bros. to MGM he brought Mother with him. She came to admire her new boss, Louis B. Mayer, but early on she missed being under LeRoy's personal management. She clashed with Mayer a number of times. She never did with Mervyn, whom she said was always "a true gentleman."

Visiting Mervyn on the set of his film, *Thirty Seconds Over Tokyo*, in 1944.

The first string of the University of Alabama's Crimson Tide meet Warner contractees Billy and Bobby Mauch, Mother, Humphrey Bogart, Priscilla Lane, and Wayne Morris.

At Warner Bros.

The women of Warner Bros. were known as some of the toughest ladies on the screen. Among others, Bette Davis, Barbara Stanwyck, Miriam Hopkins, Joan Crawford, Joan Blondell, Ida Lupino, and Ann Sheridan, were all set loose in Warner films of the 30s and '40s. A film like *The Postman Always Rings Twice* shows that later on Mother would have been capable of fitting into a more hard-edged mold, but she was also a natural for MGM, the studio with a history of divine cinema queens like Greta Garbo. At the start of her career, before she had grown into that darker, sultrier aura and it was just a job, being a member of the WB lineup could be fun. She was doing little in the way of acting, but she was in good company. The studio had a stable of contract players just starting their careers, some on their way to stardom. Among the array of young contractees in Mother's time at Warners were Humphrey Bogart, Ronald Reagan, Pricilla Lane, Jane Wyman, and Mother's big crush, Wayne Morris.

Warner Brothers Portraits

Warner Bros. wasn't sure what to do with Lana Turner. She was only in her mid-teens, but she had a beautiful face and was already shapelier than most leading ladies. Hence the lace collars, hair ribbons, and even hayfields of some Warner Bros. photos of her, and dramatic lighting, smoldering gazes, and clinging gowns of others.

Miss Popularity

During production of Mother's early films, several of which featured young actors around her age, she began making friends. There was a joy about my mother in those days that attracted people. All of her friends were from the studio because there was very little opportunity for her to meet anyone on the outside. Mother was then making four films a year, working six days a week. Between publicity, radio, and a wide variety of lessons, they kept her busy, but she had endless energy. She was out on the town almost every night because she would be so keyed up from the day's activities.

Some of her best friends in the early MGM days were fellow rising actors Judy Garland, Ann Rutherford, Mickey Rooney, Virginia Grey, Bonita Granville, and Robert Stack. Their group generally went out together rather than pairing off. It was usually wholesome fun. They weren't getting drunk every night. Mother drank very little then. Most of them were underage, but they could get away with late nights in Hollywood. In a sense, they weren't children anymore. They looked and dressed older. They were in an adult business, making good money, and in many cases supporting their families.

Fittingly, Mother's first solo magazine cover was *Glamour*.

In those days, if a star got into trouble it was kept quiet. The press obliged the studios by looking the other way or providing little detail. The studios, especially MGM, didn't let their stars take a bad picture. One of the cardinal rules was never have a photo taken with a drink in hand, even if it wasn't alcohol. Photographs that showed stars smoking were often retouched, so there were doctored shots of stars with fingers poised for a cigarette and there's nothing there. The studios went over every photo with a magnifying glass to make sure they were presenting the right image.

Those first years were a low-pressure time for Mother. She didn't see what was in store for her prior to making *Ziegfeld Girl*, her first big hit, in 1941. "I thought it was all a clambake and pretty soon it would be time to go home. I came to the studio and did scenes like they told me to." Her first roles were not demanding and she could still get away with not putting her heart into the parts, though it's hardly noticeable. She shows a vibrant spirit in the early films that makes her performances nonetheless interesting.

Still a redhead, projecting the girl-next-door look in 1939.

The Nightclub Queen

In the heyday of her youth, beauty, and talent, Mother was dynamic. Based on her own stories and what others have told me, she was a ball of fire. She had come out of the Depression era into the Swing era. Poverty and death in her childhood, bad memories of her foster home, and loneliness were all behind her. She loved everything and everybody. Fan magazines and columns in the late 1930s and early '40s crowned Lana Turner the "Nightclub Queen."

Wearing a crown of sequins out in 1945.

This could be the "Nightclub Queen" on her throne.

With fiancé Tony Martin in 1941.

Surprised by a photographer as she pins a corsage to her evening dress at the Mocambo nightclub, 1951.

Before she was given the first role that she knew was important, in *Ziegfeld Girl*, Mother didn't take her work seriously because she had no sense of how long it would last. She had no qualms about staying out into the wee hours of the morning and then stepping into character. In that 1938–40 period she truly earned the title, but Mother enjoyed going to nightclubs and parties for most of her life.

She could dance all night long and she was good at it. In the '40s, the most popular nightclubs were the Palladium, Ciro's, Mocambo, Cocoanut Grove, the Clover Club, and the Trocadero. Ciro's was Mother's favorite. Head waiters would unhook the velvet rope and greet her enthusiastically. She could make an entrance like no one else. People would turn around and the entire room would hush for a few moments. After

Taking in the music of Ray Noble's orchestra at the Cocoanut Grove in 1941.

sweeping over to her table, she would acknowledge friends seated nearby. It was rare for her to tablehop. Instead, people came to her table. "You Stepped Out of a Dream," a number from *Ziegfeld Girl*, became Mother's song, and sometimes the band would lapse into a refrain, alerting all that Lana Turner had just entered the room, in case anyone hadn't noticed yet. She had a special gift. Even in high heels Mother was a small lady, so it was some quality within her that stopped a room—not something that can be learned.

To Mother, having a studio wardrobe department at her disposal was one of the greatest perks. After wearing this evening gown for a photo shoot (right), she wore it for a night out (left).

Pin-Up Girl

The two most famous World War II-era pin-ups were Betty Grable looking appealingly over her right shoulder in a white bathing suit and Rita Hayworth, tantalizing in a negligee, sitting on her bed. Mother was not tied to any single photograph, but she was nevertheless a pin-up girl of the first order. She was a soldier's dream during World War II, officially "The Girl We'd Like to Be Stranded on a Deserted Island With," "The Girl We'd Like to Find in Every Port," and "The Most Gorgeous, Spectacular, and Pulse-stirring Thing on High Heels." The 18th Bomb Squadron of the U.S. Air Force painted her on the nose of their B-17 and named the plane "Tempest Turner."

In the early '40s she was "The Girl Who Inspires the 'Woo-woos' of the Crowd," among other odd titles servicemen and fan magazines gave to her.

A pin-up shot used in publicity for *The Postman Always Rings Twice*.

Mother did as much as her work schedule at the studio allowed for the war effort. She signed up for nationwide railroad tours and would speak at rallies from city to city, tour defense plants, and visit soldiers at military camps and hospitals. In 1942 she raised $50,000 selling war bonds with kisses and her efforts altogether brought in an estimated $5,000,000. Back home Mom was a regular at the Hollywood Canteen and on the studio lot she played hostess to large groups of soldiers.

She also performed broadcasts for Armed Forces Radio, which was specifically for the boys. She did a famous bit for *Command Performance*, which was a weekly show where soldiers could have any wish come true, no matter how random, if it could be transmitted over the airwaves. They could hear Carole Landis sigh, Judy Garland sing "Over the Rainbow," or Lana Turner cook a porterhouse steak smothered with onions. That's the request that was made of Mom and she was happy to oblige. They filmed this episode of the series to send out to war zones around the world.

All of this was the energy of the times. Everybody was contributing in some way to the war effort. Visiting hospitals was the most difficult because she was easily affected by injuries and sad stories. The soldiers loved her. Convinced she was the last pretty girl they would ever see, they gave her

Greeting the boys in 1942.

Entertaining Army and Navy boys on the MGM lot, 1942.

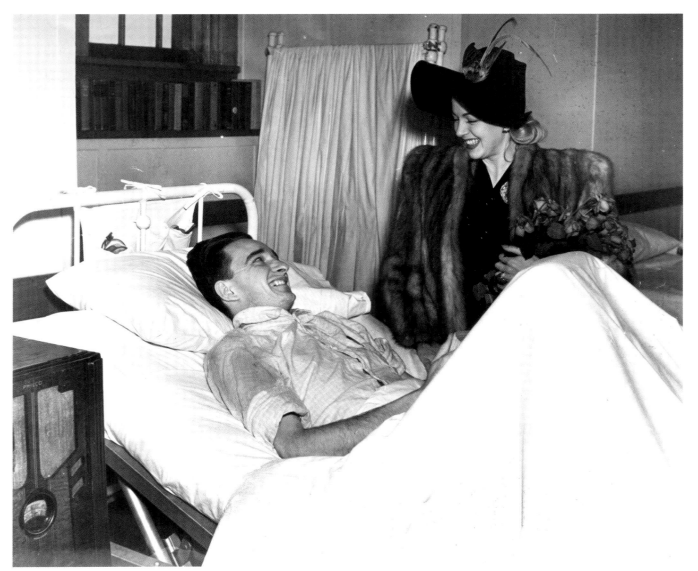

Hospital visits like these meant so much to the servicemen in those days; the stars kept their smiles bright and their emotions in check.

personal items, including the medals they'd been awarded.

Giving some measure of comfort to the servicemen always remained important to Mother. She joined Bob Hope in Korea, Guam, the Philippines, and Japan for his tour of Christmas shows in 1962. In 1967 she flew to Vietnam and hobbled around, doing everything she set out to do in spite of the sprained ankle she acquired at the start of her trip, including distributing gifts for the men and nurses in the hospitals. She came back full of stories of what she had seen—the people, the rituals, the lushness of the land. The hardships of the soldiers she kept to herself. Mother's experiences in Vietnam left a very strong impression on her.

Mother never wanted to discuss politics, which drove me crazy. There were more outspoken actors in her day, but in general, stars then were not as vocal about whom or what they supported as in later decades. Mother never leaned right or left. All anyone could tell was that she was in awe of Roosevelt, like everyone else. Vietnam was a bone of contention between us. A product of the '60s, I wanted to go out on protest marches while she went over to participate in USO camp tours. I was passionately upset about it at the time, but she said she had to do it for the soldiers.

Deanna Durbin, Marlene Dietrich, Mother, and Eddie Cantor make a soldier from Texas very happy. He was the millionth serviceman to check in at the Hollywood Canteen.

Mother would make speeches from city to city, encouraging the crowds to buy war bonds.

At a Navy party in 1940.

Les Brown, Peter Leeds, Janis Paige, Bob, Amedee Chabot (Miss USA), Anita Bryant, Mother, and Santa begin their Christmas 1962 U.S.O. tour in the Far East.

Mother and Bob Hope perform before U.S. servicemen during their 1962 holiday show at Atsugi Naval Air Station near Tokyo, Japan.

Hobbled from a sprained ankle she acquired during her ten-day tour near the front lines in Vietnam.

Visiting troops in Vietnam, June 1967.

The troops help her out of a jeep.

Mommy and Me

Like her relationship with Gran, the relationship between Mother and me was strained many times over the years, but never broken. I never stopped loving her. We lived through harrowing times together, beginning with my birth. Mother was twenty-two years old at the time I was born in July 1943, at the pinnacle of her beauty and just entering the ranks of superstardom. Her career was still on the rise. The studio worried that a "Mother" image was not right for Lana Turner, but as it turned out, it only increased her popularity.

Privately my birth was almost fatal. The fact that her blood was Rh negative was life-threatening both to her and

My parents planned to name me after my father, but a month before I was born, Mother's friend Joan Bennett named her newborn Stephanie, so my name was switched to Cheryl.

any children she carried. I was born ivory white due to anemia and they had to completely transfuse my blood. Mother too was extremely anemic, but they were able to stabilize her while she prayed day and night that they would allow her to hold me. She was never again able to carry a pregnancy to term. The miscarriage and stillbirths to come were devastating.

Remembering her loneliness and fear as an only child, Mother's strict instruction to my nanny was that I never be left alone. (FBI agents were added to the vigil during a kidnapping scare in 1945.) She hoped to spare me what she had felt, but the reality is that even surrounded by people I was lonely without her. Mother provided what she truly believed was the best any child could have—the most beautiful house, clothes, toys, and the best English nanny to look after me.

I cherished my time with Mother. When I was a toddler she used to take me for drives in her convertible, with top down and music *up*. I liked it loud, she would later tell me. What I mostly remember of our together time when I was little is that it often consisted of me watching her as she prepared to go out. I would admire her dress all laid out and she would tell me what she was doing with makeup and where she was going. Mother was affectionate with me. She liked hugs and kisses. Kids, however, have a gift for mussing hair and rumpling dresses, so I was pre-warned

Mom wrote the captions to this photo in her customary red ink.

by my nanny not to muss Mommy when she was all made up.

I missed her company during the day, but she had to go to work, six days a week in the MGM years and Sundays were my days with Dad. That was common for us star babies. My mother was the breadwinner for the family. That part was unusual in those days. All the other kids at school had a mother who stayed home and a father who worked. It made me feel different from the other kids. I felt closer with other star babies, like Stephanie Wanger (whose mother was Joan Bennett). Our sensibilities were alike and we had similar upbringings.

Pony Land was a fun photo shoot because I got to go on all the rides and eat popcorn and hotdogs.

I brushed her hair; she brushed mine. We had our differences over clothes. I wanted play outfits, but "No daughter of mine is going to look like a peasant," so I got organdy dresses, puffed sleeves, and Mary Janes instead.

On a trip to Santa Barbara in 1951.

As a teenager I would be arrested for speeding, infractions like staying out past the state curfew for minors (10 p.m. weeknights, midnight on weekends), or for being caught with "unacceptable" company. In the wake of the "Stompanato Scandal" that would change our lives, I was sent to El Retiro reform school for six months and then spent nine months in the Institute for Living, a psychiatric clinic in Connecticut. My life turned around when I went to work for my father, Stephen Crane, at the age of twenty. He was by then one of the country's leading restaurateurs. As I matured into a young adult, Mother made me feel her pride in me always—proud that I went to business school at Cornell, had a head for numbers, went into real estate, wrote a book. She would express herself in a way that said she was downright astonished that someone who could do those things came from her.

Mom and me in 1946. I was a well-behaved child, though I do remember one tantrum as a little girl. Mom ventured to take me out to Saks with her and I threw a fit.

Mother, Gran, and me at the press preview of *Madame X* in 1966.

"Are you Lana Turner?"

I didn't know who "Lana Turner" was until first grade. My discovery of Mommy's alter ego began one day at school, when some of the girls crowded around me saying, "We know who your mother is . . . She's La-na Tur-ner, isn't she?" "No she's not! She's my mommy," was all I could say. I had no idea what they meant, but it couldn't be good. No one talked about the other kids' parents in that tone, which I came to realize contained a mix of envy and resentment.

After school I waited anxiously all afternoon for Mother to get home from the studio so that I could ask the question that was on my mind. I was frightened about what it would mean if she was indeed "Lana Turner." When I asked if she was, she became visibly distressed, which only upset me more, as she said, "Yes I am. Do you know who that is?" As tears welled up, I asked, "But are you still my mommy?" I found it impossible to comprehend that she could be

At Laguna Beach during the filming of *The Postman Always Rings Twice*.

Watching Mother at work on *The Prodigal*. I'm seated at right.

"Lana" as well as my mother. I didn't know the names of my classmates' parents, but they knew her. That was hard for me to take. Mother hastened to say that she was still mommy and tried to explain that people go to the movies and see her and that's how they knew her. At least I felt secure that she was still Mommy, but it took years for me to understand who Lana Turner was and how people knew that name.

I was rarely taken to the movies as a small child. When Gran took me to *Bambi* I thought there were people behind the screen doing the voices. I saw my first non-Disney film when I was five, on the ship home at the end of a trip to Europe. It was a French version of *That Lady in Ermine*, a Technicolor fantasy starring Betty Grable. I had no idea what it was about, but even in French, it was fascinating. Even watching Betty, another blonde movie queen, did not make me connect what I was looking at with what Mommy did at the studio all day. The first movie of Mother's that I watched in its entirety was *The Merry Widow*, when I was nine. Before that I had seen only bits and pieces. If I was on the set, Mother would take me with her to view the day's rushes, which is the footage of the film in production. *The Merry Widow* left a great impression on me and after that I saw almost all of Mother's films.

Nana and Me

Mary McMurphy, "Nana" to me, was employed by Mother before I was born so that she'd be there when I arrived. She presented the very picture of a proper English nanny, which was considered fashionable in film families of the day. She dressed almost all in white: dress, stockings, cap, shoes, topped off with a navy blue cape; her uniform was so highly starched that she crinkled when she hugged me. Mother felt very strongly that I should never be left alone, so Nana never left my side.

I came to adore Nana and was inconsolable after returning from school one day to a home without her. I had gotten an inkling of her imminent departure the same way many seven-year-olds find out anything—by overhearing adult conversation. Nana was retiring and going home to her native Scotland. On her last day, to calm me Gran made the mistake of promising she'd still be there when I got home. She wasn't, so I never got to say goodbye. We did visit her later, however, during a trip to England when I was ten years old. After Nana's departure, my governess, Irene Hulley, came to me from the home of Gary and Rocky Cooper, where she'd had charge of their daughter, Maria.

Star Baby Birthdays

Another turning point in my realization of who Mother was came as my sixth birthday approached. She asked me what I most wished for. "I want to meet Lucky," was my considered answer. She had no idea who "Lucky" was until I pointed him out on my very favorite television show, *Hopalong Cassidy*. She said "I know him. That's Russell Hayden." I always felt that Mommy was a special person in some way, but this was the first time it was made somehow palpable to me. She knew Lucky and she produced him at the party she was planning for me. When we were introduced I literally almost fainted. Mother caught me as my knees buckled.

In the months before that birthday, Mother had been away from home for so long (on an extended honeymoon with third husband Bob Topping). I wasn't alone, but I missed her and took to playing with an imaginary friend named Elizabeth. What I didn't know was that Mother had been planning a party for me while she was away. She

Taking tentative steps on my first birthday.

At my zoo-themed third birthday party, there was a monkey present for the celebration.

Cutting the cake at my
third birthday party.

and Bob returned just in time for her to throw me my most memorable birthday party.

Elaborate birthday parties were probably Mother's biggest indulgence for me. For my seventh, she planned a pirate and luau combination, with the boys in pirate costumes and girls in Dorothy Lamour sarongs or grass skirts. There was a treasure hunt with a chest of candy and coins to be discovered. Other kids had the standard clowns. My circle of friends included the children of Mother's friends, like Stephanie Wanger, Evie Wynn's boys, Vanna Heflin (Van Heflin's daughter), Missy Murphy (George Murphy's daughter), and Missy Montgomery (daughter of Dinah Shore and George Montgomery).

Milk and cake with the star babies at my fourth birthday party.

My western-themed sixth birthday.

I could not believe Mother got Russell Hayden to come to my party. (I was addicted to *Hopalong Cassidy*.) That's him seated left of Mother, with his wife, actress Lillian Porter. My present from Papa Topping (at right) was one of Hayden's own ponies.

My seventh birthday had a Hawaiian theme.

Mother threw a grand party for me on my twenty-first birthday. She rented the Galaxy nightclub on the Sunset Strip and hired the Righteous Brothers to entertain. That's my dad, Steve Crane, at right.

The Image

It was "presence" that got Lana Turner into films. She was totally riveting to a Hollywood veteran like Billy Wilkerson while sipping a soda at age fifteen. One's eyes gravitated to her when she appeared and her image lingered in the mind when she left. Beginning with her first film, she had spontaneity and a personality that made audiences care what happened to her. She also had style and exceptional beauty while remaining approachable (if unattainable), and not seeming as utterly ethereal a screen goddess as Garbo. The dichotomy of sweetness and luscious sex appeal she projected on the movie screen made her a multi-dimensional star who could be loved by both male and female audiences.

Lana Turner enjoyed watching Lana Turner movies. There were certain ones she could never watch, like *They Won't Forget*. The shame she felt at that preview in 1937 was indelible. Likewise, you couldn't pay her to sit through *Mr. Imperium* because she thought both the film and her co-star were intolerable. Unlike many stars, Mother could remove herself completely from that shadow on the screen that looked like her. She would react with laughter or tears like anybody else. I found it frustrating to watch movies with her because it meant there would be a running commentary. She told anecdotes, critiqued the performance, and pointed out bits of business, like playing with her lipstick or tossing a lighter in the air in *Postman*. "That was good"; "Did you see that?"; "Oh, why did she do that?" From a modern perspective, I wish I'd had a tape recorder. It would be priceless commentary. At the time I just wanted to watch the movie.

She called some of her early films "silly," but she enjoyed them. *Dancing Co-Ed* was one of her favorites. She loved musicals and comedies, both watching and acting in them, but she won the most acclaim for her dramatic roles in *Ziegfeld Girl*, *The Postman Always Rings Twice*, *The Bad and the Beautiful*, *Peyton Place*, *Imitation of Life*, and *Madame X*. She was proud of them. More of her favorites were *Johnny Eager*, *Green Dolphin Street*, and *Cass Timberlane*. Others she particularly liked for specific reasons, like *The Three Musketeers* because she adored acting with Vincent Price.

At the beginning of her career, Mother played variations of herself as a teenager and then she eased into more substantial roles. Over the years I think she became a fine actress, conscious though she was of the camera. She didn't have any stagey mannerisms. Her style was quite natural because Mother put a lot of her everyday behavior into her acting.

"Jobs are landed in Hollywood through brains, ability, beauty, talent, hard work, or through a combination of features and figure that stack up to a photogenic accident. I was one of the photogenic accidents."

When I first noticed this it was so startling that I wondered how much of the behavior was genuine and how much was an act. Later I began to realize that those looks I knew so well at home and her ways of expressing herself with her body were as real to her off screen as they were onscreen, so I knew that she was genuine both in performance and in life.

Mother completely immersed herself in roles. The fact that movies were shot in random sequence didn't phase her. Not being an actress myself, this standard practice always seemed impossible to me. What I could understand is that Mother had the fantastic imagination of an only child. It allowed her to put herself in the shoes of whatever character she was playing and give sincere reactions to the events happening around her.

The glamour, beautiful clothes, and jewels intrinsic to Mother's screen persona were a shield for her. Without them she felt vulnerable. She would experiment with a dizzying array of hairstyles and colors in an effort to make every character she portrayed have a slightly different look, but she had a tough time with makeup tricks whose purpose was to make her look older or less attractive; hence, the black veil she insisted on wearing to and from the set when she was made up for *Madame X*.

Rita Hayworth, Betty Grable, Ann Sheridan, Jane Russell, Veronica Lake, Dorothy Lamour, and others might be considered Mother's "rivals" in that they were the leading glamour girls of the World War II era, but each of them was unique in looks and personality with images influenced by the distinct studios that they bankrolled. Since the studios designed roles around them rather than the other way around,

A true movie star shot of Mother waiting for her cue on the set of *By Love Possessed.*

they didn't compete for the major parts they played. Mother was friendly with many of the female stars of her era, but as most of them faded from the spotlight, she kept on going.

I think Mother's career success outlasted the other glamour girls because her image evolved over the years. She went from being the giggly good-time girl, through a seductive bombshell phase, to powerful roles as struggling mothers. From the youthfulness of her early days she went into a sultrier look as the years progressed, followed strikingly by a perfectly coiffed, regal style. You can catch glimpses of it in earlier films but this great elegance didn't truly take hold until *Imitation of Life*, released in 1959. I thought it made her look and act older than she was, but it certainly worked for her. The films of that era in her career were some of her greatest successes.

Early on, being in movies was pure fun and off screen it was the height of her "Nightclub Queen" phase. Getting into movies had been so easy for her that she felt no sense of permanence about her career. She hadn't worked hard to get where she was and it wasn't until the part of Sheila Regan in *Ziegfeld Girl* was dropped into her lap on 1940 that she gained a sense of responsibility and appreciated the fact that a great career had been handed to her on a platter.

Pre-*Ziegfeld Girl* she didn't look at a script to prepare for a scene ahead of time. She approached her work "with the same sort of indifference I used to have going from one class to another at school." Only seventeen, eighteen, nineteen, there was an innocence to her in this time. She wasn't yet a star, so she didn't feel the pressure to maintain her standing. However, the minute the studio showed that they believed in her by giving her a meaty role, she began to try to understand her characters and work at giving a good performance. Playing Sheila made her feel that she could be "something besides just pretty."

Those who saw her only as a glamorous star would be surprised to learn how seriously Mother took her work from then on. She used to view the rushes at the end of each day. Up on the screen, ten times larger than life, everything wrong looks ten times more wrong; she was a perfectionist, critical of every minute detail while a film was in production. Through study and experience, Mother grew ever more knowledgeable about her craft beyond acting. She knew camera angles and lighting. She was able to feel if the light

Actress in training, trying to capture various emotions.

Mother had to go from a spunky girl-next-door (left), to *Ziegfeld Girl*, which portrayed a slide into alcoholism as Sheila Regan (center and right).

on her wasn't right as soon as she stepped on the set and she would ask a crewmember to make an adjustment.

Mother was a director's dream because usually she gave herself to them completely, with a few rare exceptions when he didn't instill confidence in his abilities. The man in charge (she only had male directors) always loved having an actress

Laughing with the crew, including cinematographer Sidney Wagner (center) and director Tay Garnett (right) at the *Postman* wrap party. Whereas some stars retreated to their dressing rooms between scenes, Mother always had music going and played card games, dominoes, or backgammon with prop men, script girls, and gaffers. The crews on her films liked her. On the set I could see how protective they were of her.

show such faith in him. They also appreciated that she knew her lines. Mother had an amazing memory. In her everyday interactions there was power in this. Her knack for remembering names blew people away—it made people feel special. In her work such a memory was a major asset as well. Sometimes she would study her script in the evening and be letter perfect for the next day, only to be handed pages of rewritten dialogue in the morning, which she committed to memory quickly. In private, of course, she complained about constant changes ("I just wish they'd make up their minds!").

Once Mother reached a certain point in her career, she carried the responsibility for the success of the film, the series, the play. If she was difficult, it was because she wanted everything to be the best. But because she never barked orders and was tactful, she usually got her own way.

Mother's grand goal was to become the studio's highest-paid star. From a $50-per-week contract player in 1937, she matched Clark Gable and Spencer Tracy in 1947, and went on to earn $5,000 a week in the '50s. She was also the only star kept on salary for a full fifty-two weeks out of the year. Mother insisted on respect in her profession and nothing made Mother feel more respected than a large paycheck. She was much more competitive about money than she was about supposed rivals. Elizabeth Taylor got the first million-dollar salary for *Cleopatra*, but the share of the profits earned by Mother's deal for *Imitation of Life* added up to more than any actress's salary for a single film up to then. Realizing that was a proud moment for her as an actress.

Studying the action on the set of *By Love Possessed*.

Behind the scenes of *The Survivors*, 1969.

Entourage

The entourage—the definitive star accessory. The members of Mother's essential group of aides weren't people she saw only on the set or in her dressing room; they were also her dearest friends and seemed to be at our house anytime they weren't at the studio. Her entourage changed often over the years, but key members were the all-important Del Armstrong and Helen Young, makeup and hair, respectively. Alyce May was Mom's stand-in for most of her career. The aforementioned three all lent an extra dose of reality to *The Bad and the Beautiful*, in which they appeared on-screen in their own jobs.

Mother and Johnny Hyde at Mickey Rooney's birthday party in 1941. Known later for launching the career of Marilyn Monroe, Hyde was Mother's agent and a dear friend for years.

With Ben Cole, her business manager.

Ben Cole, Mom's business manager, had been Artie Shaw's band manager and was Gran's best friend and bridge partner. Ben was later replaced by Jess Morgan and then Roberta Turner (no family relation). Sara Hamilton was a reporter who traveled with Mother often, until she found out that Sara was untrustworthy with her secrets. Glenn Rose was Mom's publicist. Lillian Rader had charge of her hair into the mid-'40s, before Helen Young. Larry Germain was another frequent hairstylist, particularly early on, and he was close with Mother for years. He and his wife were my godparents.

Many agents came and went over the years. When she was fifteen, Billy Wilkerson gave my mother a letter of introduction to agent Zeppo Marx, who passed her on to another man in his organization, Henry Willson. Willson almost immediately turned her over to a third agent, Solly Biano. Biano connected her with Mervyn LeRoy and she was under his personal management until they moved to MGM

My father, Steve Crane, is at left, seated beside Mother and publicist Glenn Rose.

in 1938. Johnny Hyde, and later Stan Kamen, were her agents during the Metro years. In the '50s, as more and more stars found themselves in an uncertain position independent of studios, agents assumed a huge amount of power. After MGM there was Paul Kohner for Mother; and then back to Kamen in the late '60s. She also had Ray Stark for a time and Jac Fields in the '70s and '80s.

Helen Young

Helen Young worked with Mother for the first time on *Green Dolphin Street* in 1946. She had a salon in Beverly Hills but whenever Mother needed her, she was there. Then she closed the salon and went to work with her exclusively, until Helen's retirement in the early '60s. When I was on the set it seemed every time the director yelled "cut" she would run over and fix the hair slightly. Mother was lucky—she had a great head of hair that could withstand all of her and Helen's experimenting.

Del Armstrong

Dear Del Armstrong was probably the best friend Mother ever had. He was her closest confidante all the years they worked together, from late 1943 until the mid-'60s. He taught her how to do her own makeup. Del acted in a larger capacity during the making of *Another Time, Another Place*, in title at least. She brought him with her for location shooting in England, acting as both her makeup artist and assistant producer, as it was produced by her company, Lanturn. Otherwise, British union rules would have prevented him from working as makeup artist.

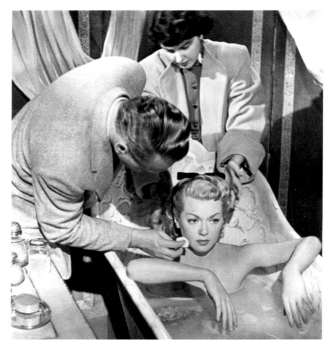

Helen Young attends the hair and Del the makeup before beginning a scene from *The Merry Widow*.

Mom and Del together for the first time on *Marriage Is a Private Affair*.

Playing cards on the set of *Green Dolphin Street*, 1946.

Lorry Sherwood

Since various studio workers handled correspondence, travel arrangements, etc., Mother didn't employ a personal secretary until after she left MGM. The longest-lasting was Lorry Sherwood. Lorry impressed Mother because she had worked for director John Huston. Mother said, "Anyone who survived John Huston should find me a breeze," so Lorry was hired in the early '60s. They were a perfect match, sharing the same sense of humor.

A birthday party for Lorry (center) on the set of *Who's Got the Action?*.

Alyce May

Alyce May had a bit part in *They Won't Forget*, but she wasn't Mother's stand-in until *Rich Man, Poor Girl* in 1938. This was not for stunt work. A stand-in needed to have the height and coloring and similar body type of the star they worked with in order for the camera crew and cinematographers to set up shots and direct lighting. Setting up shots could take hours on special occasions, so stand-ins saved the stars a lot of time. Alyce had been a ballet dancer but an injury forced her to give up her career. Alyce was Mother's companion on trips occasionally, to Palm Springs, New York, and once trailing through the Colorado Rockies. Mother was known to be lavishly generous with her dearest friends. Because they were the same size, Alyce could get Mother to give her the mink coat off her back if she admired it. Alyce said in an interview about her famous friend, "the things in her heart are keyed, all of them, beyond the norm. She is dyed in richer colors than the rest of us."

Stand-in Alyce May sits in for Mother while a photo shoot is prepared.

A portrait of Mom from the session Alyce helped set up.

Mother loved being a star and everything that went with it. She even cultivated a particular kind of independence based on who she was. As an older woman living by herself, she knew how to get along using "Lana Turner" whenever she, or her family, needed something. The trappings of fame were bearable until her later years, when the paparazzi started turning up everywhere. She came to hate it and preferred to shield herself in the "Ivory Tower" (her last home) instead of going out.

Outwardly Mother gave the appearance of being tremendously confident, but in reality, the famous entrances that attracted all eyes at nightclubs and restaurants were part of her act. "I try to camouflage it by throwing my head up high and walking in as if I own the world, but I'm scared." Every popular actress I've known has been insecure to a certain degree. Their fans seem to sense it and that vulnerability becomes part of their appeal. The only people with whom Mother felt completely comfortable were family and very few dear friends.

Mother was notoriously late for everything. Some thought it was bad manners or affectation, but it was really insecurity and innate shyness. If she had to appear before a crowd, she would be overcome with terror. Little things would suddenly go wrong. She might insist on a last minute fix to her dress or an entirely new hairstyle and then lock herself in the bathroom complaining of a stomachache. I found it remarkable that she was known for her punctuality on the set. That was her professionalism but it had nothing to do with the private woman.

Mother and Lex Barker arrive at the opening of *Knights of the Round Table*.

Mother and Gran, last arrivals at the opening of *Wilson* in 1944.

Tony Martin escorted her to the opening of *Meet John Doe*, March 1941.

With James Stewart at Grauman's Chinese Theater for the premiere of *The Women*.   The premiere of *An American in Paris*, with Fernando Lamas.

The Fans

Mother's connection with her fans was special. On the whole, their devotion to her, even when the headlines were unflattering, didn't waver. In fact, her ups and downs seemed to endear her to them all the more. They saw that she had her problems, too. There were some stars that seemed unreal, but for all her glamour, Mother retained an approachable side that her fans sensed. I think she was seen by them as a Cinderella, who through a combination of luck and beauty of face and form, landed in movies. These qualities, combined with her personality, were embraced by the public and produced an enduring star.

For her part, Mother respected her fans and recognized that the public makes a star. From the time she was very young, she appreciated the fan letters sent to her from people all over the world. In the beginning she read and answered as many pieces of mail as she could herself, but it quickly got out of hand and had to be managed by studio personnel. During a nine-month period in 1944 in which MGM monitored the fan letter flow to each of the stars, Mother and Judy Garland were shown to be ahead of the rest by far, each receiving close to 200,000 letters. After she left the studio, Mother hired a personal secretary for the first time and she dedicated a certain part of every day to signing photos, reading the mail, and dictating responses to her secretary. She took this very seriously. There were rare occasions when she was scared by a bizarre fan, but more commonly, there were special fans with whom she became comfortable enough to strike up regular correspondence, or even make telephone friends.

Signing one of her latest portraits in 1950.

Mother stopped giving out autographs in 1974 when she was on tour with *Bell, Book and Candle*. After exiting the stage door of a theater in Chicago she signed a piece of paper that was thrust in front of her by one of the waiting autograph seekers. Soon her business manager at the time, Jess Morgan, was on the phone asking, "Lana, did you make out a check for $25,000?" She said, "Of course not." Fortunately, they were able to stop payment on what turned out to be a counter check that Mother signed outside that theater in Chicago. Jess said we got lucky, but that if she ever signed another autograph he would quit. That's when she started telling fans, "I'm so sorry, but I can't," when they approached her for an autograph. Of the man with the check she said, "He got greedy. If it had been one less zero I wouldn't have been so upset!"

Clowning for a friend's camera in 1944.

On a shopping trip on Rodeo Drive.

"Sometimes I wish people could really know me, not just believe the junk that has been written."

Stopped by a fan outside of Romanoff's.

A candid shot from her 1962 trip to servicemen in the Far East.

Outside of Dad's restaurant, the Luau, in 1968.

Lana and the Press

In Hollywood's Golden Age, the fan magazines were very different than they are today. Because they were controlled by the studios, for the most part they were celebrations of the stars—truly *fan*-oriented. But in the early '50s, the infamous tabloid magazine, *Confidential*, appeared and went on a spree of spreading foul rumors. Some of their articles had a grain of truth in them, but many more were sheer fabrications and some were proven false in court. *Confidential* folded within a few years. After the headlines of the notorious Johnny Stompanato case, Mother finally dismissed the newspapers altogether as trash and stopped taking them.

As far as I knew, Mother didn't read printed reviews of her performances. She was so sensitive about her work that a bad review would have hurt her feelings. Billy Wilkerson of the *Hollywood Reporter* discovered her and his paper sang her praises from then on. Good or bad, she never kept any reviews in her scrapbooks, which were usually maintained by Gran or sent to her by fans. They were primarily filled with photos and magazine pieces.

Louella Parsons and Hedda Hopper were the doyennes of Hollywood reporting in the studio era. These two women wielded outrageous power and everyone was afraid of them.

Mother's South American "vacation" included press conferences.

Mother preferred Louella, which naturally caused friction with Hedda, who used to annoy Mother by mispronouncing her name purposely, with a flat A. Mother never liked her and she told her as much.

Neither Louella or Hedda got as far with Mother as a less intrusive publication like *Woman's Home Companion*. The magazine featured an article she wrote with one of their writers in 1951. In the closing words, readers were brought up to date on the recent end of her marriage to Bob Topping. It's interesting that this indicates the article was written at her lowest ebb—a time when she thought, however briefly, of ending her life. Approaching this state of mind she wrote the most revealing portrait of herself that she ever gave the public. The article's most glaring flaw is

A really unique shot; I love it because it was a face Mother would make—but never in the presence of cameras.

the manner in which she describes her time with Tyrone Power—as a friendship. She wasn't yet open to discussing their relationship, but still, I got more from this piece than I did from her 1982 autobiography.

Mother was the movie magazine cover champ of her heyday.

When Mervyn LeRoy relinquished Mother's personal contract with him to MGM, Mother began her eighteen-year tenure as a key member of the MGM family, headed by Louis B. Mayer. The leading production company during the studio era had an illustrious history and was known as the home to "more stars than there are in the heavens." Female stars in particular seemed to shine under the MGM banner. There was Greta Garbo, Jean Harlow, Norma Shearer, Joan Crawford, and Myrna Loy in the 1920s and '30s. Mother arrived at just the moment the studio needed a captivating new actress to continue its tradition.

Known above all for producing the highest quality family entertainment, did they make the best use of her

During the making of *Ziegfeld Girl*. Her dressing room at MGM was cottage-like; it was a separate, freestanding building. She decorated it in floral prints.

abilities? She did make her greatest impression in *Postman*, a film of uncommon theme and style for Metro, and she was more at home in modern settings than in the studio's epic period films with epic costumes. The question is open for debate, but whatever the conclusion, she didn't do badly at MGM.

Metro for as long as she lived if it had been possible, but their entire concept had begun to change by the mid-'50s, along with the rest of Hollywood. The studios were crippled by television and the loss of their theater chains. In the changing world of the industry, they couldn't afford Lana Turner anymore. Or, for that matter, the magnificent

"I don't want to know how the cake is made—but I want it!"

The studio era was a magic time in the film industry that created magnificent faces and incredible illusions for the rest of the world. They guided up-and-comers in the development of a technique on the screen that made many of them legends long after their time. Soon after her arrival at Metro, Mother was receiving lessons in poise; learning hair, makeup, and lighting techniques; and drilled in speech exercises, how to dress, and how to take photos. If she was cast in a role that called for a particular skill, she was taught how to do it for six weeks prior to filming. This was how she learned to fence, tap dance like a professional, flip pancakes, and prepare a banana split blindfolded.

In that era it was worth the time, money, and effort the studios put into these lessons because their actors were still working all the time and they had them under long-term contracts. There was the promise of them making a lot of money for the studio in the future. It was a commitment on both sides for Mother. I'm sure she would have stayed at

backlot, the massive training of actors, and full-time employment of skilled technicians who invented new methods of filming and built anything that was needed for use in a film.

I had such fun running around the MGM backlot. They had stables, a western town, city streets, a zoo, and a commissary that featured a specialty named after Mother, the Lanallure Salad. In spite of the menu tribute, I think Mother's favorite department was Research. The staff could answer questions on any subject in the world. If she was playing a game of Scrabble and someone played a questionable word, Mother would yell, "Call research!" The staff would look into it and phone back shortly with an answer. I think of it as Mother's version of Google in those days. Much of this had to go by the late-'50s.

Many stars fought their studios tooth and nail for years because of the enormous amount of power their contracts gave to the studios, but when it was over, most of

Mother was the consummate MGM star.

them missed the studio system. Mother did. Metro, in particular, pampered their stars. After being taken care of for so long, it took a long time for the stars to learn to operate on their own. Up to then they had been shielded in a sense, though many, including Mother, lived colorful lives and managed to get in trouble in spite of the watchful eye of Big Brother Metro.

If you wanted a reservation, a ticket of any kind, needed to hire a maid, cook, or gardener, it was all taken care of by the studio. For much of her time at MGM, Mother was queen of the lot. As long as she kept up her end and remained a box-office personality, they took care of everything else. I can't imagine how she ever came out of this as unspoiled as she did. But where my mother could be overly grand at times, she was never rude. And she was appreciative. I'll never forget how many bouquets of flowers from admirers or friends filled her dressing room. She began sending them to the hospital to give to patients. After all the expensive gifts and banks of flowers, something as simple as a seashell picked up off the beach pleased her as much as jewelry. She would hold it in her hand and study every corner.

With very little effort on her part, people always gave in to Mother. I remember as a child being very upset by this. I didn't feel it was fair and I couldn't understand *why* everything seemed to be weighted in her favor. As I grew older I understood the why was because she was Lana Turner. Once I realized that she was who she was and not just my mother, I could deal with it. But she managed not to let this treatment make her an unreasonable person.

Louis B. Mayer

As Mother told it, Mervyn LeRoy had shown her such care and personal attention that when she came to Metro, Louis B. Mayer seemed coarse and quick to anger by comparison. I think she was always a little afraid of Mayer but on the other hand, when she got together with Judy Garland, they made a game of testing how far they could go before they got into trouble. Mayer's desire to control his stars' actions in and outside of the studio caused immediate clashes between him and Mother. He didn't want her to gain a "playgirl" reputation by going out as often as she did. One day she was summoned to his office with Gran and he told her, "The only thing you're interested in is . . . " and pointed to the crotch of his pants. My normally meek Gran said, "How dare you!" and she took Mother by the hand and they marched out of his office.

But as she matured and looked back on the glory days of MGM, Mother came to have the highest esteem for Mayer. His love of stars and movies showed in the way his company treated its stars and in MGM's reputation as the Tiffany of film studios. When he lost his position in 1951 and was replaced by Dore Schary, Mother missed Mayer terribly.

"I have wonderful memories of him. I have some that if he were here I'd like to kick him in the pants . . . that's what memories are made of."

A visit with L. B. Mayer on the set of *A Life of Her Own.*

Dore Schary took over Louis B. Mayer's post as top man at the studio in 1951, after Mayer lost a power struggle and left MGM. If Mother's transition from being managed by Mervyn LeRoy to Mayer took getting used to, the transition from Mayer to Schary was impossible. They clashed immediately. Schary's outlook for MGM was the opposite of what Mayer's had been. Mayer wanted to continue the glossy,

With Dore Schary in 1953.

Mother sits at the head of the table with director Robert Z. Leonard; Lillian sits second from left at this story conference for *Marriage Is a Private Affair*.

star-driven entertainment for the family that his studio had become famous for. Schary was more interested in stories with a message and social conscience, and he had no respect for glamorous stars like Mother.

She tangled with Schary for the first time on the set of *A Life of Her Own*. Their encounter over the casting of her leading man was resolved quietly, but it set the tone for their relationship. She used to call him Mr. Numbers. Everything was about the bottom line with him. He didn't care about MGM's glossy past or "studio family." She felt that under his direction, the studio didn't support her anymore. That feeling lasted until 1956, the year they both left MGM. It was ironic that I was going to school with Schary's daughter and I found her to be similar to her father, not friendly, as though she wanted no contact with the movie star babies.

Lillian Burns

Lillian Burns and her husband, director George Sidney, were "Aunt Lillian and Uncle George" to me. To Mother, Lillian was "Burnsie." Much credit for the development of Mother's technique in the early transition from party girl to actress to a woman of talent and dedication to her craft should be attributed to long hours of training with Lillian Burns. The head MGM acting coach saw something in Mother when she began working with her on *Ziegfeld Girl*. Lillian's whole focus was the great art of acting and she projected all of her knowledge and dreams and desires onto Mother. Lillian wanted her to be an actress first and foremost, not a star.

The MGM Girls

I always attached more meaning to the title of one of Mother's films, *Slightly Dangerous*. I thought it described a side of her. In all of the great MGM ladies of her time, I saw an element of danger—to themselves and other people in their lives. Mother, Judy Garland, Elizabeth Taylor, and Ava Gardner all had it in spades.

They also had such charm that they could compliment a person on an article of clothing or an object like jewelry

Mother and Lucille Ball (here at a premiere) were friends from Lucille's early days as a glamorous MGM comedienne.

or a pen, and it would be theirs in a minute. The MGM girls were masters at getting anything they saw and liked. It made people feel good to give them things. "If you like it so much, I want you to have it," was the attitude. Mother

and Ava even worked their magic on each other. She had a box of Ava's jewelry and I'm sure Ava had one of Mother's. As Lana's daughter, it mortified me, but it was fascinating to watch. One of the more memorable examples of this phenomenon was when a handyman came over to fix a light switch and for some reason Mother loved his tool belt. He took it off and gave her the belt that was essential to his job. I was so embarrassed every time I thought about the poor handyman who left Mother without a tool to his name.

Mother really didn't have rivals among the bigger female stars who worked at MGM at the same time she was under contract. The studio always had more parts intended for Mother than she could possibly play. Actresses in similar situations were all kept busy and their bosses saw to it that each woman had her own unique appeal. Among others there was the inimitable Katharine Hepburn; Greer Garson, lovely and heroic; the exotic Hedy Lamarr; June Allyson, the sunny girl next door; Esther Williams, the swimming star; Ava Gardner, the sultry, dark beauty; Elizabeth Taylor, from child star to sophisticate; Lucille Ball, a firecracker before her TV fame. Judy Garland, Debbie Reynolds, Ann Miller, Kathryn Grayson, and Jane Powell offered their distinctive talents to the studio musicals. Just a taste of the studio roster in Mother's day was remarkable—and that's just the women.

The MGM Boys

It would take some formidable actors to stand alongside a female lineup such as MGM could boast of having. On the studio's roster of male stars in the '40s and '50s were Clark Gable, Spencer Tracy, James Stewart, Robert Taylor, Mickey Rooney, Gene Kelly, Frank Sinatra, Peter Lawford, Van Heflin, Van Johnson, Walter Pidgeon, Ricardo Montalban, and Howard Keel. Mother was lucky to have some of the best leading men in the business, and her co-stars felt even luckier to have her. When a national poll of box-office attractions gave top-ten rankings to Clark Gable, Spencer Tracy, and Van Heflin, with Mother number one on the list, the men took out an ad in the trades thanking her. All three of them had been her recent co-stars.

Clowning with one of MGM's top male stars, Gene Kelly.

"Lana, Thanks a million. Love Clark, Spence, and Van."

"Camera Ready"

t's interesting that Mother never thought of herself as beautiful. To her, the great beauties were brunettes. Dark was beauty, while women like herself and Betty Grable were bubbly, popular, and pretty, but not beautiful. The epitome of beauty to Mother was Hedy Lamarr. She was so impressed by an entrance Hedy made at Ciro's, glamour personified and wearing a single diamond on her forehead at her widow's peak. Years later Mother was still impressed, telling me she had never seen anyone look as magnificent in her life. Nevertheless, Mother didn't do badly with what she had.

On the screen all our movie idols are larger than life, and many people who met her commented that they imagined her much taller. In her bare feet I measured Mother at just above 5'2". She added to her height by wearing high heels (usually four inches), often with platforms or taps and lifts inside. In her youth she was buxom and very curvy. Twenty-two-inch waist, broad across the shoulders, and narrow hips. She wore size six shoes until the last twenty years, when she

At the peak of her beauty in the mid-'40s. Even in unretouched photos, her look was flawless.

was more comfortable in a seven. Her driver's license said her eyes were blue, but depending on what she had on, they could be light or dark blue, violet, or emerald green.

Her appearance, whether for the screen, at home, or in public, was always "camera ready." She was serious about being presentable at all times. That was MGM training taken to heart. Makeup on, hair done—no matter the time or place. "Camera-ready" was even the rule into her last few months of life, when she never left the house. I remember one time we were just going to watch a movie at home and I found her wearing a blue silk Chinese robe with her diamond and pearl broach as if she was going out to meet Mrs. Astor. She never let herself go.

Being disciplined was one of Mother's leading characteristics. She had the self-control to give up something that she liked if it was affecting her appearance (yet, unfortunately, she never tried to quit smoking). She trained herself not to like sweets. One day she cut them out of her diet and never

Quite often it's noted that Marilyn Monroe wore a size twelve, as though it meant the same in her day as it does today. A size twelve in her day would be about the equivalent of a size six today. Back then, a size ten or eight was considered very small. Mother was an eight, and then much later in life, when she got very thin, she was a two (probably a zero today). A good, healthy weight for her frame was 110 pounds. This was the weight at which she got into movies and it kept her curvy, with no unwanted bulges. Years later, with changing fashions, she came to think that was a bit too heavy and maintained herself around 100 pounds. She put on extra weight only twice in her life—when she was with Bob Topping and for a while in the mid-'70s, but in both cases, she slimmed down as soon as she put her mind to it.

Like any woman, Mother felt she had problem areas. She was conscious of not having a long neck. She also wasn't happy with her hips. They were slim, so she felt her backside was

"No one who adored her in movies would be disappointed to meet her in the flesh."

—Dorothy Kilgallen

missed them. If a food she liked was high in fat, she allowed herself to enjoy one bite. She was a devoted coffee drinker all her life until she realized it was beginning to stain her teeth. After that she switched to tea. It was deeper than vanity. It was strict discipline, training, and the desire to look at herself in the mirror and feel good about what looked back at her.

inadequate. In the case of Gran, who was tall and willowy and even slimmer, Mother tried to help one day by bringing home for her a pair of underwear with built-in padding. Gran was so embarrassed she never even tried them. Neither did Mother, for that matter. Instead, she specifically directed part of her daily stretches toward building up the bottom.

Mother used very simple products on her face. She believed in ordinary soap and water and moisturizers. She also had her own concoction of water mixed with Boraxo, a grainy soap normally used by mechanics to remove grease from their hands. Declaring it the world's greatest exfoliate, she used it faithfully once a week. Watching from the sidelines I was amazed her skin endured. I was not the only one shocked by Mother's cleansing routine. She shared her secret with Kathryn Grayson and Grayson became angry and accused Mother of trying to sabotage her complexion.

Mother hated the heavy "pancake" makeup that was necessary for film. It was so thick she could run her fingernails through it. It would crack and required a lot of touching up. As a reaction, when not filming she wore no base makeup at all. Clear skin and good coloring allowed her to get away with it. She was usually well tanned from sunbathing. An eyebrow pencil was essential, however, because from the time her eyebrows were removed for her role in *The Adventures of Marco Polo* in 1937, they never fully grew back. She had only a quarter of an inch of hair on the insides, and I can count on one hand the number of times I saw her without the rest penciled in. When she was working with Del on a film they applied fake eyebrows that had hair in them. Offscreen, she had simple but stringent requirements: lipstick was always in place, mascara and eyeliner on.

Mother experiments with a mole for an evening.

Making up for *Two Girls on Broadway*, 1940.

Beauty Ads

Whether they were devoted to Max Factor face powder, Cover Girl lipstick, or Woodbury cold cream, the ladies of the silver screen endorsed these and a myriad of other products. Cigarettes were advertised by famous faces then, but not the MGM stars, if Louis B. Mayer could prevent it. In fact, Mayer ordered that cigarettes be retouched out of photos that were in the studio's control. Mother's lifelong smoking habit kept the photo retouchers on their toes. Another Mayer rule regarding ads was that his stars would not be diminished by anything they endorsed, and it should befit their images. Columbia Pictures had Rita Hayworth endorse spark plugs, but MGM would never place a glamour star in that position. Mother could sell shampoo, stockings, or cola drinks (after all, a soda brought her into movies) but primarily, she was the studio's queen of beauty products—never mind that she didn't actually use them.

A cover girl in the making. The portrait in the background, painted by the artist Bradshaw Crandall (pictured), became a *Cosmopolitan* magazine cover.

"Be Lovelier Tonight!"

"My Beauty Facials bring quick new loveliness"

Lana Turner

Lovely star of Metro-Goldwyn-Mayers' "The Postman Always Rings Twice"

● Feels like smoothing beauty in when you cover your face with Lux Toilet Soap's creamy Active lather the way Lana Turner does. Work it well in, rinse with warm water, then cold. Pat gently with a towel to dry. Now skin is softer, smoother, takes on radiant new loveliness.

Don't let neglect cheat you of Romance. This gentle beauty care screen stars recommend will make *you* lovelier tonight!

In recent tests of Lux Toilet Soap facials skin specialists, actually three out of four co plexions improved in a short time!

9 out of 10 Screen Stars use Lux Toilet Soap—*You try it!*

38

An ad for Lux soap.

Advertising "Woodbury-wonderful" skin.

A Woodbury makeup ad in three stages. Above, Mother prepares her pose. At right is the final ad. On the opposite page is the photographic image.

The Mane Ingredient

Mother and Helen Young came up with amazing hairstyles for her movies, but some of the most elaborate up-dos were created for Mother's off-screen appearances. After the style was in place Helen often decorated Mother's hair with flowers, bracelets, or even diamond necklaces weaved through the curls. A pin for clothing became a hair ornament. I remember the green can of Aquanet, but before then, they resorted to other products, including a type of wax once used by men to shape handlebar mustaches. Invisible netting shaped to precisely match the style was also put to use.

It was long one moment, short the next. Platinum, dark blonde, or red, Mother was constantly changing her hair. It was very easy to style. When she went brunette and got one of the Italian haircuts for her role in *Flame and the Flesh* it was too short to style very much, but Mother found ways to

Her hairdos even inspired photographers at events to shoot the back of her head.

With pearls sewn through her hair. Her sharp hairline looked like it had been shaped, but it was natural, similar to her father's.

toy with the look. She put in highlights, lowlights, streaks, then went back to a single color again. After all of that, in later years she settled into a pale blonde color and a cropped style brushed back and to the left with her natural wave.

Even when she was no longer making public appearances, Mother's hairdresser continued coming to the house once a week to wash and set her hair. Coloring was done every two weeks. She did let her natural hair color grow in at the end of her life and kept getting haircuts until it was all back to its original shade, which was brownish red. There wasn't a single gray hair. That magic gene came from Gran. After decades of bleaching and constant styling, I don't know how she was left with a hair on her head, but it remained healthy-looking.

After the much-adored *Postman* look, Mother's hair was totally altered to long, lush, and dark, for *Green Dolphin Street*.

Mother's hair grew so fast that two years after her "Victory Bob" for *Somewhere I'll Find You*, her hair had grown far down her back again.

An intricate hairstyle described in detail: "Lana parts her hair in the center. Then she waves it gently outward and backward over the sides, which have been brushed smoothly in back of the ears and held close to the head by a black velvet band. The chignon effect is created by drawing the ends of the page-boy upward and around until they all but form a circle. A pearl ornament completes the coiffure."

Diet

Mother's taste in food was wide-ranging, from macaroni and cheese, hotdogs, and barbeque ribs to Italian (particularly spaghetti with meat sauce and garlic bread); traditional Southern plates of fried chicken and mashed potatoes; to Mexican dishes with tamales and chili—the spicier the better. She carried hot sauce in her purse and added it to virtually everything. She believed chili peppers cleaned the toxins out of the body. In Acapulco we would eat in some frightening-looking places, but Montezuma never took his revenge on Mother.

When she was at home and by herself, after the husbands, she wasn't regimented as far as meals; she picked at her favorite snacks all day. Her maid would arrange a plate of cheeses, vegetables with hot sauce for dipping, salami and crackers, or egg custards. One peculiar favorite was cottage cheese with steak sauce. She didn't sit down for a meal at home unless there was company. Having dinner with her could be maddening. She ate very, very slowly. It took a full hour to get her through a meal.

There were only two things Mother could cook. One was a fabulous turkey gravy, which she was always in charge of at her favorite holiday, Thanksgiving. It was a recipe learned from Gran. Her other dish was filet mignon. She would coat the steak with French's yellow mustard and season it with salt and so much cracked black pepper that it would form a crust. Then she would broil or barbecue the steak.

She stopped drinking sodas when she was very young. Obviously, she was drinking one the day she was discovered, but later on she wasn't fond of bubbly drinks, not even champagne. She drank distilled water, which was only used for ironing in those days. A cold, tall glass of milk with ice in it might come in between meals. Black coffee flowed all day long for years, then stopped cold one day (because it was staining her teeth) in favor of herbal tea. Conscious of eating or drinking anything that might stain after that, she drank white wine instead of red. As far as alcohol, she went from scotch and water to vodka and cranberry; she liked a Ramos Fizz at Christmas, then gave up liquor and had only a glass of wine with dinner.

Lunchtime during the making of *Flame and the Flesh,* 1953.

How to Be Lovely

Stand straight; head up; walk with a book on your head; descend the stairs without looking down. She had mastered these points as a teenager at MGM and tried to make them second nature to me as well. Like most children, I tired of hearing them. Meanwhile, I know she would have liked to put a bar down the back of my shirt to make me sit up straight when she would find me slumped on the sofa, reading, feet up.

As I watched Mother over the years she tried to impress upon me a number of her beauty hints, like moisturizing the entire body with Nivea cream after every bath. She always held up a handheld mirror to check the back of her hair and her full-length three-way allowed her to view the back of her clothing because another rule was, "More people see you leaving than see you coming. You better look at your back."

Some of her tips took more than others. Most of all her cardinal rule, "*Never* sleep with makeup on. I don't care if you have to hang onto the sink at the end of the night, take your makeup *off*." This became so ingrained in me that the few times I let myself slide, I would wake up in the middle of the night under the weight of the makeup and have to scrub my face clean.

Inspecting every angle of an Irene suit for *Cass Timberlane*.

She got her beauty rest. Nine hours of sleep when her schedule permitted, though she was naturally a night person and hated waking up for early morning calls at the studio. She didn't do any strenuous aerobic exercise, saying the human body wasn't meant to have its innards thrown up and down. What she did do without fail was twenty minutes of stretches in bed every morning, but that only started in 1971, when she was preparing to go into the play *Forty Carats*. It was theater in the round and she was required to make entrances and exits from ramps. She found the inclines strenuous and decided to start toning the body. A trainer that came recommended by the show's costume designer, Nolan Miller, started her doing stretching exercises. She stuck to them to her last days. Not long before she passed away I recall her excitedly saying, "Feel my butt. I bet yours isn't that hard."

Mom learned poise and perfect posture posing for fashion layouts for MGM.

At home in lederhosen.

The casual look—for a movie star in the '40s.

Lana Style

Mother's personal style reflected her peak era of the 1940s and '50s. She didn't show a lot of skin. She wore form-fitting gowns, but plunging necklines were not typical for her. This was her own preference as demonstrated by her personal wardrobe, but it was also the times. As with love scenes in films of her day, things

Dramatic yet sweet in black, 1941.

were left to the imagination regarding costumes. Fortunately, this coincided with Mother's tastes (except when it came to *The Prodigal*, but that's another story).

There was a store on Rodeo Drive called Jewel Park, owned by the aunt of a school chum of mine. Her father was our local butcher, her mother was a housewife, and her aunt was the flamboyant Jewel Park. All of Mother's lingerie and handkerchiefs came from this shop, where every article was handmade.

Specific outfits for specific activities, always. Jodhpurs for horseback riding. Tennis, of course, was played in tennis outfits. If she was going to meet someone for lunch or shopping at Saks or I. Magnin's, she would dress impeccably for the daytime. In the summers, I remember her often wearing shorts or pedal pushers and Italian thong sandals. Before air conditioning, Mother got creative to keep cool. She came up with a variation on cotton rompers that she called "bubble" dresses. She had them made in all colors. More comfortable than a bathing suit and and just as cool, they were always worn with a belt. Without one, a bubble dress resembled a beach ball.

She would never wear "off-the-rack" clothes for professional appearances. That way nobody could find her gown in their local department store and there was no chance anyone else at the event would dress the same. She thought it was poor taste to wear the same gown twice to an event with

Mother liked the outrageous ensemble and wore it to a party at Ciro's celebrating Judy Garland's marriage to David Rose. Mom's date was Tony Martin.

MGM's original caption for this explained, "Of white crepe, the shirred peplum front forms deep pockets which are banded in sable. The straight skirt and long sleeves are important fashion notes for 1941. A tiny bow of sable in her hair and a matching scarf completes the charming ensemble."

Mom loved to dress all in white and all in black, which went well with her skintone and hair coloring.

At home in the comfort of white sharkskin shorts and a candy stripe blouse.

photographers, though I can think of one or two instances when she made an exception to her own rule. Her shoes were Ferragamo and she would have them made to match specific gowns.

Mother had beautiful casual clothes too, but everything was precisely tailored to her shape by a dressmaker. She did buy from Don Loper's salon, sweaters from Saks; cashmere cardigans and mock turtlenecks. More often she would look at the latest issue of *Vogue* or *Harper's Bazaar,* and then put her dressmaker, Wilma, to work on a version of the styles she liked. One peculiar adjustment had to be made to every pair of pants she owned because her left leg was slightly shorter than the right. When she was standing in them, the one-inch difference in the length of her pant legs didn't show.

Perfectly arranged for a night out in 1944.

Wearing ermine and silk brocade in 1948.

Exquisitely fashioned for traveling to London in 1957.

Stylish during her promotional tour for *Madame X*.

Wearing one of her "bubble" dresses.

A Nolan Miller design for her stage debut in *Forty Carats*.

Wearing a dress from her *Falcon Crest* wardrobe
to the Thalians event for co-star Jane Wyman, 1982.

Don Loper decorates his creation for Mother to wear to the Ribbon Ball, a charity event, in 1951.

A fitting with Irene (left) in 1942. Irene was an enormously talented but very troubled woman. Gran was friends with her and she was devastated when Irene ended her life by leaping from a window of the Knickerbocker Hotel in Hollywood in 1962.

Mother's perfectionism caused trouble during fittings. It was not unheard of for a dressmaker to walk out because she was so detail-oriented. She didn't mind standing in high heels, sometimes for hours, not moving, eyes seldom leaving the mirrors that were all around during fittings so she could view every angle. She never fought with the masters. Jean Louis was her favorite designer and later, Nolan Miller. They clicked and she loved working with them. Mother's childhood passion for clothing design never left her.

With Oleg Cassini in 1946. His career hadn't quite taken off yet and he was best known as the husband of Gene Tierney, but he dressed Mother beautifully.

Inside Lana's Closet

Mother had many closets, of course, but the grandest of them all was at the big house we had in the '50s on Mapleton Drive in Holmby Hills. It was the length of half the house. It started as an outdoor porch but she had it closed in and remodeled. French doors on either side of her bed led into this dressing room. There were windows at the far end and long panels of mirrors by the two-and-a-half-foot-high platform where she had her fittings. Furs were locked in a walk-in climate-controlled vault. It might be unthinkable today, but everyone wore furs then and she had everything from fox to mink to monkey fur.

Mother wears knit gloves and brings Mexican flair to the Los Angeles courts, carrying a hand-tooled leather purse and matching shoes on the day she had her name legally changed to Lana Turner, March 13, 1950.

Across from the fur vault was a revolving closet the length of the dressing room. Clothes were separated into evening wear and daywear and, within that, grouped by color and weight of the clothes. Slacks were another sector. Sweaters and blouses rested on massive shelves opposite shelf upon shelf of hats. A twenty-foot jewelry vault held precious diamonds, pearls, and emeralds, alongside imitation pieces from MGM.

On the other side of the revolving clothes closet, what was once a sewing room was filled with shoes stored in floor-to-ceiling racks. You could spend days looking at all of her clothes and shoes. Mother's affinity for footwear amounted to a passion. When she liked a style, she bought the pair in every available color. At one time she accumulated 698 pairs.

A maid kept these rooms and their contents in impeccable order. All of this was necessary for the upkeep of a star like Mother. She was naturally inclined to present herself well, but she also felt it was her duty to maintain herself as befits a star—"camera-ready."

The Mad Hatter

Spanish influence at a party hosted by Elsa Maxwell.

Even she wasn't serious about this hat, worn at the Mad Hatters Ball during her vacation in Aspen in 1953.

Mom had a face that allowed her to wear any hat.

With Gran at the Academy Awards dinner in March 1946.

She seemed to wear her strangest hats when out with her husband Fred May.

In general, low cut was not typical of Mother's style, yet this fuchsia frock cut down to her navel was a favorite. It was described in a studio caption: "Cut with long full sleeves and an extreme shoulder line, the dress features a low neckline that extends to the waist, where it is met by a wide waistband accented by appliquéd gold kid. The skirt is full in front and boasts a drape hemline. The actress wears gold kid pumps and gold hoop-rings to accent her gown."

The gown of "mermaid" sheath and white lace Mother wore to the Academy Awards when she was nominated for *Peyton Place* may have been her very favorite. Wilma, Mom's dressmaker, created gowns for me and Gran that night as well.

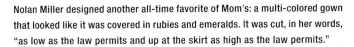

Nolan Miller designed another all-time favorite of Mom's: a multi-colored gown that looked like it was covered in rubies and emeralds. It was cut, in her words, "as low as the law permits and up at the skirt as high as the law permits."

With stage director John Bowab at a benefit for the Phoenix House in New York.

"I Got My Own Poils"

When a friend told her that if she married Bob Topping he'd give her all the jewels she wanted, Mother's quotable response was, "I got my own poils." From the first time she had money to spend, she spent it on jewelry. She had a cus-

Displaying the wealth of her character on every finger for *The Survivors*.

tom-made, twenty-foot-long dresser made up of two and a half inch drawers filled with jewelry and nothing else. Mother was no snob about the jewelry she wore. "MGM rings," which were imitation, rested alongside the real thing. Whether it was genuine or costume, if a piece of jewelry caught her eye with a brilliant sparkle, she would wear it, not only around the neck, wrist, or ankle, but woven through her hair or as added adornments to simpler neck-

laces and clipped to her clothing ensembles. On mornings after she had guests over, her jewelry could be found draped around the cocktail shaker.

Mother was usually associated with diamonds, but she actually preferred wearing colored stones—turquoise, rubies, emeralds, amethysts, star sapphires, and black and gold jewelry combinations. She wore diamonds too, but not as much as the colored jewelry. Back then nobody wore diamonds in the daytime. They were strictly for after dark, but she was one of the first to wear them any time of day.

Even when wearing sweats she had jewelry. One time, when she visited me in San Francisco, we rented a car to take

Notice the long gloves and bracelets. "No dress, however startling, can stand alone," was a rule of fashion for Mom. She could coordinate jewelry with anything she wore. This is the premiere of *An American in Paris* with date Fernando Lamas.

Adorned with a $350,000 necklace and turquoise and diamonds earrings at a *Madame X* party given by producer Ross Hunter (left).

Mother began collecting earrings after *The Postman Always Rings Twice*, when her ears were pierced for the first time. Prior to that she wore screwbacks, the equivalent of clip-on earrings in those days. The pair worn on this night (with fashion designer Luis Estevez) have infamy attached to them in our family. At an event one of them was ripped out of her ear by a fan. It tore through her earlobe, which eventually healed with the help of stitches.

a drive through the wine country and she wore her pink sweats and tennis shoes with a long strand of pearls and dangly earrings. When our rented car broke down on us, we were stuck on the side of the highway with a trunk full of wine. Mother walked over to the road decked out in pink and pearls, stopped the first car and said, "Hi, I'm Lana Turner. My daughter and I are stuck. . . . " It worked. We soon piled all the wine into the back of the car and made it home. Mom knew the power of pink sweats and pearls— and the name of Lana Turner.

These photos show Mother's creativity with jewelry. She uses a set of diamond clips in different ways a decade apart, embellishing an evening dress and her favorite necklace.

Lanamours

At first glance her list of *amours* looks a little shocking, but many of them were just fun dates. She dated many attractive men (almost always actors or musicians) in Hollywood, some for a single night of dancing, others for a month or more. She went beyond the goodnight kiss with just a few. In her own words, she was very sensual, but not terribly sexual. That's why she could never comprehend being called a "sex symbol." Not that she was indifferent to the act of love, but her whole being was geared to the promise of romance, the early bloom of love, the excitement, and then the fade-out—just like a movie.

She always said she wasn't looking for her father, that the loss of him so early in life did not influence her choice in men. She didn't go for her father's looks, to be sure. He was a redhead, short, pug-nosed, and built like a prize-fighter. Grownup Lana liked her men tall, dark, and handsome. But beyond looks, Mom's memories of Virgil Turner were that he was a good dancer, a charmer, and had a great sense of fun. These were qualities that made her weak in the knees in men.

"I think men are exciting, and the gal who denies that men are exciting is either a lady with no corpuscles or a statue." That was a well-known quote of Mother's. The fact that she had seven husbands is partly a reflection of the times in which she was living, when it was taboo to just live together. But being married was also a sincere desire within her. Simply put, when she fell in love, she married. The danger was that Mother tended to fall in love with her eyes—with the courtship and the promise of the façade. Or if she was lonely, a particular man may have appeared to be her savior. But it wasn't enough. In most cases, she didn't get to know them well enough until it was too late. As she would say, although a person learns from their mistakes, their characters essentially remain unchanged. She was always impulsive, romantic, and optimistic about a new relationship.

Mother had this surreal, very large and odd-shaped ring that she called her "cracked ring" because she said it reminded her of all her marriages. She also had a notion that something should be done with the rings from the husbands. "I should gather all of my wedding rings and have them made into something so that they're not wasted in a drawer." She never hesitated to poke fun at herself, even about her marriages. That sense of humor helped get her into trouble in the first place. "One thing I have to say about my husbands. All of them were able to make me laugh—at least at the beginning. I couldn't have married them otherwise." Mother didn't brood over her marriages or even think of them as failures—not for longer than was good for her.

Fidgety around the man she loved best, Tyrone Power.

"My definition of love is— believing in dreams."

The Love, Lana Club

Giving gifts to friends was one of Mother's greatest joys. In the early 1940s she had customized bracelets made that spurred a group of men to form what they good-naturedly called the Love, Lana Club. These tokens of affection were fourteen-carat gold-link men's bracelets with a plate for an inscription that read, "I Love You," with her name set below the sentiment. On the reverse side was a blank area on which would be engraved the name of the gentleman she was giving it to. After a time there were a number of these bracelets in circulation. The young men about town who realized this took it in stride. It was part of her playful nature and her friends understood.

Mother's close confidante Del Armstrong said she had a man's view of dating, but she didn't think herself so different from others of her sex. She would always say she loved to party with handsome men and dance with them while wearing expensive clothes—"just like any average young woman." In between marriages and more serious relationships, Mother had an assortment of attractive dancing partners with whom she was guaranteed a good time. That seemed to be the case with beaux like Peter Lawford and Robert Stack. Mother remained on good terms with these men, who might be called "fill-ins" between more serious relationships.

With Robert Stack in 1940.

"I liked the boys and the boys liked me."

Studio Dating

The studios, Warner Bros. and MGM for Mother, would set up dates for their unmarried actors and actresses. That way their pictures would be taken with "suitable" companions at parties or industry functions and both careers would benefit from the publicity. Among the men considered appropriate escorts for Mother were Ronald Reagan, Jackie Cooper, James Stewart, and assorted up-and-coming actors including Dan Dailey.

Then there were a great many men who courted her. The columns linked her to Rex Harrison, Roger Pryor, and Tim Holt. When asked about the old days at MGM, actress Marsha Hunt, who made *These Glamour Girls* with Mother, remembered that most of the men at the studio were after Lana. William Powell, the suave star of MGM's *Thin Man* series, courted her by making her a present of a beautiful art deco glass case that stood five feet tall. It had mirrored shelves on which sat the finest perfumes and came with a note attached that read, "Lana, please have dinner with me. W. P." The cabinet actually stood in the living room of the house she shared with Artie Shaw during their marriage and was featured in an article *Look* magazine did on their home life. They finessed it by saying that the cabinet came from Lana's mother.

At the Trocadero with MGM actor Alan Curtis in 1939.

Lucky Peter Shaw, who later married Angela Lansbury, got to be an escort of Mother's by way of studio matchmaking. They attended the premiere of *The Yearling* in 1946.

Wayne Morris

Mother said actor Wayne Morris was her "first big crush." He was under contract to Warner Bros. at the same time Mother was on the lot under contract to Mervyn LeRoy.

Ronald Reagan

They started at Warner Bros. at about the same time, so the studio tried to arrange a little romance, but the most Mother and Ronald Reagan ever did together was go horseback riding at the Warner ranch. Mother was close with Nancy Davis long before she became Mrs. Reagan. The couple came to parties at our house in the '50s. After Reagan became president, Mother couldn't help always thinking of him as the young guy from Warners. For me the most memorable moment between them occurred in the '80s when I accompanied her to an event. When Mother came face-to-face with Mr. Reagan she said pointedly, "Well if it isn't *El Presidente*." Everyone thought it was perfectly charming of her to say. As her daughter, it was an "Oh Mother" moment of the highest order in which I wanted to crawl under the red carpet.

Mother and Ronald Reagan in 1937.

Don Barry

Don Barry, like Mother, was just starting out when they began seeing each other in 1938. Barry played one of the interns in *Calling Dr. Kildare*. It was a bit part, like most of his roles of this period, but he would later go on to fame and acquire the nickname of "Red" Barry when he began starring in the Republic Pictures western series based on the Red Ryder comics. Barry was short, only about two inches taller than Mother, not quite her type, but they had a good time.

With Don Barry.

Mickey Rooney

When Mickey Rooney's autobiography was published in 1991, he claimed that he and Mother had a love affair that resulted in her becoming pregnant and then having an abortion. Mother was livid and adamantly denied it. I know that it was very important to her to fight this accusation because she even phoned her attorney, which was completely opposed to what she always told me about dealing with false stories being printed about us. She would say not to fight it because it only brings more attention to the issue that you're trying to refute. If Rooney's story had been true and she wanted to keep it a secret, it would have been more like her to act as though he didn't exist. But she never avoided his mention in the years before his book came out.

He was well on his way to becoming the number one movie star in the country when they met in 1938. They ran around with the same group of friends at the time they made *Love Finds Andy Hardy*. She was very particular about the physical type of the men she dated, and it was the complete opposite of Mickey Rooney. The ultimate word on the subject of their supposed relationship is that he says it happened and Mother said it absolutely did not.

Mickey Rooney gets his cake from Judy Garland and Eleanor Powell at his birthday party at the Cocoanut Grove. Ava Gardner, Mickey's first wife, is the brunette seated to the right of Mother.

Robert Stack

Robert Stack and Mother dated on and off from the late 1930s to the mid-'40s. She liked him very much, as he did her. She saw him in between more serious romances. He served as a Navy lieutenant during the war. When he was on leave he made a beeline for the set of *Keep Your Powder Dry*. They goofed around for photographers on the set and moved the party to the nightclubs after working hours.

Fun in the pool with Robert Stack.

Greg Bautzer

Mother was about seventeen years old when she fell in love for the first time. Greg was a well-known attorney and a ladies' man in his off-hours who shared her passion for dancing. He was Mother's first lover and she fully intended to marry him after he presented her with a beautiful star sapphire engagement ring. She had no idea that one of the other women on his list was Joan Crawford, who set out to nip Greg's new relationship in the bud. Joan told Mother how serious her relationship with Greg was, that they would soon be married, and that Mother ought to disappear if she knew what was good for her. But Mother wasn't intimidated by the formidable Miss Crawford. In spite of their "heart to heart" exchange, Mother remained convinced that she and Greg would be married.

But it turned out that Greg simply wasn't ready for a commitment yet, with her or Crawford. He was enjoying his bachelorhood and not making enough room in his life for Mother. He stood her up once too often. After she married Artie, Mother and Greg never rekindled their romance, but he remained in her life for many years, helping her out of more than a few tight spots in his capacity as an attorney. Greg was her first love and her first heartbreak, impossible to forget.

"I learned how to be hurt from Greg."

Greg remained in Mom's life long after their breakup. It was usually in a professional capacity, but here Mother and Greg, then a naval Lt. Commander, are shown nightclubbing at the Mocambo.

This is Mother and Greg at the premiere of *The Women*. She said, "He was going to be the greatest attorney in the world. . . . He had an energy and drive, yet was fun and handsome. Very. And I was just totally like the little puppet, just gaga, but so in love."

Artie Shaw

Six months before they married, Mother made *Dancing Co-Ed* with Artie Shaw, who made his big screen debut in the film. There was no love lost between them during production. At first Mother was thrilled to be working with him. He was a great clarinetist and one of the nation's top bandleaders. Then when she got to know him she thought he was arrogant and too serious while he viewed her as a senseless Hollywood doll. Artie turned up his nose at the movies in general. Appearing in them was something he did for the money. But he had to admit this Hollywood doll had a way about her because he phoned her house a few times asking her out on dates—which Mother always declined.

Mother's and Gran's birthdays were four days apart. On Gran's birthday in 1940, Greg Bautzer was going to take them both out but cancelled at the last minute, saying he didn't feel well. Mother was upset and then the story turns into one of the movies she'd enjoyed on Saturday afternoons, something a Joan Crawford character might do. Boyfriend stands up Girl. Unwanted Suitor calls. Girl goes out with him to spite Boyfriend.

Artie took her out to dinner and then they drove out to Santa Monica beach, sat in the car, and talked for hours about his philosophies, about what was wrong with the world and how life ought to be. Artie was a terrific spinner of tales. He put images in her head of a perfect married couple nestled in the living room of their white-picketed cottage, reading together and playing music. At nineteen years old, Mother already had marriage and children on her

This was how Artie Shaw found Lana Turner, but he expected marriage to turn her into a hausfrau. She said, "I was not ready for a combination of Nietzsche, low-heeled shoes, no lipstick, and an ironing board."

mind because of Greg. She ate up every word and told him, "That's what I want, too." Before long, she and Artie boarded a plane, flew to Las Vegas, and were wed at four o'clock in the morning of February 13, 1940. He removed a cat's-eye circlet from his own finger and gave it to her as a wedding ring. When it was over, Mother sent Gran a telegram: "Got married in Las Vegas. Love, Lana." Gran thought Greg Bautzer was her new son-in-law, but after the previous night she wasn't sure, so she called his house. To her dismay, Greg answered, so she knew it wasn't him with her daughter in Vegas. "Who did she go out with?" Greg asked. Gran told him Artie. "Then it's him." That's how Lana's mother and fiancé found out about her marriage.

Within days, the weight of what she had done was overwhelming to Mother. It dawned on her that she was married to a stranger. She didn't even know that he had been married twice before. Once it was done, she did try to make

A happy moment with Artie in 1940.

it work. I know they had some good times because she adored the music scene. They had parties and did broadcasts from his charming house up on Summit Ridge, and in moments of joy she was the inspiration for one of Artie's signature compositions, "Summit Ridge Drive."

Artie was indeed a gifted musician but he could be a very difficult man. He made it his duty to improve her mind.

He said she was dumb and that's exactly the way she felt. When they fought, Artie could use his intellect to twist her words in a way that made her feel inferior, which would make her dissolve into crying fits. Looking back on it, he expected a lot of her at the age of nineteen. She was just a kid who worked hard and then liked to go out with friends, not read Nietzche or the other philosophical volumes found in their book-lined living room. Mother finally just got tired of being schooled.

What Artie was thinking is a mystery because from the moment they were married he wanted to change everything about her. He wanted a hausfrau. Although Artie and Mother had a maid, he wanted her to iron his shirts and do the dishes after she came home, and he insisted that she wear flat shoes, plain dresses, and no makeup. He later tried to repeat the de-glamorizing process on Ava Gardner of all people, when he married her in 1945. Poor Artie was fighting a losing battle because no matter what you dressed these women in, they looked beautiful. Artie and Mother even fought over whether the toast at breakfast should be light or dark. Doomed from the start, the marriage lasted only four months and eleven days.

After a bad fight with Artie she called Greg Bautzer, who told her to leave the house. In a way he was responsible for bringing them together and when the marriage was over, it was Greg who started the divorce proceedings. Mother and Artie, two music lovers, kept musical souvenirs of the other. Much to her annoyance, Artie would not part with a baby grand piano Gran had given them as a wedding present, but she walked off with his clarinet. Also, she and the maid

MGM was not pleased about the marriage, but they tried to turn it to their advantage with a photo shoot at the Shaw homestead.

had come to like each other very much. When Mother left, Maybelle went with her.

While Greg arranged her divorce, Mother sailed to Hawaii for a four-week rest. On the way over she found out that she was pregnant. Artie floored Mother by telling her he didn't believe it was his baby. Still in her teens, she was faced with an impossible marriage and a burgeoning career that would be ruined. She and Gran had no other means of support. Mother came to the decision to have an abortion. Artie said nothing to change her mind. Like everything else, it was arranged by the studio. It was a poorly executed operation that caused her excruciating pain and she was lucky to have come through it alive.

Mother allowed herself to be pressured into this decision, but I know it took a great toll on her emotionally. Here a bit of disillusionment crept in and she began to grow up. Dreamer that she was, this was just one of many hurts to

lock away. In later years there was never any real communication between Mother and Artie. And yet, she kept up with the music she loved and bought his records. She came away from her marriage to Artie with a little more than a clarinet and a maid. She used to say, "Artie was my college education."

At court divorcing Artie Shaw, 1940.

Victor Mature

Both Mother and Victor Mature did a lot of dating in 1941. He soon went into a serious relationship with Rita Hayworth. Mom and Victor performed a radio version of her film *Slightly Dangerous* in 1943 and later co-starred in the movie *Betrayed*.

Tony Martin

Life imitated art and gave Mother and Tony a cinematic start to their romance. He gave her a signature song by introducing "You Stepped out of a Dream" as she took the stage in *Ziegfeld Girl*. Tony's three-year marriage to Alice Faye had ended shortly before he came into Mother's life in November 1940. Gran adored him for her daughter. I think at the time Mother's relationship with Tony Martin meant more to her than she later let on, but he was certainly her most steady boyfriend of the early '40s. Indeed, they were engaged to be married for a short time. They were out all the time and the photos speak volumes about how much

fun they had together. Her jewelry collection contained many lovingly engraved pieces from him.

After Tony found his lifetime partner in Cyd Charisse and they married in 1948, the pair became one of Mother's favorite couples. There were past beaux, like Tony, who she later came to adore as part of a couple. George Montgomery and Dinah Shore, Robert and Rosemary Stack, James and Gloria Stewart, Ronald and Nancy Reagan, and Tony and Cyd were some of Mother's favorite married couples. They were friends she thought were perfectly matched. Once a former boyfriend became part of what she saw as a great couple, she downplayed her past with him.

Mother always had a great time out with Tony Martin, whether at industry events, nightclubs, cafes, or the races.

The Boys in the Band

Mother was a bit infatuated with all of the incredible musicians whose talent thrilled her. She loved being in on their late-night jam sessions and they loved having her present. There were a number of big band names whom she dated occasionally, primarily in the early '40s, after Artie and before my father. They were all young, talented, busy people. Whoever was in town and not on the road might become number one in her date book.

Desi Arnaz was a rumored romantic interest. He was certainly the type to which she was drawn. He and Lucille Ball fell in love so quickly when he came to Hollywood in 1940 I'm not sure where Mother might have fit in, but there were a number of other musicians of the day that certainly were in her life—Buddy Rich, the fantastic drummer; Benny Goodman, the "King of Swing" and a world-class clarinet player. More popular with my mother as escorts were Tommy Dorsey, and above all Gene Krupa.

Gene Krupa

Mother's relationship with the leading drummer of the swing era, Gene Krupa, turned into quite an affair. He was in the midst of a divorce, but I think ultimately Mother was plain scared away by his drug use. It was well-known that Krupa smoked marijuana, particularly after he was arrested in a drug bust in 1943. As much as Mother enjoyed being around musicians, this habit terrified her. She was first exposed to it during her marriage to Artie Shaw. Artie and his friend, comedian Phil Silvers, spent one late night smoking marijuana. Mother was shocked—also ill. The smoke that filled the room made her so sick she wanted nothing to do with any kind of drugs again, even by association.

Seeing Tommy Dorsey off at the train station. One of Mother's prized possessions was a trombone from Dorsey that read, "Lana, Happy New Year, The Boys in the Band."

All eyes on Gene Krupa, who sits with Mother and Roger Pryor at a table at the Palladium.

Errol Flynn

Did notorious ladies man Errol Flynn and Mother, who also had a lot of energy when it came to dating, ever get around to each other? He was one of the best-looking charmers in town. Women loved him and it's not difficult to imagine Mother might have been a bit smitten as well. She never mentioned him to me as anything more than a friend. She did have his cigarette case though, which she had held onto since the '40s, as well as an oversized publicity portrait of him, one of very few she had of anybody.

Mother kept the gossips guessing as much as Flynn did in those days. Advertising executive Adrian Samish was in her date calendar at this time too, as was Alexis Thompson, a millionaire playboy from New York who was very popular with the ladies in Hollywood.

Mother and Errol Flynn at the radio recording of *Mr. and Mrs. Smith* in 1942.

George Montgomery

Actor George Montgomery, whom Mom dated before his marriage to Dinah Shore, tries to keep her entertained by playing tricks with his utensils.

Robert Taylor

Mother and Robert Taylor's chemistry in *Johnny Eager* is electric, and these two beautiful people got carried away during the filming of their passionate onscreen kisses. This was a rare time in which Mother indulged in the occupational hazard of falling for her co-star. As is often the case in romances between co-stars in films, it lasted only as long as filming. It was as though the actors fell in love with the character they were in love with in the movie and once they weren't supposed to be in love with that person anymore, it ended.

Mother said she resisted Taylor because he was very much married to Barbara Stanwyck at the time. Still, they did fall into what she described as a heavy flirtation. Barbara got wind of it and visited the set one day, to remind Lana to tread carefully. Mother got the message. She locked

Dancing with Robert Taylor at the Palladium.

herself in her dressing room and refused to come out until Stanwyck was gone. Louis B. Mayer was consulted and, Mother told me, he ordered that Stanwyck be barred from the set for the rest of the shoot. Whatever happened, Stanwyck didn't return.

I think Mother got to be afraid of Stanwyck, who actually placed at least one angry telephone call to her. Mother said she kept herself from becoming too serious about Taylor because of his wife. Taylor was less in control of his emotions and one day he announced to my mother that he was in love with her and that he intended to leave Stanwyck. It was like a chandelier had crashed to the floor. Mother had let things go too far, so she backed away completely and that was the end. Meanwhile, on the screen their personal flirtation lives forever as one of the steamiest love affairs on celluloid.

Frank Sinatra

Mother never fessed up to this in public, but she and Frank had an on-and-off love affair before I was born, while he was married to Nancy, and before and after his marriage to Ava Gardner. Frank's popularity as a singer landed him in Hollywood in the early '40s. He and Mother hit it off from the time they met in 1942. They adored each other as friends always, but there was another kind of attraction between Frank and my mother that kept them in each other's lives romantically at different times over the course of many years. I can almost chronicle the times by the flow of gifts coming into the house. I can still see them as late as 1970 dancing at the Candy Store on Rodeo Drive. They weren't kids anymore, but there was still a spark between them. Why they never admitted to any romantic involvement I can only speculate. It was likely just an unspoken agreement between the two of them. And there was Ava. Mother and Frank

At the Clover Club in 1944.

Preparing to give a radio performance.

Mother and Frank always denied any romantic involvement—in public.

never had an affair when Ava was in the picture. She was the love of Frank's life and one of Mother's best friends.

Frank and Mom shared much in common: love of nightclubs, glamour, music, food—and generosity. He gave Mother some of her favorite gifts over the years: jewelry of all kinds; a treasured paint set; for her twenty-first birthday a Sommeliers silver wine tasting cup from the "21" club on which was engraved "21." She kept every gift Frank gave her, and many of them were on display, not tucked away. During an awful period in Frank's career in the late '40s Mother gave him money to help his family stay afloat. If one could ever do anything to help the other, they did.

Frank gave both Mother and me all his love and support during the Johnny Stompanato scandal, when everyone said Mother's career was dead. After her next film, *Imitation of Life*, became her biggest hit yet, Frank gave her an incredible clock that had a globe on it with a note that said "You're back on top of the world." He didn't forget me either. He lifted me out of my gloom by sending me a record player with a set LPs containing all of his music and the hit records of my other favorite musicians. He understood the healing power of music.

"Uncle Frank" was someone I remember from my early childhood, yet he and my father could not stand each other. Frank wouldn't go to any of my father's restaurants, even when they were the most popular places to go. They got into public fights over Mother a few times, before and after my parents married. Frank thought that Dad was some sort of gigolo, not good enough for Lana. The first time I know of them ever being civil to each was at my twenty-first birthday party, in 1964.

Stephen Crane

My father was a fascinating character and as much of a dreamer as Gran and Mother. He even dreamed up a whole new existence for himself, so it wasn't Joe Crane from Crawfordsville, Indiana that Mother met one night at the Mocambo, but J. Stephen Crane III, tobacco heir. He asked her to dance and it was not long before they were, in her words, "heels-over-chin, pinwheels-on-fire in love." He was charming and debonair. Where he cultivated his polish I don't know. The Cranes were from a tiny town in Indiana, where he was born five years and a day before Mother. My grandfather owned a combination pool hall and tobacco shop and that was as close as Dad was to being heir to a great tobacco farm. At age twenty-one he married Carol Ann Kurtz, a pretty girl from his hometown, but it didn't last long. My father possessed the same wanderlust the Turners had.

In Crawfordsville Dad wasn't known as Stephen, he was known by his given name, Joe. Dad and his brother Bill set out for California and when they arrived they had decided to go by the names Stephen and William. If Hollywood was the place for reinvention, Dad fit right in. He made friends immediately and one of his closest was Virginia "Sugar" Hill, the girlfriend of the underworld figure Bugsy Siegel. Dad

My parents on their wedding day.

was going to be an actor, so Sugar loaned him money when he decided he needed plastic surgery (still experimental in those days) to refine the shape of his nose and chin.

He was a struggling actor when he and Mother met. She had just returned from a war-bond selling tour. They had known each other anywhere from a few weeks to a few months (depending on who's telling the story) before July 17, 1942, when they flew to Las Vegas and got married. Their union was sealed by the same justice of the peace who joined her in wedlock to Artie Shaw. "Tie it tighter this time, Judge," said Mother to Judge Marshall.

Late in 1942, Mother found out she was pregnant with me. She thought her life was perfect until Dad dropped the bomb. His first wife, Carol, had been in touch with him to inform him that he had re-married before his first divorce was final and his second marriage was therefore invalid. As far as Dad was concerned, he'd been divorced from Carol and he hadn't any given thought to technicalities. Mother's initial reaction to the news was to run to the bathroom and get sick. She could just see the headlines:

Mr. and Mrs. Stephen Crane at their wedding reception. Among the party guests were Judy Garland and David Rose, George Sidney and Lillian Burns, Linda Darnell, Johnny Hyde, Ben Cole, Alyce May, and Dad's brother, my Uncle Bill.

Linda Darnell and publicist Alan Gordon went along as witnesses to the Crane marriage.

"Lana Turner Marries Bigamist!" and "Louis B. Mayer Collapses!" Mother gathered her strength, ordered Dad to leave the house, and applied for an annulment, which was granted immediately. Then she dashed to Palm Springs to regroup for a time.

Dad was abject from the moment the news broke. He pleaded with her to remarry him, but Mother had become so furious that she never wanted to see him again. Dad thought a grand gesture might do the trick. When she refused to see him in the middle of the night he pointed his car in the direction of the bushes outside their home and smashed through them. A few days later he was in the hospital, where, Mother was told, he was being protected from attempting suicide. Around this time he was drafted into the Army and she softened toward Dad, but the most important issue to Mother was the baby she was carrying. Dad's blunder would not cause her child to be illegitimate. That conviction finally trumped her anger, so in March 1943, my parents snuck across the border to Tijuana and were remarried. A sign on the door of the magistrate's office read, "Legal Matters Adjusted."

Meanwhile, the latest film Mother made, *Nothing Ventured*, underwent an identity crisis as its name kept changing to coincide with her recent press. *Slightly Dangerous* was finally decided upon. It was a fun film and a big hit at the box office. Dad's career was put on hold as he answered the call from Uncle Sam. He became the best-dressed private in the Army. The regulation uniform chafed his skin so he had nothing but specially tailored gabardine uniforms (paid for by Mother). Dad had foot and back injuries that prevented him from going into overseas combat. He was stationed at Fort MacArthur, a military camp near home for six months and then honorably discharged.

By the time Dad was out of the Army, I had entered their world. I spent three extra months in the hospital and Mother was ill because of complications during the pregnancy. When I was safely at home and she had bounced back, Mother went to work on *Marriage Is a Private Affair* (nobody who heard the title could keep a straight face). But Dad hadn't found his way yet. At the end of her day she would come home from work and find him still in his pajamas, robe, and monogrammed slippers.

On the Ciro's supper menu at the height of his fame as Lana Turner's husband was the Steve Crane Special: a triple-decker sandwich of tongue and cheese on rye toast, served only from midnight to three A.M.

My parents, an Army couple in 1943.

Mother receives her legal separation from my father in court.

Mother was also thrown for a loop by a trip they took to Crawfordsville, Indiana. Dad enjoyed taking his gorgeous movie star wife around his hometown, but it was there Mother realized that Stephen had presented a totally false front about himself and his upbringing, which he had led her to believe was rather privileged. But it was a more comfortable and settled home life than hers had been and she couldn't understand his need to reinvent himself as a dashing *bon vivant* who was trying his hand at acting. It came as a shock and she felt betrayed again. She filed for divorce a little over a year after their second marriage. For my sake, my parents tolerated each other, and years later, after they went through all the traumas, they became good friends again. Dad did get a contract at Columbia Pictures which landed him two bit parts (one in a Rita Hayworth musical) and one co-starring role, opposite Nina Foch in *Cry of the Werewolf* (1944).

Dad's acting career didn't pan out, even if his charm was undeniable. In those days the accomplishment that most wowed the town was his taking out, on three consecutive nights in 1944, Mother, Ava Gardner, and Rita Hayworth, all observed by a Ciro's manager. In time he would reinvent himself again. In the post-war years Dad got into the restaurant business and ran Lucy's, a popular spot across the street from Paramount.

In 1953, after spending a few years in Paris, the doors opened to the Luau, a Polynesian-themed restaurant that soon became *the* place to be. It launched Dad on a hugely successful path as a restaurateur and he made millions. Dad led quite a life up until his death in February 1985. He fulfilled his professional ambitions, but his private life was less settled. He married five women in total. I remember Mother sitting me down when I was about three years old and telling me that my father had married again and that he and his new wife were in faraway France. That was when he married Martine Carol, a well-known French movie

My parents had already separated, but Dad was back home with us on my first birthday, July 1944.

star whose blonde bombshell exterior gave her a passing resemblance to Lana Turner.

I think Mother always had a hold on his heart. My father never said a word against her. He was always very protective to the point of getting into fights with her suitors, long after they split. After her divorce from Bob Topping and his from Martine Carol in 1953, I recall him asking at the end of one of our Sunday outings if she ever asked me about him and if I thought there was a chance they might get back together. "Well, I don't know," I said. I was thrilled, but Mom wasn't interested in reuniting with Stephen. After he passed away, I found a couple of scrapbooks he had. Of all the press he received over the years, all he had held onto were those from the time of his marriage to Mother.

John Hodiak braids Mother's hair . . .

. . . and feeds her tea on the set of *Marriage Is a Private Affair*.

John Hodiak

Mother and John Hodiak made two films together; *Marriage Is a Private Affair* and *Homecoming*. While making *Marriage*, this sweet and unsuspecting man was caught up in a messy situation when Mother was trying to get my father to agree to a divorce. She told Dad a baldfaced lie—that she was in love with another man. When he didn't believe her, Mom decided to make the story sound more authentic by naming the mystery man. The most convenient and believable was her latest co-star. She heard herself say the name of John Hodiak. The story convinced Dad. Next she had to tell John Hodiak. "Suppose he comes gunning for me?" was John's startled response and he had to be convinced that Stephen would not come after him for revenge.

Mother never spoke to me about Hodiak except to say that, for his sake, she felt bad that she had used him as a reason to give to my father for why the marriage was over. There is sufficient photographic evidence to show that they did actually date, while photos of them on the set of *Marriage Is a Private Affair* show him looking positively smitten, even braiding her hair.

Turhan Bey

The romance with Turhan Bey began not long after her separation from my father. The two men got into a big fight over her when my father caught up with them at a party in hopes of retrieving a Crane family heirloom. A three-carat diamond engagement ring he had given Mother

At the height of their romance and before his entrance into the Army in 1945, Mother went to Turhan Bey's studio, Universal Pictures, for their one and only joint portrait sitting.

At the *Ice Follies* with Turhan.

was still being kept warm on her finger. My father interrupted them on the dance floor and asked for the ring. Bey, protecting his lady, took Dad out to the terrace and they got into a fistfight. Mother, looking on in horror, snapped the ring off her finger and threw it into the bushes. After waiting for the morning sun to shed light on the shrubbery and extensive searching on his hands and knees, Dad walked away with his treasured Crane Diamond—and a black eye. Turhan came through with scratches and bruises, and they all made the morning papers.

Regarding why their romance ended, Mother told a reporter, "I don't know whether I did something or someone told him something or what." The "someone" was his

mother, who did not approve of Lana Turner. Turhan was never married in his long life. Fifty years after his romance with Mother, I ran into Turhan Bey at a party given by George Sidney. Turhan wanted to know all about her. "She was so beautiful. I'm sure she still is." He went so far as to call her the love of his life. Everyone knew she was ill by then. I told him that she was doing okay but she wasn't leaving the house very much. The dear man still wanted to take her out to dinner. I knew she wouldn't accept his invitation, but I promised to give Mother all of his messages. She didn't go, but she was charmed by the story. I could see the deep feelings Turhan had in the way he spoke about Mother. It was terribly sweet.

Howard Hughes

Gran use to refer to Howard Hughes as a "strange bird." Still, he was irresistible in his day. Seemingly, every glamorous actress of a certain period from the late 1920s through the '50s not only dated Howard, but fell in love and was convinced that they were going to be married. Howard, like Tony Martin, was a man that Gran came to be very fond of and hoped to call son-in-law. She got to know Howard because of Mother's famed lateness. While he waited for her to finish getting ready, Howard would sit and talk to Gran.

One of the idiosyncrasies Howard was known for was his shabby attire when he showed up to take out his beautiful women. He wore sneakers or scuffed shoes with no socks, and his slacks were too long so the bottoms of his pant legs were always frayed. Gran thought he would have a better chance with her daughter if his pants were neater, so she would ask him for them and ended up hemming many a pair of Howard Hughes's pants while he waited with a towel wrapped around his bottom half. Tidy pants could keep Mother and Howard together, but the relationship ended on a laugh. It was Gran who always ordered Mother's bath towels. In her amateur attempt at playing matchmaker, she ordered a set monogrammed with the initials L. H. "What do I do with these towels?" Mother asked Howard, and he replied, "Marry Huntington Hartford."

The punch line about Huntington Hartford was not the last of Mr. Hughes for our family. Howard was one of the most celebrated men of his day for his achievements in aviation, including setting the record for flying around the world in ninety-one days in 1938. Mother suffered her first miscarriage in early 1949 when she was married to Bob Topping. She was at the Topping estate in Round Hill, Connecticut, far from her mother. It was a terrible time for her and she wanted Gran to come immediately, but it was impossible to get a flight. Howard was the owner of TWA, so Gran called him to help her get to Lana. When he heard what had happened, he arranged for her to get on the next available flight. When they landed, Howard Hughes came out of the cockpit. He had flown that commercial flight himself to make sure that she got where she needed to be, and that a car was there to meet the plane and take her to Mother. There are a million ways to describe Howard—as an eccentric, a pioneer, or what have you—but to our family, that act of kindness made him a romantic hero.

This is the only photo that I am aware exists of Mother with camera-shy billionaire Howard Hughes.

Peter Lawford

Peter Lawford seemed to be more enamored of my mother than she was of him, even though he was impossibly handsome with a light British accent and a good dancer. In the times she spoke of him later, the conversation always came around to how sorry she was about the break in his friendship with Frank Sinatra in the early '60s. Sinatra dismissed Lawford from his life when Lawford was unable to deliver his brother-in-law, John Kennedy, to Sinatra's home in Palm Springs during a trip to the West Coast. Instead, the president stayed with Bing Crosby. Mother's theory was that this broke Peter's heart and led to the decline of his career and downward spiral into drugs and alcohol.

At the height of their beauty she and Peter made quite a pair. They enjoyed each other's company on dates in the mid-40s, but both were popular with the opposite sex. He had other dates, while Mother had recently split with my father and was far from settling down again.

Mother and Peter Lawford attended a sneak preview of *Since You Went Away* at the Carthay Circle Theatre, and danced afterward. She looked startlingly glamorous in a full-skirted strapless gown of sheer black net sprinkled with sequins, paired with lace-up satin slippers, a fur wrap, rubies, and diamonds.

Lawford and Mother at the Clover Club in June 1944.

Robert Hutton

During the making of *The Postman Always Rings Twice*, and for a time after, Mother saw actor Robert Hutton. She liked Hutton (the cousin of Woolworth heiress Barbara Hutton), but he was not her main focus at the time as she was wrapped up in her most exciting role to date.

In New York after the film was completed, she was seen out with radio executive Charles P. Jaeger. Back in Los Angeles again after the trip east, Mother and Hutton continued to date until she went on a trip to South America. Making her way back home via an excursion to Palm Beach, she was linked with Huntington Hartford (of A&P supermarkets and heir to a tea fortune). He had been the man Howard Hughes suggested she marry to go with Gran's towels for her daughter monogrammed "L. H." Mother and Bob Hutton didn't resume dating again. When she was back from her travels it was 1946. That year Hutton married model and actress Cleatus Caldwell. As an odd postscript to their relationship, Bob Hutton was co-author of the original story and screenplay for her unfortunate 1974 film *Persecution*.

With Bob Hutton at the premiere of *Leave Her to Heaven* in December 1945.

Mother and Hutton were a closely watched twosome in 1945.

With Charles Jaeger in New York. She was quoted as saying that the ABC radio executive proposed to her. Jaeger gave reporters the standard, "We're just good friends."

Rory Calhoun

At the premiere of *Spellbound*, with Laraine Day and Rory Calhoun. The budding actor gave Mom a lovely anklet that she wore often.

The One That Got Away

Tyrone Power was the love of Lana Turner's life. Individually Tyrone and Mother stopped traffic. As a couple, they inspired awe. He's one of my earliest, if hazy, memories. I recall sitting on his lap in our den at home in Brentwood. I was only about three years old, but I remember his face. Tyrone was one of the biggest stars in films, the most valuable male actor at Twentieth Century-Fox—which meant he was property of Darryl F. Zanuck, who also happened to be one of Tyrone's best friends.

Mother and Tyrone had been acquaintances for a few years and of course she thought he was wildly attractive, but Tyrone was married to the French actress known simply as Annabella. By the summer of 1946 the Powers were separated. One evening he invited my mother to his house for a cocktail. When they said goodnight he kissed her and Mom went weak in the knees, never to recover.

Mother and Tyrone were separated at Christmas and she missed him so terribly that for New Year's she flew to Mexico, where Tyrone was filming a movie. She was in the middle of making *Green Dolphin Street* and wasn't supposed to leave, but at this point I don't think she cared. It just meant that much to her to be with him. Things were

At the Chanteclair nightclub. This was the first time they were caught out together by the press in Hollywood.

At the Mocambo in July 1947.

looking up back in Los Angeles. Annabella agreed to make their separation official by granting Tyrone a divorce. He and Mother might soon be free to marry.

Mother discovered she was pregnant. She was thrilled and didn't see, or didn't want to see until she looked back on it years later, that Tyrone didn't share her exhilaration. He seemed happy initially, but the light in his eyes faded quickly. It wasn't just their careers at stake. They were living in a different world. People didn't have children out of wedlock, especially not in the public eye, and Tyrone was still legally married to Annabella. Dreamer that she was, Mother toyed with the idea of going off to an island for nine months and coming back with a baby that she'd "found" (that happened to be the spitting image of Tyrone Power!).

Meanwhile Tyrone, who loved to fly, was still planning on taking a twelve-week airplane trip with stops in various countries across the Atlantic. He'd been arranging it for some time, without her.

The night before he left, Mother spent $10,000 on a lavish *bon voyage* party at Ciro's. She had orchids flown in from Hawaii and Jimmy Dorsey and his boys were in the bandstand. In September 1947, they parted with Mother pregnant. She was to let him know what she decided to do about the baby by a prearranged code message to be used when she and a group of friends were going to talk to Tyrone via a ham radio as he traveled. As their friends listened in unaware, she spoke the words that signaled to him that she had decided on an abortion, "I found the house today."

On a Sunday of tennis with friends.

At the airfield with Tyrone Power, who was preparing to take off on an extended tour across the Atlantic. She watched until his plane was out of sight.

Giving up the child of her greatest love was the hardest thing Mother ever did in her life.

Mother thought when Tyrone returned they would resume their relationship, he would be divorced, and they would have a baby under the proper circumstances later on. She flew to New York to meet him on his arrival. There she waited as days turned into weeks and he didn't come, as he said he would. While in New York, she was seen in the company of Frank Sinatra. The rumors reached Tyrone. Instead of landing in New York on his way back, he flew to Los Angeles. Mother returned home at once as soon as she learned where he was but there was no warm reunion. Tyrone was distant and finally worked up enough courage, with the help of brandy, to tell Mother that he'd fallen in love with another woman while he was in Europe. He had met Linda Christian in Italy. The actress had played a small role in *Green Dolphin Street*, the movie Mother was making when she dashed to Mexico for a rendezvous with Tyrone.

Mother did a lot more growing up then. By her mid-twenties she had already been through so much that when she found love like no other she'd known she was shattered by the loss of it. Mother talked to me about Tyrone as I got older. She blamed everyone else for their breakup, with Louis B. Mayer and Darryl F. Zanuck heading the list because they disapproved of a star from one studio dating a star from another. She wasn't angry about the way her relationship with Tyrone Power ended—just a year and a half after it began. She was hurt. But still more than that, later on she was just happy to have experienced that love, and to have spent that magical time with Tyrone.

This photo breaks my heart. He was going on a trip and she sensed that she was losing him more than just physically. Mom never got over him. She was very saddened by his death in 1958, at the age of forty-four.

"No man except possibly Tyrone Power took the time to find out that I was a human being, not just a pretty, shapely little thing. That could have been my fault—I didn't know myself."

Bob Topping

After Mother and Tyrone Power parted ways, she took refuge in New York in late 1947. That was when she began seeing Bob Topping. He courted her as only a millionaire could, culminating in his dropping a fifteen-carat marquise diamond ring in her martini glass by way of a marriage proposal. Bob made his first attempt to catch Mother's interest by filling her dressing room with roses and orchids during the making of *Cass Timberlane*. At the time she was wrapped up with Tyrone, so he got nowhere then. But when that relationship broke up, Bob reappeared to pick up the pieces.

Henry J. "Bob" Topping, Jr. was well-known for having family wealth from steel, railroads, and above all, tinplate. They called him the Tinplate Heir and his doings were always followed by the press. In the short time since those first flowers from Bob were delivered to Mother, he had been married and separated from actress Arline Judge (who seven

"If you want a blueprint, here it is: lose one love, snap right back and catch another."

Mother and Bob at a party following the premiere of *The Bishop's Wife*. This was their first date and Bob made it even more memorable by giving her a pair of diamond earrings on the way to the theater. She pointed out that she had her own, but he insisted and she switched earrings just before stepping out of the limousine.

years earlier had been divorced from Bob's brother, Dan). Mother was hurt and lonely and got caught up in the idea of marrying a millionaire and the notion of his glamorous social life, but she was not in love with Bob when he proposed. She told him so. He didn't care.

Bob didn't have the typical looks she went for, but he was a sweet man. Mom felt sure she could come to love him, and she actually did. He invited Mother, Gran, and me to Dunellen Hall, the Topping estate in Round Hill, Connecticut at holiday time. Bob's maternal grandfather, Daniel Gray Reid, had built the home as a wedding gift to Bob's parents. The twenty-eight room Elizabethan Mansion had stables, tennis courts, a greenhouse, a farm, a lake and was more luxurious than anything we had ever been exposed to. When I was there it was a six-hundred-acre property. It was later subdivided as Bob and his two brothers were forced to sell off acreage to continue their way of living.

At El Morocco in New York in 1948.

Surrounded by stars at the premiere of *All About Eve* in 1950. Although she was Hollywood royalty, Mother never had the kind of life the Toppings had in East Coast society. One perk was sitting in the owners' box at Yankees games. Bob's brother, Dan, owned the baseball team.

After the holidays we went back to California, where Mother made *The Three Musketeers* and decided that she would marry Bob. They were united in wedlock on April 26, 1948 at the home of Billy Wilkerson, the *Hollywood Reporter* publisher who discovered Mother in 1937. Befitting their deluxe courtship period, Mother and Bob's wedding and subsequent honeymoon were done in high style. After her early quick marriages in Las Vegas and Tijuana, she at last got her Big Event wedding, complete with police officers to control the media blitz. She bubbled over in champagne satin and lace, an original creation by Don Loper. I was the flower girl in an itchy little costume Mother ordered made for me in early nineteenth-century style.

The decorations at the reception were decidedly over the top. The guests were heady from the overwhelming odor of banks of flowers. Huge ice sculpture doubles for the bride and groom stood on a pedestal, locked in an embrace. I was most attracted to an immense buffet table on which was arranged a miniature European village fashioned out of food. Caviar hills were positioned on either side of little rivers complete with live goldfish. I don't recall if anyone dared eat the precious town, but I got to take the goldfish home.

Me in what Mom called my "1835 dress." She had a custom of giving objects little names that made sense to her. For instance, she had a silver powder box that had little pink "feet" that reminded her of a pig, so it was her "Piggy Box."

Reporters set upon the bridal party of best man Billy Wilkerson, the bride and groom, and matron of honor Sara Hamilton.

The marathon honeymoon vacation that followed started with Mother and Bob departing for the east coast. From New York they set sail aboard the *S.S. Mauretania* en route to England. From London they went to Paris and then to the French Riviera, where Gran and I joined the party. We made our way back to the United States on the *Ile de France* at the end of the season, when it was time for me to resume school. From the port of New York, we carried on to the Topping estate in Round Hill, but soon Gran and I went home to Los Angeles. Mother and Bob stayed for a few months, then went down to the Caribbean to fish and relax aboard Bob's yacht, the Snuffy, which he named after his favorite comic strip character. They finally made their way back to Los Angeles in June 1949.

Bob and Mother arrive at Southampton in May 1948.

Mother and Bob went deep-sea fishing on the Caribbean waters from Bob's yacht, the Snuffy.

While honeymooning, Mother went on suspension from MGM for refusing parts. For a time she was so enthralled by her new world that it took her away from the "work" mindset. But then I think she eventually got to be appalled by the life of the "idle rich," who seemed to her to be wasting their youths. Many movie people had a certain degree of wealth but they led entirely different lifestyles. They worked.

Keeping Mother's mind off work in the early part of 1949 was the fact she was pregnant with what would have been her and Bob's first child. After the baby was stillborn, they tried to brighten their spirits with the trip to Florida. This whole period lengthened their honeymoon by about five more months. Whatever the exact time frame, to me it was an eternity. Finally Gran basically told her, "You have a child back here. Come home." And they did. As a start to our new life together, we moved into a house on Mapleton Drive in the stylish Holmby Hills section of Los Angeles.

I called Bob "Papa." My own father was living in Europe at the time. I felt Bob really tried to become a father to me. He made me a gift of a boxer called Topper, not after Bob, but after Hopalong Cassidy's white stallion. Where my vision of Tyrone Power is vague, Bob was the first man in Mother's life that I was able to relate to one on one. He was generous and fun.

But when Bob drank, he turned into a completely different person. Bob adored dogs; he even raised them. When he was himself, he presented Mother with a diamond necklace by clasping it around the neck of my poodle, Tinkette, and sending her to Mother. During an episode of drinking, he picked up that same poodle and threw her across the room. No one would have believed that the biggest shadow on Bob's life concerned finances. He would blow $5,000 on a golf putt—he bet on anything. The appalled trustees of the Topping estate put Bob on a strict allowance, like many of his friends who lived on inherited wealth. They'd borrow from each other until their next check came.

It was Mother who ended up paying the bills at Mapleton. As she mulled over finances one afternoon, Gran sighed, "You just cannot afford to keep a millionaire." Mother certainly couldn't support all of us while on suspension from MGM, so she went back to work. Meanwhile Bob stressed about the financial constraints on him and drank. Mother tried to keep up with him and fights would

Bob and Mother on the location set of *Mr. Imperium*.

erupt. I never saw any of this. It was a big house. One day in 1952 I came home from school and Papa was gone. We spent the summer in Lake Tahoe to establish residency for a period of time required before one was able to file for divorce.

Life in this period was no easier for Mother than it was for Bob. She felt she was a failure for not being able to help his drinking problem. She suffered through two tragic stillbirths during their marriage. Both times she carried the babies for many months before going into premature labor. At age thirty-one she had just lost her third husband and experienced the loss of two babies she wanted desperately. Emotionally she was at her lowest point and she attempted

suicide by slashing her wrist and ingesting a handful of sleeping pills. The failure of her attempt made Mother bounce back quickly. She felt ashamed by it and regained a sense of value. Life went on.

Mother once summed up her marriage to Bob Topping in a single line: "Let's just say that I enjoyed being Mrs. Henry J. Topping, Jr." For a country without aristocracy, it was like gaining a title. She and Gran had always read about the doings of New York high society in magazines and newspapers. For a time, Mother blissfully lived the scenes of the exclusive world in which they once imagined themselves, until she realized it was all smoke and mirrors.

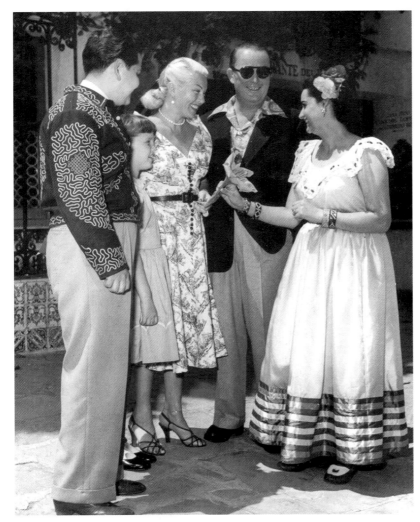

When we were Toppings, on a trip to Santa Barbara in 1951. Bob remarried later and settled into the life of a country gentleman on a farm in Idaho.

Bob was always game for attending movie industry functions with Mom.

Fernando Lamas

Tall, charming, and Latin, Fernando was typically someone Mother would adore. The attraction was instant. Already a star in Argentina, he had arrived at MGM in 1951, a year before he and Mother made *The Merry Widow* together. Theirs was a volatile relationship and when their tempers flared she might be given to take the next dance with another man, as Fernando fumed. That's exactly what happened at a party given by Marion Davies in 1952. Seated at the table with Mother and Fernando were the married couples Arlene Dahl and Lex Barker and Esther Williams and Ben Gage. Lex, who had just met Mother, asked her to dance and they danced. Fernando looked on, furious, and when they came back to the table he said something outrageous, suggesting Mother and Lex continue their affair in the bushes outside.

Mother and Fernando had an ugly argument that night, which led to the end of the romance. She never talked about him again. He was set to co-star in her next film, *Latin Lovers*, but Mother absolutely refused to work with him, so Ricardo Montalban was cast. Fernando moved on and married Arlene Dahl in 1954, a few months after Mother married Arlene's ex-husband, Lex Barker. Fernando, of course, later married the third woman at their table at the Marion Davies party, Esther Williams.

Mother and Fernando became intimate while making *The Merry Widow*.

In the fall of 1952, Mother and the recently divorced Argentinean sensation were the talk of Hollywood.

Lex Barker

Lex Barker came from a society background in New York. To his family's dismay, he left Princeton University to become an actor. Reaching Hollywood in the post-war years, he played numerous bit parts until donning a loincloth for the first time in 1949 to portray Tarzan in five installments of the adventure series.

Lex was married to Arlene Dahl at the time he invited Mother to dance and sparked the fight that broke up Mother and Fernando Lamas. A short time later, Lex's marriage to Arlene had come to an end and Fernando began a romance with Arlene that lead to their marriage in 1954. Lex and Mother began seeing each other in late 1952. The next year they took a vacation in Aspen and then continued to raise eyebrows by traveling together in Europe. Mother was to make *Flame and the Flesh* in Italy and Lex was also filming a movie. I spent my summer vacation with them, as did his two children, Lynne and Alexander (called Zan).

The press were onto the fact that we were staying at Lex's villa and they kept a vigil, knowing that a wedding was imminent. Mother had become a brunette for *Flame and the*

A serenata for the newlyweds in Italy.

Flesh, but she wasn't as unrecognizable as she hoped to be when she married Lex in Turino in September 1953. Lynne, Zan, and I were sent with the governess to the movies to watch *The Greatest Show on Earth*—in Italian, which none of us spoke. This was supposed to throw the reporters off the trail so that Mother and Lex could marry in privacy. The reporters weren't fooled. They followed Mother and Lex's car and converged on the town hall, where the vows were exchanged amid a throng of reporters. I was already late for the start of school so I returned home with Gran while they stayed in Europe, where Mother was going to make *Betrayed* with Clark Gable.

When they returned from abroad later that fall of 1953, Lex and his children moved in with us on Mapleton. Mother still desperately wanted another child of her own. She became pregnant, but the baby girl was stillborn after seven months. It was the third and last time Mother experienced the loss of a child. Nobody knew because people didn't discuss women's health issues openly in those days, but Mother suffered from endometriosis. She was required to have a hysterectomy late in 1956. The operation was anguishing to Mother because in the back of her mind she clung to the hope that one day she would have another baby.

Now and then Mother and Lex would take vacations, to Acapulco, Palm Springs, and Hawaii for the filming of *The Sea Chase*. I came to treasure their time away from home. He sexually abused me until I worked up enough courage to tell Gran. Gran called Mother over to her house and she learned what Lex had been doing to me. Back at Mapleton that night, as Lex lay in bed, Mother removed a gun from her nightstand and pointed it at his head. As she

One of Mother and Lex's first photos at home after returning from Europe.

Attending the wedding reception of Alan Ladd's daughter Carol in 1955.

held the revolver, poised at a distance, she thought of how pulling the trigger would destroy our lives and decided he wasn't worth it. She backed away and sat awake all night staring out the window, smoking and waiting. After he awoke with the early morning light she told him to get out of the house. He said, "Whatever your daughter told you, it's a lie." Mother had not even mentioned me. Lex was out of

From one of their trips to Acapulco Lex returned with a black German Shepherd named Pulco. He was fearsome to all but me. He's supervising the card playing at my side. At left is Lex's son, Zan.

our lives that February morning in 1957. Not long after, he went abroad and made films in Europe for many years. He came back to the U.S. in the early '70s and then died of a heart attack on the street in New York in 1973. Mother's comment: "It wasn't soon enough."

During a trip to Mexico.

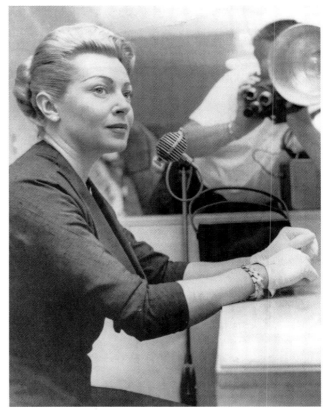

Separated since February, Mother obtained her interlocutory decree of divorce from Lex Barker on July 22, 1957. Officially, she attributed the split to his "uncontrollable temper" and physical abuse during an argument.

Johnny Stompanato

"The Paragraph" became our euphemism for the events of 1958 that made Mother and me notorious the world over. No matter what we accomplished in later years, just about everything ever written about us by the media had to include a paragraph about what happened on Good Friday, 1958. There is no gentle way to put it: at the age of fourteen, I stabbed and killed John Stompanato, my mother's boyfriend, during an episode of physical abuse. After decades of trying to suppress the memories and blotting out the mistaken information constantly printed, Mother and I both attempted to set the record straight in our respective autobiographies.

"John Steele" began his courtship of Mother by sending flowers to her at Universal while she was making *The Lady Takes a Flyer* in May 1957. After what had happened with Lex, Mother was "weak, lonely, persuadable"—always a dangerous mix of emotions for her. He was mysterious, terse, and powerfully built, but gentle and soft-spoken with both Mother and me early on. And generous. He gave Mother many pieces of jewelry and me a red Arabian mare named Rowena.

By the time Mother learned from friends that John's last name was not Steele but Stompanato, she was already too deeply involved. Everyone knew Johnny Stompanato was bad news. He had served in the military and once had a wife and son. When he got involved with Mother he was notorious as the bodyguard of mobster Mickey Cohen. He was also known by police for his specialty of winning

the trust of wealthy, lonely women, then draining their money. The more Mother learned of his lies and confronted him with them, the more possessive and threatening he became. Although her situation was ever more dangerous and he was soon extending his threats to include Gran and me, Mother remained confident she could handle it without intervention from the police. That would

With Stompanato in Acapulco, early 1958.

A month before Good Friday, Gran and I greeted Mother and Stompanato on their return from Mexico. Gran stayed away from the cameras.

bring reporters and horrible publicity down upon us. The thought of that still frightened her more than Stompanato did.

He traveled with her to England for the filming of *Another Time, Another Place*. There, Mother's makeup man, Del Armstrong, intervened after having to cover up the marks of physical abuse on her face. He contacted Scotland Yard and John was sent out of the country. After filming in England, Mother went to Acapulco in January 1958. Stompanato followed her there, and she had no way of

stopping him. She was frightened, and it was a terrible time for her but he insisted that she put on a happy front while they were there.

They were still in Mexico when Mother received word that she had been nominated for an Academy Award for *Peyton Place*. Gran and I attended the Oscar ceremony with her. She was darkly tanned from Acapulco and looked like a dream, while I felt great in my first grown-up dress. Mom didn't win, but it was still a wonderful evening. At the end of the night, Stompanato lay in wait for Mother at our bungalow at the Bel Air Hotel. From my own room I heard the blows.

I finished out the week of school before Easter vacation, when I would move into the house Mother had rented on Bedford Drive. By Good Friday Mother had told me of Stompanato's abuse. I had already heard too much and could see it in her face under the heavy makeup that poorly camouflaged the bruises and puffiness. She told me he was coming to the house that night and she was getting rid of him once and for all.

After John arrived, I sat in my bedroom writing a term paper while I heard his vicious threats carry though the house. In a panic I ran downstairs and into the kitchen, where on the sink counter lay one of the knives Mother had bought earlier in the day. The thought of scaring him away flashed into my mind. I went back up the stairs to Mother's bedroom and stood outside of her door for a few moments as Stompanato continued threatening to disfigure her. Suddenly Mother threw open the door. John came up from behind, his arm raised as if to strike. I took a step forward and he ran on the knife in my hands. Stompanato looked at me and said, "My God, Cheryl, what have you done?" before falling to the floor. He was dead within moments.

I ran to my bed, curled myself into a ball, and moaned as Mother tried to revive him. Soon Dad, Gran, doctors, Beverly Hills Police Chief Anderson, our attorney Jerry Geisler, followed by the press, were all on the scene. Amidst a swarm of reporters we were taken to the police station to give our statements. Everything was done stringently by the books out of fear it might be reported that the daughter of Lana Turner had received special treatment. I was booked on suspicion of murder and taken to juvenile hall. There were court hearings, an inquest, threats from Mickey Cohen (who arranged the publication of love letters from Mother to John), an unlawful death suit filed by Stompanato's brother, and custody battles between Mom, Dad, and the State of California. Through it all, the crush of the press was unprecedented. The coroner's inquest was a spectacle,

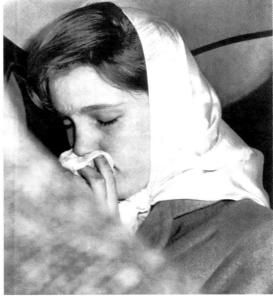

Comings and goings at Bedford Drive and the Beverly Hills police station on April 4, 1958.

I was brought to court hours before the hearing to avoid the press. When I drifted to a window a staccato of camera clicks shot my way before I jumped back.

televised and broadcast live on radio a week after Good Friday. It was ruled justifiable homicide and I was released into the custody of Gran.

I took a life and that is something that remains with me always, but it is a nightmare that my family and I lived through together and survived. The memories, in time, did not prevent us from moving on. Still, for nearly twenty years we took great pains to avoid all references to Good Friday, never really mentioning the horrible incident. Years later, on Thanksgiving Day in 1986, Mother said, "Cheryl, have I never told you how you saved my life? Gran's life? Your own life? How if it wasn't for you, I wouldn't be here today? Didn't I ever tell you how grateful I was?" She had never said so in words, I told her, but hearing her say them made me acknowledge that I had always felt in her a sense of gratitude.

At court with my father.

April 11, the coroner's inquest, with Gran, reporters, and a testimony to give. The crush looks like a movie, but it was our reality.

Mom smiles for the first time since Good Friday, after my custody hearing.

Fred May

Fred saw all sides of Mother, from the country wife to the glamorous movie star with a passion for crazy hats.

Mother radiates happiness with Fred at the Bal Montmartre, a benefit for the Los Angeles Music Festival, in 1959.

Mother was fonder of Fred May than any of her husbands. I, too, adored him. When Mother began seeing him, the press tried to make out that he was one of the May company family, but he was just a down-to-earth, stubborn German who brought much happiness back into our lives. Though Mother's friends had shown compassion and support through the Stompanato aftermath, she refused all social invitations and had not seen anybody outside of work for months.

One day a persistent friend talked her into joining a casual party at Malibu beach. It was there she was introduced to Fred May. He reminded her of Tyrone Power. He was also strong and stabilizing, and true to form, she fell in love quickly. They went ahead and obtained a marriage license, but they didn't take the next big leap because ultimately Mother was spooked about remarrying. Instead, she took the still daring move in those days of living openly with Fred. They got married over a year later because I was coming out of the reform school in which the courts had place me and they feared the judge would take a dim view of her living arrangements and not let me live with them.

Mother and Fred's wedding took place at the Miramar Hotel in Santa Monica on November 27, 1960. Gran and I were in attendance, with Fred's best man and Virginia Grey, Mother's friend since the early MGM days and her maid of honor. Fred, a real-estate broker, was not threatened by Mother's fame even though he preferred privacy to the limelight. He fell in love with the true woman and not the iconic Lana Turner. It is one thing for a daughter to see this, but it is nothing short of a miracle that he made a movie star like her feel that she was loved for herself and not for her image. That feeling of comfort and security freed her up to let her hair down again and show hidden sides of herself.

Fred brought out new interests in Mother, such as horseracing and running a ranch. He had a ranch in Chino where he housed his racehorses. They bought and sold horses. At one memorable auction, my very Southern Gran daintily bid farewell to a foal by waving her handkerchief, unwittingly raising the bidding price way up as the auctioneer misunderstood her gesture. Gran made the ranch her place to rest, but it was Mother who surprised all of us, herself included, with how she changed when she was there. She worked outside, painting, planting, and mowing the lawn. That was life at Fred's ranch. The makeup came off and she put on blue jeans. Fred was just what Mom needed then.

It is difficult to say what went wrong between them. For lack of any more tangible answer, Mother blamed the startling purchase of a car in her name by Fred shortly after she had given him a hefty financial loan. But in her heart she said that she regretted having let that break them up. "It was a stupid thing to get all upset over," she said. Their lifestyles were so opposite from each other. It sounds trifling, but I know that the fact that Mother was perpetually late drove Fred up the wall. He let her know it, which made Mother accuse him of acting like the Gestapo. They ended up being great friends and shared business interests long after their divorce, but ultimately they could not live together as man and wife.

I am thrilled to say Fred went on to a happy life. He continued to run a successful real estate business and later

One of my favorite shots. Mother is in curlers, giving Fred a fresh buzz cut.

Fred May and Mother enjoy Pacific lobster tail in Cabo San Lucas.

became mayor of Malibu. He also had a wonderful marriage to an artist named Julie that lasted the rest of his life. Mother and Fred maintained their friendship until his death in 1994.

Mexico and the Bullfighters

In Mexico during the filming of *Love Has Many Faces*, with Teddy Stauffer, Hugh O'Brian, and Gran.

As a rule, Mother liked to keep bullfighting a spectator's sport. Here she is tussling with a mechanical bull.

Mexico was Mother's top-rated vacation spot—Acapulco, Mexico City, Cabo San Lucas. She loved the people, the food, the music, the art, and the relative peacefulness of the resorts in those days. Among her friends there she was "Lanita," a nickname given to her by Teddy Stauffer, a well-known figure in Mexico who was once married to Hedy Lamarr. He owned the hotel where Mom always stayed in Acapulco, the Villa Vera.

Mother enjoyed the bullfights and of course the *matadors* in their glittering *traje de luces*. The bullfighters loved her, too, and they would make quite a ceremony of dedicating the bull to her. She occasionally dated the famous matadors of the day, in the way she was attracted to the musicians of the swing era. El Cordobes, known as "The Wolf," was an up-and-coming bullfighter when we met him. His career soared in Mexico and Spain. There was Jaime Bravo, who made an appearance in Mother's 1965 film *Love Has Many Faces*. Luis Miguel Dominguín was still more famous; handsome and dashing, his name was linked with Hollywood stars like Rita Hayworth and Ava Gardner.

After the bullfights we would go to a restaurant-nightclub where everyone gathered, including the *toreros*, the *picadors*, and the *banderilleros*. There was a small, semiprivate room with half walls around it where we always sat, near the matadors who would come and pay homage to Mother. We had a lot of fun making trips to Mexico in the 1962–65 period, but once she got caught up with Bob Eaton, our season in the sun of the bullfight arena was over.

Robert Eaton

In the mid-1960s, Mother was living in the Malibu Colony and socializing with a new set of friends that included Kem Dibbs, Peter Lawford, Carol Burnett, and Clint and Maggie Eastwood. Bob Eaton was part of this group as well. He was an attractive man who wined and dined her. Mother married Eaton at his family's home in Arlington, Virginia on June 22, 1965. He was ten years her junior, which made her hesitant to marry him, but to my dismay as her daughter, she didn't hold back about saying they had a great relationship in bed.

Eaton had come to Los Angeles to get in the movies, but never made it as an actor. After they married he wanted to try his hand at producing films, so she put him on an allowance and set him up in business with a huge suite of offices. Alas, no film productions materialized. I believed he was nothing more than an opportunist who was taking all he could get from her, but Mother didn't want to hear it.

Because of my distaste for Bob, she and I had our share of disagreements. As I was busy working with my father by this time, my solution was simply to stay away.

In 1967 she went on a USO tour in Vietnam. Later she went to Europe for several weeks to work on her television series, *The Survivors*. When she came back she found out that Eaton had been with other women and was squandering her money while she was gone. In 1969, she finally showed Mr. Eaton the door.

At a charity event in 1965. His glass eye, the left, is noticeable in this shot.

I attended a party given for the newlyweds by the furrier Abe Lipsey and his wife. Mom had worn the same pale coral dress on the day they wed.

With Bob Eaton at the Academy Awards in 1966.

Ronald Dante

Once Bob Eaton was out of the picture, Mother and I began seeing a lot of each other again. Sometimes we would go out together to the popular nightspots, like the Candy Store, the Whisky a Go Go, or the Daisy, but I was not with her the night she met Ronald Dante at the Candy Store. The hippie scene was all the rage. Dante had long hair, rode a motorcycle, and worked as a nightclub hypnotist. They married in Las Vegas in May 1969. By way of explaining how she got involved with him, Mother always wished she could prove that he had hypnotized her.

The answer, I believe, is that he made her feel young at a time when her pride had been dealt a profound blow by Eaton. The one and only thing I liked about her time with Dante was that he got her to wear blue jeans, fringe jackets, and boots. The sight of Mother riding a motorcycle was a hoot. She acted and looked younger and more "hip." It fit right in with the era.

Mother and Dante's relationship was over almost as quickly as it began. From the window of a restaurant of my father's, I had a view of the driveway of the apartment across the street that Dante still had from before they were married. I watched in amazement one night as police cars surrounded the building. Next I saw Dante being arrested. I got on the phone to Mother and told her what was happening. Hysterical, she asked me to rush over to her, which I did. Finally, he called her. There was reportedly an ambush with five shots fired at Dante. He gave little detail, but she arranged for his bail. I was never sure what had happened and she didn't discuss it, but she remained with him.

A few months after the wedding, Mother flew to San Francisco to do a charity event for the Presbyterian Children's Hospital, accompanied by Dante. He disappeared that night. Shortly after, we learned that he had flown back to Los Angeles and robbed her house. Then he actually returned later for jewelry that he missed the first time around. When the divorce came to trial the court found that, "Dante carried out a pattern of acts maliciously designed by him to defraud, oppress, and victimize Turner and to take advantage of her trust in him." Thankfully, we never heard from him again.

Mother said it best: "Husbands six and seven are best left unmentioned, except to say of the latter that he could have charmed the birds out of the trees—but so could a snake."

Of her marriage to Dante, Mother said, "I was ripe for it, and the wrong person came along and gave me this snow job and it was like, 'Oh, the savior,' which turned out to be worse than the inferno."

Though still beautiful entering her fifties, after Mother's divorce from Dante there were absolutely no more romances. That was her choice. Thereafter, secretaries, hairdressers, or friends acted as her escorts if one was needed. I knew Mother was lonely at times, but she didn't want to fall into her old pattern. She knew she loved to be in love. The idea of moonlight and roses and music and the fade out of the movie screen encapsulated the beauty of romance. But real life interfered with her dream. So one day she decided to fade-out that part of her life. And yet she was a perfectly content woman for her remaining twenty-five years.

I always got a kick out of the fact that some of the gentlemen that didn't make it into Mother's date book when she was young came sniffing around in the last few years. George Murphy, her co-star in *Two Girls on Broadway* and future U.S. senator, shocked Mother with a phone call sometime around 1989. She hadn't spoken with him in such a long time, so when he said it was George Murphy she said, "The senator . . . the dancer . . . my friend?" After standard pleasantries, he explained he was only visiting California for a short time and asked her out on a date. Mother, who hadn't heard from him in years and was not interested, said, "George! We've been through all this in 1940. Are you out of your mind?"

She didn't accept this invitation, or those other non-amours of the past who saw their chance now that she was a single older woman. They didn't know that Mother had discovered that the fulfillment she was looking for all those years was not in a relationship with another person, but within herself.

Practicing dance moves with George Murphy in 1940.

"My plan was to have one husband and seven children but it turned out the other way. I didn't plan seven husbands."

Friends

other's friends were funny, outgoing people. They would play card games, charades, croquet, have cocktails. Every game had to have a bet or a forfeit. And they entertained each other. I remember the voices of Billy Daniels, Sammy Davis, Jr., Frank Sinatra, and Judy Garland filling the house at Mother's parties. Some of the greatest talents of the day would sit around and entertain in their inimitable style. There was always laughter. She preferred people who didn't take themselves too seriously. Boredom was death to Mother. She pretty much lived her life not getting bored.

There was a certain naïveté in Mother that made her accept people at face value. She got in trouble for accepting people as friends too quickly numerous times, and yet she didn't become hardened. It always totally surprised her when she was proven wrong about someone because of her innate faith in people. If Mother trusted a person she was often generous to a fault. Consciously she knew it caused trouble, but the fact that she recognized this doesn't mean that her basic characteristic of believing the best of people ever changed.

If you were Mother's friend, you had her complete loyalty and she expected the same in return. When she felt she'd been betrayed, the door could close on a friend of years. This was a trait she shared in common with her great buddy Frank Sinatra. There were cases when she had the ability, mentally and emotionally, to completely wipe out of her world a person who had hurt her so she had no

Making waves with Judy Garland, Bonita Granville, Jackie Cooper, and on-and-off boyfriend Robert Stack. They were all part of her social group.

Mother was an expert at charades, a game played at most parties in those days. Her friend Ann Rutherford is behind her to the right.

Roller skating at a party in 1942 with Linda Darnell, Bud Abbott, and Lou Costello.

"I don't like to be by myself. I like to be where people are; like things going on around me. It's cozier."

Mother (in costume for *The Bad and the Beautiful*) visits Debbie Reynolds on the set of *I Love Melvin*.

Linda Darnell creates a pastel of Mother. Linda went along as a witness when Mother skipped off to Las Vegas and became Mrs. Stephen Crane.

more feeling for them, good or bad. It wasn't vindictive. The person was simply out of her life.

No one was to talk against those she loved. Having been the subject of gossip too often, she wasn't into that kind of chatter, but she was inquisitive. She had to know about everything her friends were up to. Mom asked a lot of questions and really listened to your answers. She could make someone feel that they were the most important person in her life. But she wasn't phony. Good or bad, she wasn't afraid to let friends know what she was thinking.

Most of Mother's friends during her MGM days were from the studio talent pool. Among the men were Gene Kelly, Van Heflin, Van Johnson, Jimmy Stewart, and Vincent Minnelli. Among the ladies the closest were Ava Gardner, Judy Garland, and Virginia Grey. Other MGM friends were Jackie Cooper, Ruth Hussey, Ann Rutherford, and Debbie Reynolds. Holmby Hills neighborhood friends were Sonja Henie, Joan Bennett and Walter Wanger, Humphrey Bogart and Lauren Bacall, among a star-studded list. Of her glamour girl "rivals" she was closest to Betty Grable. At the height of their fame, fans who ran into them would mistake

Mother adored the telephone, especially in her last years, when it became the all-important connection to her friends. When I bought her a cordless phone in the 1980s she reacted as if she'd been handed a million dollars.

them for each other occasionally and Mother happily obliged them with a "Betty Grable" autograph.

Other close friends were Susan Hayward, Evie Wynn Johnson, Vincent Price, Cesar Romero, Dean and Jeanne Martin, Kirk and Anne Douglas, Fred MacMurray and his wife, June Haver. Ross Hunter and Jacques Mapes became part of Mother's circle after *Imitation of Life*. Among her Malibu beach friends were Carol Burnett and Clint Eastwood, and Lily Tomlin at the end. Mother's greatest friends were the people she worked with every day—hair and makeup artists. She built a crew around her that shared her sensibilities

and she was most comfortable with them. But she wasn't outgoing with people she didn't know. When she went out she was always with friends and wasn't interested in meeting strangers. Reaching out to new people was always difficult for Mother, but especially in her later years.

Mother spent the end of her life in her condo in Century Park East. She was ill, but kept in touch with people by telephone. It made her feel she was still in her friends' lives. When she became too ill to talk, I told her many "telephone friends" to continue calling and leaving messages. She enjoyed listening to the voices of her friends to the end.

With Ann Miller during the Punta del Este film festival in Uruguay, 1957. Mother thought "Annie" was the best dancer MGM had and terribly underappreciated.

Visiting with Dean Martin on the set of *Flame and the Flesh*.

John Garfield and Mother became friends while making *Postman*. I can dispel rumors that they didn't like each other. They socialized outside of work. I remember him at my birthday parties.

Clint Eastwood became a good friend of Mother's when she was living in Malibu. Here they dine with her husband, Bob Eaton, in Rome in 1966.

Laughing it up with Frank Sinatra, Peter Lawford, Xavier Cugat, and Carmen Miranda at Cugat's party following the premiere of his film, *Holiday in Mexico*.

She's Funny That Way

I can still hear the sound of my mother's laughter with a group of friends. If I needed to find her at a party, I could usually follow the sound of the laughter. One of her greatest joys was when she could get a friend to do a true belly laugh. It could usually be accomplished in the way she told stories, complete with imitations of people's voices and mannerisms. Laughter and Mother were a constant in my memory. Once the panic of a problem was over she breathed a sigh of relief, moved on, and laughed about it. Our whole family could laugh at anything once the trouble was over. It maintained our sanity.

Virginia Grey

Rich Man, Poor Girl was the first movie in which Mother and Virginia Grey both appeared, though Mother was not in Virginia's one scene. It's possible they met on the set of this film, but more likely they met through mutual friends on the MGM lot. Virginia was beautiful and a terrific supporting actress, but never became a star, though Mother certainly helped Virginia's career. Any movie she could get her into, she did. As a result, Virginia appears in nearly every one of Mother's films of the '60s.

There was a small group of people with whom Mom remained friends all the while I was growing up. Virginia Grey was among them. She was a staunch Catholic, had an angelic face, but swore like a truck driver. Apparently that is how Clark Gable liked his women. Carole Lombard was known for this as well. After Carole's death, Virginia and Gable had a long relationship through the '40s and '50s, and many, including Virginia, were surprised when he married Lady Sylvia Ashley in 1949, and then Kay Spreckels (Williams) in 1955. Virginia was heart-broken. She never did marry and she drank more than was good for her, but she was a terrific lady. Virginia was maid of honor at Mother's wedding to Fred May, and she was considered part of the family.

Virginia and Mother posed for a series of photos showing old fashions versus new. The girls are ready for afternoon tea and cocktails, respectively.

Virginia Grey was one of Mother's dearest friends since 1938.

Judy Garland

Judy and my mother at the Mocambo in 1941.

Judy, who was no longer employed by MGM, visits Mother at the studio in 1952. Our homes on Mapleton looked into each other's kitchens. Judy used to come over and sit in the bathroom while Mother did her makeup.

Judy and Mother were very close from the time they made *Love Finds Andy Hardy*, but Judy was a bit jealous of her in the early MGM days for a few reasons. Louis B. Mayer called Judy his Little Hunchback, so she felt unglamorous and unattractive next to Mother. But the number one reason was Artie Shaw, whom Judy thought she was going to marry. Mother always felt guilty about that, although later she would say that she had saved Judy from a fate worse than death. Their friendship survived Artie.

Judy and Mother used to go out all the time. Both were absolutely fascinated by Marlene Dietrich. Like two giggling schoolgirls, they'd dress themselves up as sophisticated as possible to go to a gay nightclub on the Sunset Strip where Dietrich would go to see her girlfriend, who was a singer. They were intrigued by the whole scene and thrilled when Dietrich would invite them to join her table.

Lana's and Judy's mothers were both always around, as very present, but very opposite influences in their lives. Judy had a stage mother. Perhaps her mother didn't know the possible effects of pills? Looking back it's a disgrace, but nobody in those days disparaged what the studio did to Judy by starting her on the uppers and downers that led to disaster. They never tried anything like that with Mother. She showed up on time and ready to work even if she had been out the night before. She was so full of energy that she never had to take "wakeup pills." A cup of coffee was more than enough.

Ava Gardner

Mother and Ava Gardner were a dynamite pair. Of all of her friends, I think they were the closest in temperament and outlook on life. They shared many of the same tastes and even fell for many of the same men, yet they never let it affect their friendship. Both loved all things Latin. Bullfights thrilled them. They could rumba, samba, or dance the flamenco from sundown to sunrise. Even their final years were similar. Both were world-class beauties who ended up no longer wanting romantic attachments, were somewhat reclusive, and hooked on the telephone. They were telephone friends up until Ava passed away in 1990.

My favorite of Mother's Ava Gardner stories was the one that turned into a Keystone Cops comedy while Mom was making use of Frank Sinatra's Palm Springs home, Twin Palms. He had loaned his house to her for the weekend and it got her caught in the middle of one of Frank and Ava's domestic feuds.

The action began over a hundred miles west of Twin Palms, at the Sinatra home in Los Angeles, where the couple had gotten into a fight that Frank ended on a wild exit line, telling Ava that if she needed him he would be in Palm Springs, in bed with Lana Turner. He proceeded to drive off into the night and Ava proceeded to follow him on the road to Palm Springs, which with the cars and roads available in those days, was a four-hour trip.

At Twin Palms, Mother was accompanied by her business manager and friend, Ben Cole. They were about to dig into a late supper of fried chicken when they heard noises that turned out not to be prowlers, but Ava, hoping to catch

her husband in the act. Mother invited her to join them for cocktails and chicken. Before long, an enraged Frank burst through the door. Frank and Ava got into a heated argument and soon Frank was throwing everything that belonged to Ava out into the driveway. Mother and Ben ran for the door,

Ava and Mother at the Ribbon Ball, 1951.

abandoning the fried chicken spread. They drove around a while and then Mother insisted they go back for her chicken. Back at Twin Palms, the police had reached the scene. Amid flabbergasted officers, battling Sinatras, and a driveway littered with clothes, books, and cosmetics, Ben Cole walked up, meekly asking for the return of Lana Turner's chicken.

In spite of the drama, Mother had no desire to return

home. Another rental was not to be found in town. When the dust settled and Twin Palms was empty again, Mother and Ben had their stay in Palm Springs, enjoying the hospitality of Frank. Wired, without a wink of sleep and too many drinks, Ava had set off on the long road back to Los Angeles, with Frank tearing up the road behind her.

In the late '40s and throughout the '50s, Ava was a big star at MGM just as Mother was. I always wanted them to do a movie together while they were both young and vibrant. There was talk of them making a film called *My Most Intimate Friend* in 1954, but nothing ever came of the idea. In the right parts they would have been on fire together. In Mother's mind, the truly great beauties were brunettes. To

Ava, Fernando Lamas, and Mother at the Marion Davies party in 1952.

her, Ava was a testament to that belief and I was witness to the simple fact that with all that hair and not a speck of makeup, Ava was magnificent looking.

Mother was thrilled to have a friend in London, where some of *Flame and the Flesh* was filmed. Ava was in town making *Knights of the Round Table*.

I remember Mother and Elizabeth being very close, especially when Elizabeth was married to Michael Wilding in the mid-'50s. Mother also saw quite a bit of Elizabeth and Richard Burton when she was in Europe in the '60s. Mother, of course, had a thing about jewelry and she was green-eyed over the Krupp Diamond that Elizabeth flashed around in those days. "Well, I saw the Diamond," Mother would tell me. "It's large, but I have ones that sparkle more." There was a bit of rivalry in that sense but Mother liked Elizabeth and supported whatever she did over the years—with the exception of her marriage to Larry Fortensky.

In 1966, with Richard Burton and an adoring Elizabeth Taylor at the David di Donatello Awards, where she recieved an award for *Madame X*.

Mother christened our home on Perugia with a Halloween party in 1944. Gene Kelly showed up ready for a ballgame.

Costume and theme parties were very popular in Hollywood. Here she plays the xylophone at one in 1940.

At the Bal Masque, a benefit for St. Johns Hospital in 1950, with Bob Topping and Gloria Swanson.

At the Bal Masque. Loretta Young, Irene Dunne, and Mother's masks were named the first, second, and third best, respectively.

With Fox studio head Darryl Zanuck at a party Mother threw for Tyrone Power in 1947.
Zanuck and his wife, Virginia, were among Tyrone's best friends and the couples spent a lot of time together.

With Eleanor Powell and Mickey Rooney at Mickey's birthday party in 1941.

At a party in 1957 with Ronald Reagan.

Close Encounters

The Persistent Prince

There was no romance between Mother and the son of the fabulously wealthy Aga Khan, spiritual leader of the Ismaili Moslems, but her encounter with him is a great story. Aly Khan pursued her while she was in Paris with Bob Topping. He courted her with red roses, and when someone like Aly Khan sends flowers, it's no joke. Roses filled her and Bob's hotel room at the George V and spilled over into the hall.

The fact that Mother was honeymooning made absolutely no difference. The continental prince simply told her that she could bring her husband along to dinner. "No, I cannot," was her answer. He insisted until she finally convinced him that there was no chance she would ever join him for dinner, with or without Bob. Aly Khan found consolation when he met Rita Hayworth about a month later. Rita was single after her breakup with Orson Welles and traveling in Europe solo. She and Aly Khan married the next year.

Mother picked up her all-time favorite necklace the day Bob Topping took her to Cartier after their fight over Aly Khan. Here she wears the diamond piece at the premiere of *Guys and Dolls* in 1955.

Bob was furious over Aly Khan's open courtship of his bride. He wasn't familiar with the prince's reputation and found it impossible to believe that any man would pursue a bride on her honeymoon. He was convinced that Mother had encouraged him. They had a terrible fight that ended with Mother throwing a precisely aimed crystal ashtray across the room, resulting in a black eye for Bob. The contrite husband made up for their quarrel by taking her to Cartier. By way of apology he told her to pick out any bauble she desired. Mother's eyes surely lit up. "I want that, don't I, darling?" she said by the watches. "I want that, don't I, darling?" she said when they moved to earrings. Finally, she told me, "I stopped going 'I want that, don't I, darling?' because I realized that I was probably going to be paying for them in the end!"

The Copycat

The first lady of Argentina was fascinated by Lana Turner. Observing her from afar, Eva Perón copied fashions and a number of the unique hairstyles for which Mother was known. It became troublesome for Mother when she entered Perón territory in February 1946. Customs seized all of her jewelry and held her up for hours on end. She learned that every piece was photographed, to be copied later, before the diamonds and assorted precious stones were returned to her. Her last encounter during that visit to Argentina was at a party at which Eva Perón was present. Feeling Perón's eyes openly fixed on her all night, Mother couldn't wait to get away.

Eva Perón, the First Lady of Argentina, was known to model her look after Lana Turner.

The Corners of Lana Turner's Eyes

Mother took a holiday weekend to Carmel at a time when Salvador Dalí was in residence. Great artist that he was, it was a thrill for Mother to meet him over cocktails and an even bigger thrill when he announced that he wanted to paint her. "My heart was racing," she remembered in the retelling, "I could hardly keep my seat." Then Dalí grabbed her hands, leaned over and with his oiled, shoulder-length hair hanging down, looked Mother in the eyes and told her that he wanted to paint only the corners of her eyes. Mother would continue her story with gestures, "At which point, I stood up, flung his hand off of mine, and said, 'Why would you want to do that?!' to which Dalí replied, 'Oh, because you have the most beautiful corners of your eyes I have ever seen.'" It was the last thing in the world Mother expected to hear and she remained flabbergasted by the memory. "At the time I had a beautiful profile. I was known for it and he wanted to paint the corners of my eyes!" The joke in our family was that if ever you see a Dalí with two spots that look strangely familiar, they are the corners of Lana Turner's eyes.

Surrealist painter Salvador Dalí had a thing about the corners of Mother's eyes.

The Bullfighter and the Shoe

Manolete, considered by some to be the all-time greatest bullfighter, was the star of one of the great romantic anecdotes of Mother's life. She loved to tell it and had a way of acting out the story that put you right at the scene. Mom was getting ready to go out for the evening during a trip to Mexico City in the mid-'40s. Having slipped on her evening gown, she was fumbling to fasten the buckle on her ankle strap at the moment there was a knock at the door of her hotel room. She opened the door to three men whom she thought were from the hotel. She asked the dashing man at center who was carrying a bouquet of flowers, "Can you help me with my shoe, please?" The men at his sides tried to stop him but he bent over and struggled with the buckle as she had a moment earlier, while she balanced herself with her hand on his back. Meanwhile, the men flanking him seemed very uptight and stood ramrod straight through what was apparently an offensive scene to them. She finally realized this man, who spoke very little English, was not from the hotel but a guest coming to pay his respects with a gift of flowers. His men squired him away. The following afternoon she found out the identity of her handsome cavalier as he walked majestically to the center of the ring at the bullfight. The matador dedicated the bull to her. The celebrated Manolete was the gentleman who had fixed Mother's shoe.

Happy Birthday, Mr. President

When she traveled to Washington D.C. with a contingent of stars invited to Franklin D. Roosevelt's fifty-ninth birthday ball in January 1941, Mother's greatest thrill was meeting her idol, the president himself. She stood by while First Lady Eleanor cut the cake, but Mother only met Franklin Roosevelt briefly. Her heart raced as they were introduced. He seemed impressed by her, too, when he admired and complimented her on her gown, which she had borrowed from the MGM wardrobe department. He sighed about being incapable of dancing with her, but putting a twinkle in FDR's eyes was a memory Mom cherished all of her life.

This was the gown that impressed Roosevelt.

The president's gala. Mother and Deanna Durbin assist Eleanor Roosevelt with the birthday cake.

More Milk for Lana

Andy Warhol, a great fan of Mother's, met her for the first time at the Deauville Film Festival in 1981. He put his signature stamp on Lana Turner in two of his silkscreen printings. The pop artist worked in many different media, including film. He made over sixty movies, including *More Milk, Evette*, which was influenced by the Stompanato scandal and is sometimes called *Lana Turner*. The 1966 underground film starred "Warhol Superstar" Mario Montez in drag. After their meeting at Deauville, Mother encountered Warhol on at least two other occasions, once during her book tour in 1982 and then at the *Love Boat* party in 1985, when she was feted as the show's 1000th guest star. Besides presenting her with a plaque, he unveiled his silkscreen printing of an image of Mother from her trip to Egypt the previous year. His more famous Lana Turner work was made from a beautiful portrait from *The Sea Chase*.

When he came back from the Deauville Film Festival in 1981, Warhol said the highlight of the event was meeting Lana Turner.

Lifestyles

Home was always Mother's haven and she had many of them, in the tradition of her nomadic parents. When she earned enough money from her movie work for her and Gran to move out of the home of Gran's friend Gladdy, where they had been staying since their arrival in Los Angeles, she rented a Spanish-style house on Kirkwood Drive in Laurel Canyon and they furnished it exclusively in white. In 1939 they leased another Spanish-style dwelling that was memorable for a strikingly ornate staircase that led to the upstairs of the split-level home. Mother lived here with Gran for only a short time before her marriage to Artie Shaw.

At home on San Ysidro Drive.

"I was always the one who bought the house."

When he married Mother, Artie Shaw owned a picturesque ranch house secluded in Coldwater Canyon, overlooking Beverly Hills. A reporter came over for a Sunday afternoon with the Shaws at home. For reasons that have always been a mystery to us, Artie's mission was to de-glamorize Lana Turner. It is evident in the modest gabardine suit and plain hairstyle she wears in some of the photographs that accompanied the magazine article. The write-up itself is positive, per custom of the day, but in retrospect it is littered with hints to their inevitable separation. Artie inexplicably dropped lines before the reporter like, "I hardly know whether I'm married to you or to MGM." He clearly did not want her to be the only thing he had ever known her to be in their short period of acquaintance, which was a busy MGM actress.

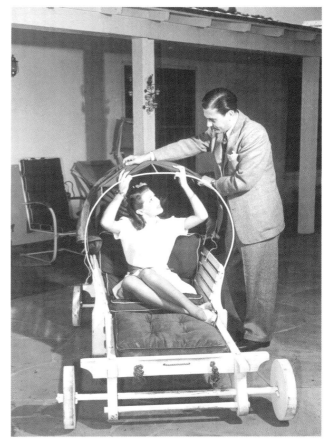

The Shaws at home on Summit Ridge Drive.

Mother took the maid, Maybelle, with her when she moved out of Summit Ridge.

Mother did indeed love yellow, as shown by her bedroom in 1942. The room had Priscilla curtains and plenty of organdy ruffles.

The first home Mother ever owned was a small ranch-style house that sat in a cul-de-sac at 662 MacCulloch Drive in Brentwood. Greta Garbo, Irene Dunne, and Deanna Durbin were her neighbors. This home was a favorite of hers. It held warm memories of parties with musicians and simpler times in her life. She shared it with Gran, a Pekinese named Puchin, and her Great Dane, Billy. My father moved in when they were first married and it was here he crashed his car into the front hedges in a show of desperation to win her love.

When Mother's salary hit $4,000 a week, she invested in a large Georgian-style house on Perugia Drive. She would discover it was too close for comfort to the ninth hole of the Bel-Air Country Club, but it was not stray golf balls but growing pains between Mother and Gran that triggered our next move in 1946.

The residence on MacCulloch, where she lived with Gran, and later my father, was a favorite.

At twenty-five, Mother wanted to live in her own house, apart from Gran, as do many women in their twenties. But this was Hollywood and she was Lana, so she went about getting her desired housing arrangements in a slightly outrageous fashion. She decided that the only way to get Gran out was to sell the house and buy a smaller one so Gran clearly wouldn't fit and would move into her own apartment. This problem and all of the details were left in the hands of Mother's attorney and ex-fiancé, Greg Bautzer, while she went on her trip. Eventually Greg found us another Spanish-style home on Crown Drive in Brentwood. There was just room enough for Mother, my nanny, and me. Greg followed through with the second part of his duty, finding a nice apartment for Gran, to which Mother paid the rent.

I can still close my eyes and walk through the grand house on Mapleton Drive that we moved into in September 1949. Situated on four acres of the posh Holmby Hills neighborhood, it was christened "Mapletop" during Mother's marriage to Bob Topping. But she had paid most of the bills and remained living there for years after they parted. Purchased for $97,000 at the time, it was the most "movie star" home

120 South Mapleton Drive

she ever owned. Our kitchen looked directly into that of our neighbors, Judy Garland, her husband Sid Luft, and daughter Liza. Other famous neighbors were Joan Bennett and Walter Wanger; Humphrey Bogart and Lauren Bacall; the Alan Ladds; and Sonja Henie (who was once married to Bob's brother, Dan Topping). Art Linkletter, the television host, lived down the street. He quipped, "I was the only person on this block that I had never heard of."

Before the Georgian facade of the two-story house was a front lawn area marked by an enormous pine tree and a circular drive. The exterior had bay windows with green

shudders and a stately red door on which was embossed "Mapletop" in brass letters. The interior of the home had a French Regency feel. I believe it was designed by Paul Williams. The floor of the entry hall was tiled in alternating rows of black and white and looked up to a mesmerizing crystal chandelier and a sweeping staircase with wrought iron banisters.

Mother's room was above the living room, facing the front of the house. In the back was a vast porch which was later converted into her closet. Hers was a sprawling lavender and gray bedroom that had a beautiful cream marble fireplace with gray veining. The adjoining bathroom was Louis XVI, pink and gold with chandeliers and gold faucets.

Downstairs, large double doors opened to the formal dining room with a long mahogany table that seated eighteen. The walls were Italian murals of foliage, rivers, and clouds, painted in soft shades of blue and green. Though this grand dining room was seldom used, the house was wonderful for entertaining. We had a loggia and bar room that featured a mirrored bar large enough for guests to sit around. This was a casual area with a fireplace, television, couches, and a dropdown movie screen behind which was a small projection room. Above the loggia was the broad balcony that later became her closet. It was opposite my bedroom of blue and pink.

Outside, the grounds had a pool and pool house, tennis court, rose garden, and play area with my swings and

The pool area and grounds of Mapleton made a personal setting for many photo shoots in the '50s, but she never let press cameras inside of Mapleton.

playhouse. When Bob was with us we also had a dog run for his boxers. At the end of the right side of the property was a vegetable garden and the wall between our house and Judy Garland's. The other property adjoining ours belonged to *Amos 'n' Andy* radio star Charles Correll.

Mother made additions to the house over the years, including three bedrooms and baths above the garages and her own remodeled bedroom. When she was single again after Lex it was really far too large for us. Eventually Mother sold it and took up temporary residence in an apartment in Westwood while I was at boarding school.

When we were getting ready to sell the house on Mapleton, Mother took a duplex apartment on Devon Drive in Holmby Hills. She had it decorated strikingly in black, white, and red. She had recently divorced Lex, her contract at MGM was up, and she had just met John Stompanato. She said the color scheme matched her mood. Then she went to England to film *Another Time, Another Place*.

730 North Bedford Drive was our next address. The home had been custom-built for Laura Hope Crews, the actress who played Aunt Pittypat in *Gone With the Wind*. This was the scene of the Stompanato scandal and we lived here for only a matter of days. Mother moved into a bungalow on Roxbury Drive that turned out to be the site of her personal and professional resurrection. It was here that she was courted and won over by Ross Hunter and Fred May. Ross brought her the biggest hit of her career in *Imitation of Life* and Fred brought her what were probably her best years of married life.

Our house at the corner of Bedford and Lomitas, the site of the Stompanato scandal. Mother's bedroom is at far left. It was all in pink, and I remember the fresh pink roses that sat on her dresser that day.

Mother, Gran, and me with Gus and Babe, the caretakers of Fred's ranch. Mother was so relaxed there, and with Fred in general, that she's actually wearing curlers.

Mother mowing the lawn! This is the paddock behind Fred's guest house, where they usually had sheep.

Mother painting a ladder.

During weekends at the Circle M, Fred's horse ranch in Chino, Mother was a different person. She wasn't a movie star but a rancher's wife, abandoning the jewelry, the Ferragamos, and most of the makeup for overalls, loafers, hoes, fishing rods, and paint brushes. She worked hard at the ranch and enjoyed it. For permanent residency, Mother and Fred bought a property in the Malibu Colony and then spent six months reconstructing it. The foyer of the house was a recreation of the Mapleton entryway, with black and white tile floors, gilt mirror, and Bombay chest.

After her divorce from Fred, Mother remained and the Malibu Colony house is where she and Bob Eaton resided during their marriage. Even after their split she had no intention of moving until a developer knocked on her door one day and offered her $350,000 cash for it. When she eventually accepted, she was given thirty days to vacate.

At home at the beach in Malibu.

Her next residence was on Fern Drive. It was a sprawling one-story house, very mid-century, with a great view. This is where Mother lived during her strange, short-term marriage to Ronald Dante. She shook off those memories by moving from Fern to Edgewater Towers. Situated at Sunset and the Pacific Coast Highway, the penthouse was later changed to a condominium and Mother wasn't sure she wanted to buy, triggering a final move.

The Ivory Tower

Like Edgewater Towers, the Century Park East penthouse apartment that Mother moved into in the early '70s was converted to a condo. This time, however, she said nothing could make her endure one more move. It had a fabulous view and was decorated as she loved by Vince Pastere. It was her "Ivory Tower" until the end of her days, the place of which she never tired.

Mexican art adorned the walls of Mom's home on Fern Drive, 1969.

At her Century City condo in 1974.

Cars

Mother got her first driving experience at the age of six, when her father let her take the wheel on the road to San Francisco. They were both steering until he nodded off and Gran shrieked at the realization that her little girl was driving alone—and actually keeping them on course. Mother said that set the tone for her future. "My life has been a series of emergencies in which I have had to take the wheel without knowing where I was going or how to run the machine."

From that momentous experience sprung Mother's love of driving and from the time she got her first red Chrysler convertible in 1939 she loved cars. Whatever the make, she always had to have the newest and the most extravagant model. Fast cars thrilled her so she racked up a multitude of speeding tickets, though I don't remember her ever having an accident. She was a good driver and liked to drive herself places rather than be chauffeured. It wasn't until the '60s

Posing by her first car.

that she began to accept the luxury of having a studio car pick her up. I recall she had Jaguars; a Mercedes with gull wings; Cadillacs, usually convertibles, from the '60s on; and a Karmann Ghia that won the Concorde de Elegance in Santa Barbara. She brought one of the first Volkswagen buses back from Germany in 1954. It was for my governess to take me to school. Oh, how it embarrassed me! No one had ever seen one before and it was a sight. I used to have her drop me off a block away from the school.

Behind the wheel in Paris, 1953.

Traveling in Papa Topping's green Jaguar. I loved its speed. Mother didn't, even though she loved to drive fast herself.

Pets

Puchin and Molly were the favorites, but over the years there was a parade of dogs, including a Great Dane, a Bedlington Terrier, a German Shepherd, a Weimaraner, a Dachshund, Toy Poodles, Boxers, and two Pomeranians.

Puchin was Mother's Pekinese, who became famous by appearing on a 1940 cover of *Life* magazine with his mistress.

Molly was my Lhasa Apso, and her "Grandpuppy." Mother loved it so much she bestowed upon it a solid gold and emerald collar of her own design. They are pictured here in 1994.

Travels

Mother had an ear for the romance languages. In France, Italy, or Latin American countries she would absorb enough of the language to get around after a couple of days. She was not very fond of Europe. London was too cold and too damp for her. She felt a great affinity for Egypt, where she went to film a segment for *Lifestyles of the Rich and Famous* in 1984. Mexico was her favorite getaway. She was a sun worshipper and tanned very easily. She loved the beach and even lived there for a time.

Taking Egypt by camel, 1984.

Posed as a work of art herself at the Louvre in Paris, 1953.

Fans in New York would always gather outside of her hotel (usually the Pierre or the Sherry Netherland). Here she is shown during a trip east in 1971.

Mother also loved Hawaii. She went there for the first time in July 1940 after her separation from Artie Shaw. Much later on, when she took trips there to visit me in the '80s, she would modify her usual "camera-ready" style to coincide with the laidback atmosphere. When it came to dining outside of home, Hawaii seemed to be the only place where we could have what she called "a simple dinner with my family." People recognized her and would wave to her on the beach, but they left her alone in restaurants.

She liked the desert too. Mother made frequent trips to Palm Springs, beginning with Artie Shaw. Later on we used to borrow Frank Sinatra's home, Twin Palms, when he wasn't occupying it. She was much more a city person than a country girl. She liked going to New York and always considered San Francisco home, as she lived there from age six to fifteen. Mother used to take Gran and me there for visits and her love of the city passed to me. I lived in San Francisco for four years and Mother visited regularly. When I was working on my book we would talk and talk and then go out together. She loved going to see the famous cabaret show Beach Blanket Babylon and wanted to join them on stage for a guest appearance.

She and Fred May loved to go deep-sea fishing in Cabo San Lucas.

Using her fishing gear to stand a beer upright.

Her first trip to Hawaii was an escape after her failed first marriage to Artie Shaw. The strain shows on her face in most of the photos, except when she got on the water at Waikiki Beach.

Winter wonderlands were not typically where Mom would spend a vacation, but she enjoyed a trip to Aspen, Colorado in 1953.

Carnival in Rio

A trip to South America, begun in January 1946, was one of Mother's most memorable. It included travels through Argentina, Peru, and Brazil, during which she was accompanied by a journalist friend of hers, Sara Hamilton. She found out how much South Americans adore blondes. The police in Rio would break up mobs of as much as two thousand people that gathered outside her hotel.

Mother reached the Brazilian pleasure capital at carnival time. She danced the Samba in the streets until dawn, intoxicated by the music and the smell of perfumed ether that the men there once carried on handkerchieves. She climbed into bed early the next morning and drifted off to sleep until being awakened by a pounding headache and a room that reeked of ether. The smell clung to her clothes so overwhelmingly that they had to be discarded.

In South America, 1946.

"This is what? I want a high rise!"

Mother always liked to stay at a certain hotel when in San Francisco. She had her standards. Once when she visited us her usual place was full, so we arranged for her to stay at a lovely new place. It was a mansion that had been converted into a hotel. When her car pulled up in front of this house she asked, "What is this? Where are we?"

"This is it," said the driver.

"This is what?"

"Your hotel, Miss Turner."

"Oh no, it's not. I want a high rise!"

On the terrace of my San Francisco apartment in 1987.

Breakfast in the dining room, with the ocean behind us. | Lunch consisted of burgers and grilled cheese by the hotel pool. | Stopping for a snack when we went fishing.

Three Little Pigs

We had a fun family weekend in Santa Barbara in 1951. I remember the drive up from Los Angeles in three cars. Papa Topping and I led the caravan in his green Jaguar. It only sat two so Mother drove behind us and my governess was in a third car behind her loaded full with luggage. "Faster, Papa, faster!" Driving fast thrilled me. Mother grew hysterical and made me drive up the rest of the way with her.

After a stop in Malibu we reached our destination, the Biltmore Hotel in Santa Barbara, where we settled in for what seemed a weekend of non-stop eating. Mother, Bob, and I had all gained weight under the tutelage of André, our new French chef. He was responsible for our nourishment and he didn't kid around about his work. Trained well by him, we ate heartily and often on this trip and brought back photographic evidence. To me this was always our "Three Little Pigs" trip.

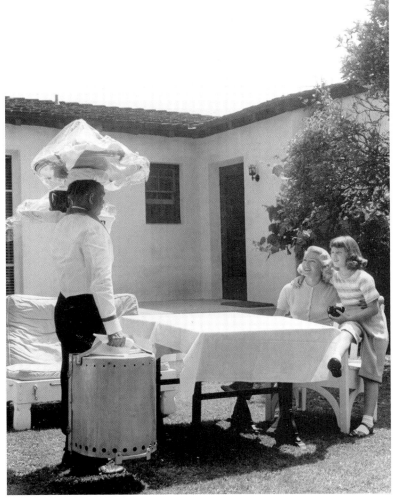

A hotel waiter brings us our next spread, on his head.

Captured outside of Ciro's in 1944.

Restaurants: Mother was known for frequenting the Brown Derby, sometimes for both lunch and dinner. It broke her heart when the venerable establishment was torn down in 1992. That was her favorite for more casual dining. Dressing up to go to Ciro's and Romanoff's was a popular occasion with her. Later on she was also a regular at the Luau; Spago's in the 1980s and '90s; the Smoke House in Toluca Lake; and Le Dome for French. Near her home in Malibu she loved Jack's at the Beach and Chez Jay's.

Perfume: Mother's signature scent was tuberose, a sweet, pungent fragrance that lingers in the air. You knew

she'd been in the room, yet it wasn't overwhelming. Fittingly, it's a night-blooming plant and native to Mexico, where Mother took so many holidays. She bought Mary Chess Tuberose by the case and wore it all her life. As a child I used to wander into her closet and pull her clothes around me to feel close to her in some way. That was the smell of my mommy when she was gone.

Art: I think her favorite painter was actually Frank Sinatra. She loved his art. Also Maurice Utrillo. She was mad about Mexican art as well. She didn't collect original paintings by well-known artists, but she did have many Mexican pieces, often of children with large eyes.

Shopping for paintings in Mexico in 1965. She brought this particular work home and hung it alongside her other Mexican art.

Actors: Given the chance Mother would have bowed down before Laurence Olivier. She revered him and always

This unusual portrait shot by Eric Carpenter as publicity for *A Life of Her Own* was Mother's favorite. It sat on top of the piano at home.

referred to him as *Sir* Laurence. Mother was also a fan of Robert Montgomery, Ronald Colman, Elizabeth Taylor, Leslie Caron, Gene Kelly, Spencer Tracy, Bette Davis, Angela Lansbury, Joanne Woodward, and Paul Newman. She also thought Marilyn Monroe was a fine actress besides being a fascinating personality.

TV Shows: We had one of the first television sets ever sold in the late '40s. I remember Gran being hooked on the story of Kathy Fiscus, the little girl who fell into a well in 1949. Mother watched a lot of TV later in life. Sometimes she would stay up long into the night watching old movies, occasionally her own. Other television favorites were game shows (*What's My Line?*, *Wheel of Fortune*, *Jeopardy*), talk shows (*Oprah*, *Phil Donahue*), *Entertainment Tonight*, *The Golden Girls*, *Star Trek*, anything *Lucy*, Bill Cosby, and Red Skelton. She didn't even mind commercials. She wanted to buy everything. As often as not she wouldn't like whatever it was when she got it and we'd have to return it. In later years I might be sent out for anything from makeup and toiletries to a chicken dinner from El Pollo Loco.

Movie: *Gone With the Wind* was Mother's favorite, even though a screen test she made for the part of Scarlett O'Hara in 1938 came back to haunt her in documentaries about the movie.

Above all blooms for Mother was the yellow rose—never red. She loved to wear flowers and was the first person I knew of who pinned them to her furs. Sinatra sang about it in "Violets for Your Furs," which I am convinced refers to Mother.

Color: Mother's favorites were bright, clear colors, like sunshine yellow. Writing in red ink was her signature.

Mixing up her signature gravy on Thanksgiving.

Holiday: From the time I was little, Mother always tried to have us together for her favorite holiday, Thanksgiving. She was in charge of the turkey gravy, using a delicious recipe of Gran's that she mastered. This, and broiling a steak now and then, was the only time she could be found cooking. Thanksgiving was also the one occasion on which she remembered her long-neglected sweet tooth. She always had a single slice of pumpkin pie on Thanksgiving.

Collectibles: Mother had many collections over the years and people would give her gifts of whatever she was gathering at the moment. She had a cabinetful of little china mice. Then one day she said, "That's it, I don't ever want to see another mouse," and she got rid of them. They were packed up to make room for other collectibles. Over the years there were compacts, powder boxes, perfume bottles, cigarette cases, and lighters. And all sorts of butterflies— porcelain, metal, china, jewelry, and fashion accessories.

Interests & Hobbies

Athletics

Athletic is not a word that springs to mind when one thinks of Lana Turner, but publicity photos tried to play up her sporty side occasionally, to present her as an outdoorsy girl-next-door. There were certain activities she genuinely enjoyed, however, like tennis, golf, deep-sea fishing, and swimming. Everyone was a horseracing enthusiast in her day and spent afternoons at Hollywood Park. She owned prizewinng racehorses named Grey Host and Cheryba.

"Favorite sport? Any as long as it's a spectator sport."

Painting

Artistic was a great word for Mother. She was sketching costumes and doing pastels from a very early age. Frank Sinatra, himself a painter, gave her a magnificent set of oil paints. She put it to use for the first time when I was about five years old. She asked me to draw a picture for her, which I did (in crayon), and I asked her for one in return. She stayed up all night doing an oil painting for me of four dwarves, named Hokey, Pokey, Mokey, and Dokey. It hung in my bedroom for years.

Painting was Mom's very private form of relaxation. She would finish a work (often of flowers) and put it in the closet. She never thought they were good. Her paintings weren't displayed, or even shown to anyone, until I dug them out years later.

Mother's favorite hobbies, painting and costume design, come together in this photo.

Music was always of great importance in Mother's life. That began in her childhood when she would dance around the room with her father to "You're the Cream in My Coffee." As an adult, there was always music playing in her home. At the studio someone was hired just to change her records throughout the day. Tony Martin, Buddy Rich, Frank Sinatra, the Dorseys, Gene Krupa—any of the swing era bands. She loved "west coast jazz," which is a slightly different jazz sound that is not as interpretive. She wasn't into the kind put out by John Coltrane or Thelonious Monk. I was. She liked Artie Shaw's more melodic style of jazz. She didn't have an ear for opera but made an event of Going to the Opera. She did have a lot of classical music and Monteverdi strings

that she enjoyed having on in the background of her everyday movements.

Sometimes she was in the mood for "movie music," referring to soundtracks, from her own films as well as a wide span of genres and decades. The Merry Widow song was played nonstop for a time, as was the famous jazz rendition of "Green Dolphin Street." Broadway musical soundtracks filled the house. *Oklahoma*, *Carousel*, *South Pacific* (she may not have liked working with Ezio Pinza, but this was Rodgers and Hammerstein). Yanni was a favorite. She loved flamenco, samba, rumba, mariachi; in brief, anything Latin. The Gershwins' "Embraceable You" was her favorite in the '40s. She was mad about Jerome Kern

Mother's passion for dancing began early in life. She believed there was power in it. In a 1939 interview she offered the following advice to her fellow teenaged girls: "If you can dance you're all set. If you have that reputation, you're popular."

She kept the rhythm going all day at the studio. There was even someone on the payroll whose sole job it was to change Lana Turner's records.

Laughter and dancing with Peter Lawford, 1944.

"The worst thing in the world is to stand still."

and Oscar Hammerstein's "All the Things You Are." Johnny Mercer's "Tangerine" was her and Dad's song.

Musicians were some of her best friends. Benny Goodman's whole band used to come over. At-home entertainment for Mother revolved around records and live music. On the morning of December 7, 1941, neither Mother nor her friends knew about the attack on Pearl Harbor that brought the United States into the war because they were still having a jam session from the night before. Then Gran, who had been on a trip to San Francisco, came home. "What are you doing?" she asked, appalled to walk into a party on the eve of war. She gave the group the news report and they broke up the party.

Mom had natural rhythm and with just a few weeks' training could play a professional ballroom and tap dancer in *Dancing Co-Ed* and *Two Girls on Broadway*. Singing was a skill she never learned well enough for film, though she did inspire a few tunes in her day. Her name was mentioned in many songs. She had her own theme, often played if she entered a nightclub or a restaurant that had live music—"You Stepped Out of a Dream," from *Ziegfeld Girl*, by Nacio Herb Brown and Gus Kahn. In jazz circles years later her theme song was "Green Dolphin Street." Artie Shaw wrote "Summit Ridge Blues" (named after the street on which they lived) for her while

Sheet music for "The Lana Turner Blues," a pop tune of the World War II era.

they were married. During World War II the U.S. military had an anthem to their pin-up girl, "The Lana Turner Blues," by Billy Hayes and Charles Gunther.

Rehearsing for *A Life of Her Own* with Hermes Pan, Fred Astaire's collaborator on the choreography of the Astaire-Rogers musicals.

With Fred Astaire in 1954. Mother could boast of having danced with him once off screen, but her dream of gliding across the floor with him in a film was too much to hope for.

The 1950s

At many times, the 1950s seemed a long series of nightmares for Mother, for Gran, and for myself. It wasn't all bad, but looking back at the major moments, our survival skills were truly put to the test. Mother's second miscarriage, in October 1951, plunged her into despair and with it her marriage to Bob Topping was ending. She was still a top star but at the moment it seemed unimportant. She felt responsible for not being able to keep Bob off the alcohol that led to their separation. She felt unnecessary to me as I had Gran, a governess, and became more involved with school. Losing all sense of worth, she felt dead inside so she thought, why not make it official?

I remember the day Mother attempted suicide, though I had no inkling of what was going on. I recall loud noises and Gran coming into my room to say that everything was fine. The next morning I was told Mother was ill, that she was being made well again, and that she would be home in a few days. This story was completely hushed up. The press was told Lana had fallen in the shower and injured her arm. Actually, she had locked herself in her bathroom, swallowed sleeping pills, and slit her left wrist. Ben Cole, her manager, was at the house. He broke down the bathroom door and saved her. Two days later she emerged from the hospital with renewed spirit. Through the dramas still to come she never considered ending her life again, for herself, and her family.

Mother was met by photographers when she emerged from the hospital after her suicide attempt, dressed in white from head to toe. Only the ghost of the recently removed second "T" remained on her car as a reminder of her third divorce.

As I look back on her suicide attempt, it was the act of someone very different from the woman I knew. Mother was the type for the grand scene, but she was never a quitter. There was also Gran, me, and *the publicity* to be considered—and she would never purposely do injury to her body. She recovered almost immediately. Realizing again how much she was blessed with, more than anything she felt shame about what she had done. They say if a person is

Reporters were told Mother's slashed wrist was caused by an accident in the bathroom in which she cut her arm on the shower door.

In Italy, 1953, Mother debuted a look that shocked her fans for her role of an Italian girl in *Flame and the Flesh*.

serious about suicide they succeed. It could have been a cry for attention, but no one can say for sure what was going on in her mind. Decades later she was still trying to rationalize it to herself.

I was growing into a spirited adolescent in the '50s. Mother was never much of a disciplinarian. She didn't believe in striking a child. Then again I was exceptionally well-behaved, until I lost trust in adults. When that mistrust really took hold is when we were in Europe in the fall of 1953, right after Mother married Lex Barker. I discovered that Miss Hulley, my governess, was being fired and they had interesting plans for me.

I had just been through a month in Italy in this new family that I wasn't particularly fond of, with Lex and his children. Gran, my safety, my rock, was being sent home with the Barker kids while I was to remain in Europe with

Mother and *him*—Lex. They planned to hire someone for me and put me in a French school. I wanted to go back to the school I had been in since kindergarten. It shocked Mother, but I was so angry I emphatically refused to stay. She said "Fine" (after a lot of other words). Gran and I went home together and waited for Mother to complete the filming of *Betrayed* in Holland.

This was a bad time for Gran too. Mother was upset and she took it out on her. On the way to Orly airport they had an argument which ended in Mother saying that when we got back to Los Angeles, Gran would have to get a job. After paying all of her bills and luxuries over the past sixteen years, she would have to begin supporting herself. That didn't last very long and they made up, but Gran actually did take a job at a store on Rodeo Drive run by friends called Gifts for Men (and Women Too).

Midway through the decade, Mother left MGM. The whole studio system was collapsing with the ever-growing popularity of television and government anti-trust laws that forced studios to sell off their theater chains. In reaction to economic cutbacks, stars had to be let go. When her last day arrived, Mother gathered her possessions and brought them home. The same had happened when Clark Gable and the other big Metro stars left; no one said goodbye to her before she drove off the studio grounds. She was deeply hurt. I remember her returning home in tears, saying that they didn't even come and say goodbye.

For the first time, I was aware of economic restrictions at Mapleton. Rooms began to be closed up and the house eventually went up for sale. Once Lex Barker was out, it was too big for just Mother and me. She felt a great sense of fear and trepidation about the future after MGM. She had never had to look for a job, though she was far from alone in this scenario. Most of the stars of the '30s and '40s were being released from long-standing studio contracts. Some found their way and others didn't. Mother had more endurance than people realized. In 1957 she was cast in one of the biggest hits of the decade, *Peyton Place*.

1958, of course, was the darkest year for the three of us—Mother, Gran, and me. After the personal trauma of Stompanato, Mother's professional career was again said to be in tatters, until producer Ross Hunter came along with *Imitation of Life*. Meanwhile, the local police kept an eagle eye on me until my eighteenth birthday. After a few run-ins with the juvenile justice system, I was put in El Retiro reform school.

Dear Gran was there immediately after the stabbing and stood up through court hearings and my assorted dramas that followed. Only when the dust began to settle did she finally buckle under the weight of it all and was close to a nervous collapse. Mother and Fred May sent her to his ranch to recuperate. Country living had a healing effect and brought my old Gran back. She came to work in my father's office with me in 1968 and lived with me in Calabasas and then Hawaii, where she passed away, with Mother and me nearby, in February 1982.

One night in 1957 I made headlines by running away to downtown Los Angeles, where I met up with some odd characters. After I was safely returned to Mom and Dad (pictured), photographers caught us at the front door of Mapleton. Lex was gone by then, but the "B" for Barker on our doormat wasn't.

In Recovery

In 1959, Mother, Gran, and I participated in a photo session to coincide with an article about how all was well again after our tragedy. Even a professional like Mom couldn't convey that impression. The images captured pain more often than they did healing. Some were posed to a laughable degree, like the sight of Mom shopping by herself in a supermarket. The casualness of other shots is equally astonishing.

This is one of the most unique photographs ever taken of Mother. The way she smokes her cigarette and the disconnect between her and the camera is unusual.

The 1960s and 1970s

other's career was revitalized by the release of *Imitation of Life*, followed up by more Ross Hunter melodrama in *Portrait in Black*. She did popular television guest spots. Her other films of the early 1960s met with varying degrees of success. She remained a leading actress, but by the middle of the decade, new stars were coming up from Europe and within the Hollywood ranks. A great many glamorous ladies of the '40s had completely fallen off the radar. Although she was doing better than any of them, it frightened Mother. I've seen it happen. When a star thinks they are slipping, they become more pronounced in acting the star. The more insecure Mother felt, the grander she presented herself; the more demanding she became, the more she felt slighted by little things.

Close friends tried to point out to her that she was still Lana Turner and didn't have to act the grand lady to be respected. "LT" was our nickname for Mother when this alter ego would come over her. She knew about it and we all understood what that meant. We could tell instantly when LT was in the room and when it was Mom. Unless you had known her for a long time, you didn't know a change had taken place and everything was fine. But she had always been happy-go-lucky, out for a good time and serious about her work without taking herself too seriously. These once outstanding qualities began to fade. It was difficult for friends who knew her for years. Some backed away, which was painful for her because she didn't see it and couldn't understand.

Many things in Mother's life were different beginning in the mid-'60s and she went into what was in some respects a very bad period. She and Del Armstrong had been dear friends for over twenty years of joy and heartache, but after 1966, they didn't work together again. Our relationship changed too because I was in my twenties, working with my father, and had my own life. Gran was living with me. The marriage to Fred May had ended and she was lonely. That opened the door for certain people to take advantage of her. When she was

At home in Malibu.

At the time she prepared to go to work on her television series *The Survivors*.

Attending a launch party for *The Survivors*.

married to Robert Eaton and Ronald Dante, they were her total focus and everyone else was largely shut out.

There were a few regrettable movies in the late '60s and '70s, but Mother's career mostly flourished again in this era. She did one great film (*Madame X*) and went into television in 1969 with *The Survivors*. The mini-series didn't survive, but it was good. She did live theater. Her tours in *Forty Carats* (1970–72) and *Bell, Book and Candle* (1974–76) were triumphs. But she was also enjoying more of her favorite vodka-cranberry drinks than was good for her and the vodka content increased steadily. I thought it was a very revealing moment when Mother later said to me, "I'm sorry, I just don't remember a lot of the 1970s." For a time it looked as though her personal life would ruin her and her career. But when did Lana Turner ever let that happen?

While touring in *Murder Among Friends* in 1980, her health was run down. She missed performances and finally couldn't go on any longer. She went to a doctor who, naturally, told her that she had to stop drinking. At that moment in the doctor's office, her survivor's instinct or as she told it, the hand of God, ordered her to quit and she did "as though

A portrait for *Forty Carats*, 1971.

Mother's portraits of the '60s and '70s continued to evoke the mystique of her MGM era.

God took the memory of drinking away." She had no love interests and she didn't want any. She said there was a wonderful sense of freedom in ending her lifelong search for a perfect romance. The woman that emerged made the last fifteen years of her life some of the best.

As Mother came to an agreement with herself regarding love, I entered into the most important relationship of my life, with Joyce LeRoy, the woman who has been my partner since 1971. She was a fashion model who was well-known simply by the name of Josh. Mother's outlook was very liberal for her time. A person's race, religion, or sexual preference made absolutely no difference to her or, for that matter, to my father or Gran. They brought me up in a way that allowed me to be honest with them and with the world about my sexuality all my life. There was no great revelatory scene about my being gay. I'd felt it since childhood and never really hid it from my parents. Josh was accepted openly as part of the Crane-Turner family.

Standing before one of the most glamorous portraits of her youth. Mother and I attended this photo exhibit, called "Dreams for Sale," in Los Angeles in February 1976.

"What a night!"

Mother said she felt she became a legend during the unreality of her reception at the tribute to her presented at Town Hall in New York in 1975. It was part of a series conducted by publicist John Springer called Legendary Ladies of the Screen.

These photos make me think of Mother's "pretty hands." She learned this from Gran, who also gave me Pretty Hands exercises—picking up a glass, holding an object, "Always arch the hands."

The 1980s

Coming out of the dark periods she went through in the 1960s and '70s, with the changes she was making in her life, she was healthy and had a sense of fulfillment that radiated from within. Her diet became impeccable and she looked better than she had in the past couple of years. She wasn't tormented by the past. Her mistakes didn't seem like mistakes to her at the time and her only regret was that she couldn't have had more children. Interviewers always asked Mother what she would do "if you could go back and change . . ." She could never give them the kind of answer they were looking for because she never thought that way. Her attitude was, "You can't change the past, so why bother?"

Mother's inner peace could largely be attributed to her spiritual side, which was always distinctly present, if not

Photographers followed Mother into a church in Acapulco, where *Love Has Many Faces* was being filmed.

clearly defined. Mother was baptized a Catholic and considered herself a member of the Church, but she had her own way of thinking. When I was going to Catholic school, I would come home and tell what I'd been taught and she would correct the day's lesson. I nearly got kicked out of school when I shared her views on the subject of Limbo. She would have been pleased that the Church has since relaxed its position to allow Catholics to hold a belief in salvation for the souls of unbaptized infants.

She felt close to God from the time she was a little girl. Shortly after her father was killed, she said the news first came to her when she was jolted from sleep and opened her eyes to the face of God telling her that her father was dead. Mom studied alternative beliefs to gain new perspectives. She explored reincarnation and decided that she was Cleopatra reborn. She felt that her belief was confirmed after a visit to Egypt during which she felt a deep connection to the land and its people. She read about mysticism and about the power of gems. Those were strange, fun times. She took from each teaching what made sense to her.

The big loss was when Gran succumbed to emphysema in 1982. Mother was in Texas on tour with the play *Murder Among Friends* when we knew the end was near. Mom came out to us at our home in Hawaii just before Gran slipped away. They shared unforgettable moments during that trip.

Mother inscribed this photo to Gran shortly before Gran's death in 1982. It was a shot used to promote her book, which she dedicated to Gran.

Out of love of her craft Mother continued to work until the mid-'80s. Amid career tributes and accolades that began coming to her in the '70s, she had television success with guest appearances on *Falcon Crest* and returned to the stage. Although she made her last movie in 1980, Mother retained the interest of a veteran film star. In general she thought the actors lacked training and the style of stars of her era. She singled out several as exceptions, however. She admired Johnny Depp, Meryl Streep, Dustin Hoffman, and Tom Hanks (especially in *Forrest Gump*).

We used to play a game joking about who could play her in a film. I thought possibly Bernadette Peters. She didn't see that. I suggested Madonna. "No way!" I thought Sharon Stone in her *Basic Instinct* period might have been suitable. That was my idea, not Mother's. Ultimately Mom continued to feel as she did at Town Hall in 1975, when she said, "The woman that plays me hasn't been born yet."

Mom did book signings, talked with fans in book shops and department stores, participated in interviews, and posed for new portraits with enormous energy in 1982.

Mother made her own fun at her penthouse home, her "Ivory Tower", in retirement. She was a fixer, the kind who would straighten pictures in other people's houses. The art on her walls was perfectly aligned with the help of a professional level. Completely fascinated, she studied a maintenance man using his level in her home one day. She never asked for it, of course. She never had to. He was thrilled to leave Lana Turner his level. This story not only demonstrates the spell of generosity she could put on people but also her appreciation for the simplest gifts. She couldn't have gotten more of a kick out of that level if it had been a diamond. She started going around the room, putting it on everything to make sure it was aligned, eyes on the gauge that showed if the surface was level. Ultimately, she decided that her whole apartment building was tilted

and deadpanned, "I'm going to end up on Wilshire Boulevard!" When Mother was finished with her toy, she gave it a permanent place atop the wall-to-wall jewelry dresser she had in her bedroom. There, as if it were a work of art, beside a fine china lamp and above her fabulous handmade dresser, rested a handyman's level.

Me, Mom, and Josh at the Rose Ball on the big island of Hawaii in 1984. Any color outside the pink spectrum was verboten.

Christmas at my home in San Francisco, 1985.

Ms. Wonderful

With Sean Connery at the Deauville Film Festival.

New rushes of adulation for her public self came over Mother at unexpected times, among them a retrospective at the Deauville Film Festival in September 1981, a National Film Society Honor the following month, and a tribute at the San Sebastián Film Festival in October 1994. San Francisco's Warfield Theater hosted a Lana Turner film festival in 1982, which Mother attended. The gala evening, which benefited a children's organization, was such a success that Mayor Dianne Feinstein named it "Lana Turner Day." There was also a series of tributes that took Mother to several key cities. Film clips would be run, followed by a question-and-answer session.

At the National Film Society Honors in 1981, Mother appeared (very late) in a Nolan Miller dress and the tiny gold cross necklace she always wore in those days.

At the 1985 Thalians charity ball, Mother was their thirtieth anniversary "Ms. Wonderful" honoree. It was a nerve-wracking night for the organizers, Debbie Reynolds and Ruta Lee, since Mother was a no-show until two minutes before the curtain went up. She had been doing her typical hellish routine before such an event of redoing hair, makeup, and getting sick to her stomach. When she finally appeared, the night went off without a hitch and they raised over $425,000 for the Mental Health Center at Cedars-Sinai, one of the most profitable evenings in Thalians history.

Mother made many public appearances in the early- to mid-'80s. Camera clicks still followed her to tributes, openings, and even to simple restaurants.

With Thalians president Debbie Reynolds and Chairwoman Ruta Lee.

Jackie Cooper, Danny Thomas, Robert Preston, Marvin Hamlish, George Hamilton, Red Buttons, Rip Taylor, and Hal Linden joined Mother on stage at the finale.

This is my favorite photo of us, taken after the Thalians gala, 1985.

No More Secrets

It shocked me to learn that Mother was writing her autobiography in 1981. In spite of—or perhaps because of—the decades of media spotlight, Mother remained a very private person. What ended up as her book started as a biography by Hollis Alpert. Fred May, Mother's favorite ex, was interviewed for it and he talked her into speaking with the writer. A two-hour talk turned into a series of interviews. "I backed into it," was her way of explaining how *Lana: The Lady, the Legend, the Truth* came about. It was published in 1982 and became a *New York Times* bestseller. An extensive tour followed that brought her into contact with fans as never before in interviews and personal appearances at bookstores.

When I told Mother I was doing my book a few years later, she was as shocked as I was when I learned of hers. She asked a few questions. "Are you going to talk about Lex?" "Yes," I said. "Oh. Are you going to talk about being gay?" "Yes," I said. "Oh. . . . Are you sure the two of you know what you're letting yourselves in for?" I told her yes, Josh and I had considered it carefully. The conversation ended with her saying, "You know whatever you do I will support—but I won't talk to anyone." And she didn't, to anyone but me.

Accolades came in her later years and her block at Grauman's Chinese Theater (left) and star on the Hollywood Walk of Fame (above) became status symbols of the movies' immortals.

At my home in 1985.

When the galleys of *Detour* came, I sent her one. She called me the moment she finished reading and told me she thought it was very well done and "I think you're one hell of a woman." Privately I think she was devastated by the book, but she never said so. What she knew was bad enough, but there were things I revealed that she hadn't known. She just retreated to her Ivory Tower for almost three years. Her memorable remark was, "I am so mad at a hell of a lot of people, but they're all dead!" When I went on my book tour she critiqued every appearance I did, offered tips, or would say, "You were wonderful." She was supportive, which was difficult for her because she was getting a lot of unwanted attention and people asking for interviews.

When Christina Crawford's *Mommie Dearest* was published in 1978, it came to be thought of as the definitive star baby book. My experience was nothing like Christina's, but I think in Mother's heart of hearts there was fear my book might have been worse than it was. In writing the book, the lines of communication between us were open as never before. We found out things about one another we had never known. Ultimately, *Detour* meant that once and for all there were no doors closed to discussion and our relationship was better than ever in her final years.

From the 1980s on were the most consistently happy years of Mother's life. Into the '90s she didn't have to work and didn't have to *show up* anywhere she didn't want to. I think in the end she lived her social life through Josh and me. She didn't want to go out with us, but she wanted a complete report on who, what, where, when, and why. Her Ivory Tower was a penthouse, but was simple compared with how she had lived. In the end she simplified her life. The apartment was everything she wanted. It was home.

After *Detour* was published in 1988, she basically closed the door and didn't go out until a sudden change occurred

At the opening of *Phantom of the Opera*, 1993.

in 1991, not long after she talked me into moving back to Los Angeles from San Francisco. Mother always said there was nothing worse than seeing an aging star who didn't look well out on the town—until her own time came. Her doctors later called it a false energy right before illness overtakes the body. I couldn't keep her at home. Constantly energized, Mother wanted to go to every show, nightclub, and restaurant. Friends were thrilled that she was out again. She was wined and dined and seated at the best tables. I saw the Nightclub Queen reemerge for eight or nine months. She was ill and so thin, but I don't regret that she had that fun. I only wished I could discourage the photographers from snapping so many pictures. She wasn't always ready for them, especially at restaurants, and it deeply upset her.

Mother suspected she was not well for some time before she went and got diagnosed. The doctor wrote six letters on a piece of paper and pushed it toward her across his desk. "Cancer." A smoker since her early teens, it was in her throat. With radiation treatments she was in remission for a time and we made a trip to Palm Springs in 1993. Then the cancer reoccurred. She was back in Los Angeles by fall. In 1994 she filmed a final television interview in which her strength of spirit belied the perceptible illness in her voice.

The year 1995 turned into a battle of wills. Mother was very weak but refused to be carried out to the hospital across the street from her building on a stretcher, and her new physician simply would not come to her. Meanwhile, she was terribly uncomfortable and I was out of my head with worry. One day my phone rang and it was Warren Beatty. He was calling about a project in which he wanted Mother to participate. Besides telling him why it wasn't possible, I poured out the story of what was happening. He said he would call me back within twenty-four hours. He actually called the White House and through President Clinton's press secretary, was connected with the head radiologist at Cedars Sinai Hospital. He called me back and said it was all arranged for the doctor to come to the house to see Mother the next day. Dr. Thompson told her, "I can't cure you, but I can make it easier for you." That was a promise kept. Warren Beatty saved the quality of her life at a time I felt helpless. He didn't want to be thanked but it was an extraordinary thing he did.

Mother lived for another six months, in good spirits, watching television, interested in everything. She became totally engrossed in the O. J. Simpson trial, firmly convinced he was innocent. (Anytime the press was against someone she was usually on that person's side.) She listened to music and messages from her telephone friends. She wasn't afraid or troubled. She had long since made peace within herself. I spoke to her on her last day. She was fine, but by the time I reached her home she was gone. Mother passed away peacefully on June 29, 1995, in her bed in her Ivory Tower, where she wanted to be.

Mom and me back at her condo after *Phantom*.

This is the last photo taken of Mom.
She is at home with Molly in 1995.

Her Last Hurrah

Actor William Hurt presented her award, which she accepted partially in Spanish. Mother, Cora, and her most famous roles projected on large screens across the stage, received a tremendous ovation from the film festival audience.

Mother hadn't made a professional appearance in seven years when suddenly she wanted to accept an award at the San Sebastián Film Festival in person as part of a segment for *Lifestyles of the Rich and Famous*. She mustered all of her MGM training to appear radiant in red for her last public event. The show itself was her final screen appearance. Taken all together it was very moving. Inspiring? Yes, it was, but it is very difficult for me even to look at these images because I know how sick she was. That's a daughter's perspective, but I too can see that her humor and inner happiness came across on the show.

She sat down with Robin Leach for a candid interview in which she spoke about her illness, "the Lana that used to be," and her life in the present. It was truly a last hurrah for Mother as a star. Between press photographers and the *Lifestyles* cameras her entire trip was covered. Mother was seen from arrival in Spain, to visiting a church, doing press conferences, going to a flamenco show, greeting masses of fans who still clamored for her, and finally, accepting her Lifetime Achievement Award to the most loving ovation a star could receive.

"An Ending is but framing the portrait of a Beginning."

Lanallure

They coined a new phrase in the 1940s, "Lanallure," which described the luscious quality of her portraits.

Recurring Film Features

The Walk: Beginning with those first memorable moments in *They Won't Forget*, from *Ziegfeld Girl* to *The Prodigal*, Lana Turner's trademark was her walk. She would try to teach it to me, but I never quite got the hang of it. It was a manner of twisting the ball of the foot with each step. One unusual feature of hers that had an effect on it was that her left leg was a bit shorter than the right. All slacks were tailored to this irregularity, the pant legs showing a difference in length of nearly an inch. She also wore high heels, usually four inches, sometimes with platforms. Hers was a rolling, subtle kind of glide, not a hip-swinging Marilyn Monroe walk. It was a way of moving that was unique to her.

Observe: *They Won't Forget*; *Ziegfeld Girl*; *Slightly Dangerous*; *Week-End at the Waldorf*; *The Postman Always Rings Twice*; *The Three Musketeers*; *The Merry Widow*; *Flame and the Flesh*; *The Prodigal*; *Imitation of Life*.

In the opening of *Flame and the Flesh*, which shows Mother walking all over town, a little girl emulates her sexy stride.

Ziegfeld Girl Sheila's stock in trade is her walk.

Somewhere I'll Find You, 1942.

Lana Turner Revealed: Many of Mother's directors at MGM came up with interesting ways of introducing her in their films. They often staged scenes, with camera movement or in the writing, to build up anticipation for her first appearance on camera.

My favorite "revealed" character is Paula Lane in *Somewhere I'll Find You*. In the film, Paula dashes into the bathroom to take a shower when Clark Gable's character enters her bedroom. Intrigued by the voice, he makes a game of putting together a picture of what Paula looks like from the bits and pieces around her room. There is an unusual hat that only a fantastic face could pull off, a dress outlines her shape for him, and a brush on the dresser provides telltale evidence that she's a blonde. Powder tells him her complexion. At this point, Gable is anxious to know how accurate he is and the audience, knowing he's right, is dying to see Lana

Turner. Then she appears, freshly scrubbed and wearing a shower cap. Great setup, great payoff in the entrance.

Her entrances weren't always so elaborate. Sometimes it was just a camera movement that put her face into the frame suddenly—or sometimes feet first, as in *Postman* or *Slightly Dangerous*. All the way up through *Falcon Crest*, on television in the '80s, she was presented like the crown jewels.

Observe: *Somewhere I'll Find You*; *Slightly Dangerous*; *Keep Your Powder Dry*; *The Postman Always Rings Twice*; *Cass Timberlane*; *Homecoming*; *The Three Musketeers*; *The Prodigal*; *Imitation of Life*.

Two features in one—she types in the tub in *Who's Got the Action?*

Typing: After the skipped typing class that got Mother into movies, typing kept cropping up in her onscreen work. It makes me a laugh to see her in these scenes because, having skipped one too many of those classes, the best she could do behind a typewriter was use the old hunt-and-peck method.

Observe: *They Won't Forget*; *Rich Man, Poor Girl*; *Somewhere I'll Find You*; *The Postman Always Rings Twice*; *A Life of Her Own*; *Another Time, Another Place*; *Who's Got the Action?*; *Week-End at the Waldorf*.

Baths: Mother covered in bubbles or photographed from the shoulders up are examples of slightly risqué scenes from her day in films that suggested sex appeal without hitting the viewer over the head with it. She enacted her scrubbed and tubbed moments in a way that was more playful than provocative.

The bath scene from *Homecoming* was cutely played by Mother and Clark Gable as Nurse "Snapshot" McCall and the doctor she's nicknamed "Useless." Worn out after performing round-the-clock operations on the African warfront, she shocks the proper doctor by breezily inviting him out to take a bath with her at the new watering hole she's discovered. He is scandalized but goes along with her and they take turns washing up. Still within earshot of each other, it's an interesting way to show the characters loosen up and open the lines of communication.

Observe: *Ziegfeld Girl*; *Somewhere I'll Find You*; *The Postman Rings Always Twice*; *The Merry Widow*; *The Lady Takes a Flyer*; *Who's Got the Action*.

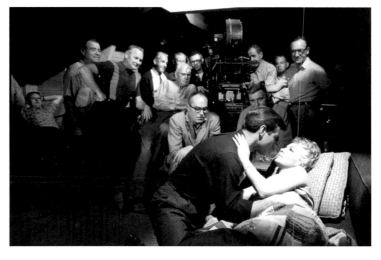

Mother's many bathtub and love scenes seemed to get her the least amount of privacy.

Fine acting makes her look relaxed with one of her dreaded feline co-stars in *Cass Timberlane*.

Cats: "Why is it never a dog?" Mother would ask herself out loud whenever she came across a cat in her script. She was afraid of cats. Professional that she was, Mother could put aside her apprehension for a role. In the play *Bell, Book and Candle* a cat was practically her co-star and she had to carry him in her arms for a good portion of the show. Pyewacket is essential to the plot of the John Van Druten play. Mother knew that going into it. I was shocked that she'd agree to do the play, but she transmitted no inkling of her fear from the footlights to the audience.

Observe: *Marriage Is a Private Affair*; *The Postman Always Rings Twice*; *Cass Timberlane*; *Portrait in Black*.

Sick in Bed: Mother spent a surprising amount of time sick or dying in bed in her movies. Once she did the "fuzzy little ducks speech" while dying in *Ziegfeld Girl* and they discovered how angelic she looked playing sick in bed, they repeated it numerous times. There was always a spotlight from the back that shone on her blonde hair and created a heavenly glow. They made her face glisten and pale "no makeup" makeup made her look younger.

Observe: *Ziegfeld Girl*; *Honky Tonk*; *Johnny Eager*; *The Postman Always Rings Twice*; *Cass Timberlane*; *Homecoming, The Rains of Ranchipur, Love Has Many Faces, Madame X, The Big Cube*.

James Stewart shows concern for his favorite *Ziegfeld Girl*.

Clark Gable cheers her up in *Honky Tonk*.

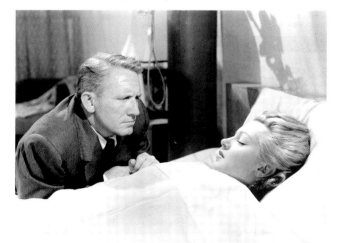

With Spencer Tracy in *Cass Timberlane*.

To-the-Core Loves: Lana Turner had a special way of showing love for a man in her movies. She could act a girl that seemed so purely in love she would do anything for her man, could forgive him anything, and would die without him. The best example of this is in *Johnny Eager*, but you can see it a number of her movies, sometimes from the start and other times as the story progresses.

Observe: *Ziegfeld Girl*; *Honky Tonk*; *Dr. Jekyll and Mr. Hyde*; *Johnny Eager*; *The Postman Always Rings Twice*; *Green Dolphin Street*; *The Bad and the Beautiful*.

With Clark Gable in *Honky Tonk*.

With Richard Hart in *Green Dolphin Street*.

With Spencer Tracy in *Dr. Jekyll and Mr. Hyde*.

A Signature Film

As her most well-known film, it's fitting that *The Postman Always Rings Twice* contains all of the recurring Lana Turner movie features. But great film that it is, the signature ingredients are presented in ways more unique than some of her other movies.

The Walk:
The big walk in *Postman* is almost the anti-Lana Turner walk, not sexy. Cora is tired, drained of energy after trying to hitch a ride for what seems to her an interminable amount of time with Frank. A lone blonde beauty might have done better but as a pair they can't get far enough from Twin Oaks soon enough to convince Cora that Frank will be able to take care of her. After they are shown walking and walking and stumbling, she's had enough and they turn back. Another tired walk occurs near the end when Cora comes out of the ocean, completely drained of energy from her swim.

Revealed:
One of the most famous entrances ever filmed is in *Postman*. John Garfield, a solitary figure, sits at a counter stool eating a hamburger. A lipstick hits the floor and rolls toward him. As he bends to pick it up, he realizes he's not alone. The camera then assumes his point of view, from the floor to the vision in white standing in the doorway, moving up from a pair of shoes to a woman's tanned legs and perfect figure dressed in white, stopping at her face. No woman ever looked as good in a turban.

Typing:
Mother doesn't use it, but a typewriter plays an important role in the movie. It is the instrument used to produce her confession to complicity in the murder of her husband. That original typed paper (and an unknown number of duplicates) first comes between Cora and Frank and then brings them back together just as they're on the verge of turning each other in.

Cora and Frank take a long walk down a dusty road.

Her most famous entrance in a film.

With John Garfield.

Baths: It isn't Lana Turner literally sitting in a tub as most of the other bath scenes in her films; in fact, no tub is ever seen in *Postman*, but again, a tub is significant to the plot. It was supposed to be the sight of Nick Smith's demise if Cora and Frank's original scheme to do away with him had worked out. Instead, it's just another domestic mishap in the place we learn is the sight of most accidents in the home, the bathtub. Nick slips and lands in the hospital with a bump on the head but soon recovers. A Plan B is in order.

Cats: "Deader than a doornail." I don't think anyone who has seen *Postman* can forget the police officer's words and the tone of his reaction to seeing the cat electrocuted when it plays with the live wire hanging down on the side of Twin Oaks. The officer intones these words to Frank a few times, until Frank begins saying it himself.

Sick in Bed: In the scene where Cora swims out as far as she can in the ocean she is close to drowning. She looks tiny with her head just above the water, struggling not to go under. The lighting produces the blonde halo effect that reminds us of her deathbed scenes.

To-the-core Love: Is Cora in love with Frank or does she just see a chance to get out of her marriage and improve her lot in life? As Frank says, she couldn't talk him into murdering a man if he didn't believe she was. There's sparks between them at first sight. After that, they show passion reflecting both wild attraction and hatred for each other, but it is in the last few minutes of the film that that they show profound love. Cora proves it by taking him to the beach and swimming out so far she knows she can't make it back without help and he can let her drown if he wants. Frank carries her back to shore for their last moments together before the metaphorical postman rings a second time for Cora.

Frank and Cora swim to exhaustion.

They Won't Forget (1937)

Plot Points: Mary Clay (LT), a young student at Buxton Business College, is killed by an unknown assailant in a classroom on the Confederate Memorial Day. The murder trial that follows garners nationwide attention. Dormant hostilities between the North and South are reignited as the prosecution, led by grand-standing district attorney Andy Griffin (Claude Rains), zeroes in on a new Buxton teacher from New York, Professor Hale (Edward Norris). If Hale's ace lawyer (Otto Krueger) saves his client from the electric chair, a group of locals are prepared to mete out their own brand of justice.

They Won't Forget was based on *Death in the Deep South*, a novel by Ward Greene for which Warner Bros. purchased the screen rights for $5,000. The novel itself was drawn from the murder of fourteen-year-old Mary Phagan by Leo Frank in Atlanta in 1913. Frank was convicted and lynched two years later by a mob after his death sentence had been commuted to life imprisonment. At the time Greene covered the case as a reporter for the *Atlanta Journal*.

It was a touchy subject in the city of Atlanta and the local Board of Review attempted to keep it from being played in the entire state. In Hollywood the Production Code Administration initially found the script "utterly impossible from the standpoint of political censorship," but screenwriter Robert Rossen's rewrites got the film the green light from the censors.

Mother, still Judy Turner, tested for the part of Mary on February 3, 1937. The first week of March, "Lana Turner" reported for her first day of filming. They started with her walk down the street. Mother's look in *They Won't Forget* is very natural. She wore minimal makeup. The eyebrows were still her own. The body was all her and contrary to what some have said over the years, she did indeed wear a bra in the walk scene. Like the character of Mary, she was totally clueless as to her effect on anybody during filming. She did what she was told, hopping from the street to the classroom to the malt shop sets and didn't know what was happening until she saw the complete movie from between her fingers at the preview (she was hiding her face).

Movie audiences and critics, on the other hand, found *They Won't Forget* tolerable and then some. It was named one of the year's top ten films by both the National Board of

Sodas with producer-director Mervyn LeRoy.

Holding her props, a compact and tube of lipstick. The title of her debut film went through many slight variations. *Deep in the South*, *In the Deep South*, *The Deep South*, *It Did Happen*, and *Murder in the Deep South* were all working titles for *They Won't Forget*.

At the scene of the crime. Besides the Mary Phagan murder, writer Ward Greene said he pulled information from "the Sacco-Vanzetti case, general books on criminology and law, *Our Lawless Police* by Earnest Jerome Hopkins, and the decisions of Justice Holmes."

Review and the *New York Times*. It could only come from Warner Bros., the studio that showed more social consciousness than any other in those days. The film garnered a great deal of notoriety because of its daring theme.

On the lighter side of the film's agenda, Mother was going to be a major part of the publicity campaign, so touches of her soon-to-be-famous discovery story were inserted. In Rossen's screenplay, Mary and the other students at Buxton Secretarial were practicing shorthand in their notebooks as the scene at the school opens. Mother had skipped typing class, so shorthand was changed to typing. After class, Mary goes to a drugstore in another mix of fact and fiction. Judy Turner sipped a plain soda, but those who saw the movie remembered Mary tell the soda jerk to make hers a chocolate malted ("and drop an egg in it, as fresh as you are").

For Mother, a soda fountain represented being in the right place at the right time. That's Hollywood. Skipping typing class set her in the place where certain innate qualities made her a star; poor Mary in the film dutifully waited until after class to quench her thirst and wound up a murder victim. It would seem that with the physical assets of the girl with the sexy walk, she is destined to create headlines either way. It's just a toss-up whether or not she gets the fuzzy end of the lollipop.

A very unusual portrait suggesting Mary's terror. The Leo Frank-Mary Phagan story also inspired the film *Thou Shalt Not Kill* in 1915, and a 1988 miniseries starring Jack Lemmon, *The Murder of Mary Phagan*.

The Great Garrick (1937)

Plot Points: David Garrick (Brian Aherne), the foremost actor of the day, is also the most arrogant—at least that's what the players of the Comédie Française believe after hearing Garrick has boasted to London audiences that he is headed to Paris to teach the French to act. The French company embarks on an elaborate hoax to get even that only they could carry out. At an unassuming inn on the road to Paris, Garrick falls into a den of dueling lovers, giggling chambermaids, and other characters so bizarre they could only be phony, with the exception of one fair gentle lady (Olivia de Havilland).

Ladies and Gentlemen, a story by Ernst Vajda, was purchased by Warner Bros. for $15,000. It took an actual English theater legend of the eighteenth century, David Garrick, and placed him in a fictional story. The stars were Olivia de Havilland and Brian Aherne, who later married de Havilland's sister, actress Joan Fontaine. Mervyn LeRoy had a test made of Mother as Auber, an actress who plays the part of a scullery maid throughout the movie. She called it, "a part I knew how to play," her difficult childhood days in Modesto still fresh in her mind.

Mother's few scenes were filmed in July 1937. In the call reports, Auber is the "third maid." Maids one and two were played by Marie Wilson and Linda Perry, to whom she is joined at the hip, giggling throughout the proceedings.

At age sixteen, Mother works her charm on co-star Craig Reynolds.

On the set with Marie Wilson.

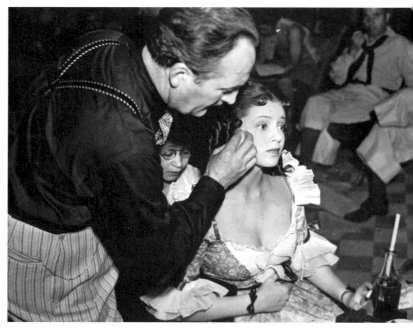

Having her makeup done.

The Adventures of Marco Polo (1938)

Plot Points: Thirteenth century explorer Marco Polo (Gary Cooper) travels to China to establish trade with the Far East, taking him into the realm of the Emperor Kublai Khan (George Barbier) and his counselor, Ahmed (Basil Rathbone). Ahmed is secretly planning to overthrow his sovereign, so Marco Polo becomes enmeshed not only in a Chinese war against Japan, but in an imminent revolution. The Princess Kukachin (Sigrid Gurie) is also in danger, betrothed to the King of Persia. With the help of the warlord Kaidu (Alan Hale), Marco Polo has a hope of saving China, and the beautiful princess.

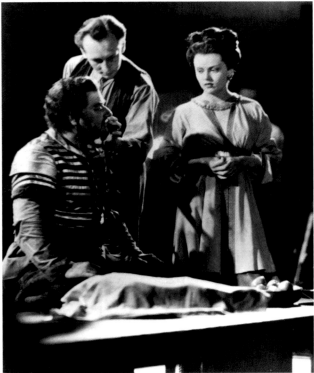

Mother observes Alan Hale get his warlord makeup touched up prior to filming. The movie had its share of problems during production. Director John Cromwell was taken off the picture due to creative differences with Goldwyn and replaced by Archie Mayo.

In terms of the size of Mother's role, this was a comedown from *They Won't Forget*, but Mervyn LeRoy agreed to loan out his rising starlet for a bit in *Marco Polo* because it was going to be a prestigious production from Samuel Goldwyn. Originally planned in Technicolor, Goldwyn was pulling out all the stops in the hope of launching his new protégé, Sigrid Gurie. Even more importantly, it was going to star Gary Cooper as the adventurous Marco Polo, which LeRoy knew meant his actress would be seen by a wide audience. It would have meant more if she was more recognizable in her role. She played an Oriental maid who is pawed by a Chinese warlord played by Alan Hale. Once again, Mother was embarrassed by being put out there as a sexual object. She thanked Hale for his kindess in helping her get through the scene.

Mom had a certain stature from *They Won't Forget*, so it was a feather in Goldwyn's cap to have her in the cast of his big movie, showing quality down the line. For her it was a memorable role because right before production began, they sat her down in a makeup chair and removed every hair of her eyebrows. Each morning on this film they would apply wax to any new growth and rip it out. It was very painful and she lived for the rest of her life having to pencil in eyebrows, except for a quarter of an inch bit of hair on the insides that grew back.

"They ruined me!" Mother never got over losing her natural eyebrows for a bit part as one of a "cast of 5,000."

Mother possibly made out better than Sigrid Gurie. Goldwyn was touting her as an exotic new European find for her big screen debut, but her aura of mystery disappeared when reporters discovered that she was in reality a Brooklyn native of Norwegian ancestry. So in *Marco Polo*, Gurie was a Brooklyn babe advertised as a Norwegian Garbo playing a Chinese princess. And, unfortunately, the film was not well received. When they reissued *Marco Polo* in 1945 it was ballyhooed as co-starring Gary Cooper and Lana Turner, who were friends by then and found it amusing.

Love Finds Andy Hardy (1938)

Plot Points: Young Andy Hardy (Mickey Rooney) is saving up to buy a used roadster. If he plays his cards right, he may have a set of wheels in time to drive his date to the big Christmas Eve dance. These are desperate times, so when a friend offers Andy eight dollars to entertain his girlfriend, Cynthia Potter (LT), while he goes out of town, Andy accepts, in spite of the fact that he has a girl of his own, Polly (Ann Rutherford). Taking care of Cynthia may be easy enough, as all she wants to do is kiss, but Polly will never understand. Luckily, Andy's good friend Betsy Booth (Judy Garland) knows how to get him out of trouble.

Mother made her debut at MGM as Cynthia, the sixteen-year-old mantrap who tantalizes young Andy Hardy in a swimsuit. It's a cute movie, considered one of the best of the *Hardy* series. This was the second of many films Mickey Rooney and Judy Garland made together. As in the movie, he and Judy were great friends, but Mickey had designs on the new bombshell on the lot. He called Mother "Baby Glamour." Mickey was the complete opposite of her type and she wasn't interested in him romantically, even if he was emerging as the biggest star in the country.

This was the fourth installment in the *Hardy* series and thus far none had featured "Andy Hardy" in the title. Not yet realizing Mickey was the breakout star, the belief at the time was that they still needed to put the emphasis on Judge Hardy or the Hardy Family. Pages of alternate titles were suggested, some very bad (*Judy Hardy's Andy*).

ONLY 5 CENT MOVIE MAGAZINE IN THE WORLD

Hollywood

5¢

FEBRUARY

Mickey Rooney and His Girl Friends

NORVELL, FAMOUS MOVIE ASTROLOGER, FORECASTS **STAR HOROSCOPES FOR 1939**

Though shown only in profile, Mother earned her first magazine cover in connection with this film.

Noting how big Mickey was becoming at the box office, they eventually went with *Love Finds Andy Hardy*.

The series was as wholesome entertainment as you could find, but the censors still had some comment on the movie. They advised Metro that "care must be taken with the kisses, to avoid objection." Of course their one warning had to do with Mother's role of Cynthia, the kissing champ.

It was a nice little showcase for her. The *Hardy* movies would also provide early showcases for Donna Reed, Esther Williams, and Kathryn Grayson in coming years.

For the present it was Mickey, Judy, and Ann Rutherford, together with young Lana Turner. Mother's scenes were shot in only five days. MGM got a lot of mileage out of them, again making use of the scenes in the final installment of the series, *Andy Hardy Comes Home*, twenty years later.

With Ann Rutherford, Mickey Rooney, and Judy Garland.

Mother's first of many onscreen smooches was with Mickey Rooney.

The Chaser (1938)

Plot Points: Ambulance-chasing attorney Thomas Brandon (Dennis O'Keefe) comes under fire for his unethical methods, from both the bar association and the unscrupulous head of the street car company, Mr. Beaumont (Pierre Watkin). Playing on his weakness for pretty girls, Beaumont hires Dorothy Mason (Ann Morriss) to trick Thomas into a scheme that would end in his disbarment. Dorothy, instead, falls in love. In protecting him she ultimately lands in jail for perjury. Thomas and his pals cause havoc with the street car company in a campaign to get Dorothy released. She even makes him begin to rethink the idea of ambulance chasing.

Blink and you miss her. In the final print of *The Chaser* she disappears in a flash, but that wasn't the original plan for Mother. At one time her character of "Miss Rutherford, a divorcee," had a meeting with lawyer Dennis O'Keefe, to whom she appeals for legal counsel. In editing stages, this superfluous scene landed Mom on the cutting room floor. Her eleventh-place billing came down and all that remained was a brief shot of her sitting in a waiting room, dressed as she is in the photo on this page, as O'Keefe rushes into his office. It's about seven minutes into the movie.

The Chaser was a remake of a 1933 Lee Tracy film called *The Nuisance* and shot in just two weeks in June 1938.

With Dennis O'Keefe in a scene cut from *The Chaser*.

Rich Man, Poor Girl (1938)

Plot Points: Rich businessman Bill Harrison (Robert Young) proposes to his secretary Joan Thayer (Ruth Hussey), daughter of a hardworking middle class family, but Joan worries that they come from two entirely different worlds and puts the brakes on their romance. To prove to Joan that he can fit in with her family, he moves in with her radical cousin Henry (Lew Ayres), starry-eyed sister Helen (LT), and the rest of the loveable Thayer clan. From then on it becomes a toss up whether Henry's speeches will talk Bill right out of his fortune or Bill can improve the Thayers' lot in life.

Working titles for the film were *White Collars*, after the play on which it was based, and *It's Now or Never*. It was a remake of a 1929 MGM film called *The Idle Rich*, which starred Conrad Nagel and Bessie Love. Franchot Tone was originally announced to star in *Rich Man, Poor Girl*, but Mother's future co-star, Robert Young, was cast instead. The same announcement indicated Tone was to play opposite Mother. The feminine lead role went to Ruth Hussey but Mother did well with her assignment. She has quite a bit of screen time in the movie and attracts all eyes when she's present. She has a nice moment as the spirited Joan Thayer where she verges on hysterical and then quickly brings it back down to earth in a sweet and effective way.

It is a joy to see and hear her in *Rich Man, Poor Girl*. The excitement in what she was doing comes across. When she was in her teens, the Lana Turner persona was different; she was much more a comedienne than she ever was in later years. Her voice was happy and girlish and she had the look of a teenager when not specifically made up to appear older. Much later on she was so elegant I used to want to muss her up. I love the playfulness of her early films.

Not yet the fashion trendsetter, Mother tentatively reaches for the door during production in June 1938.

Dramatic School (1938)

Plot Points: Louise Maubin (Luise Rainer) stands out as the most exceptional among a group of capricious pupils at a French school of drama where girls would be as happy to win praise for their legs as for their talent. Louise's uniqueness fascinates the handsome Marquis D'Abbencourt (Alan Marshall). That coupled with her habitual lying causes her no shortage of trouble with the girls. When she lands the role of Joan of Arc, it becomes a choice between her professional dream and romance. Nana (Paulette Goddard) would pick the Marquis. So would Mado (LT). Would Louise?

Luise Rainer was a delicate Austrian actress who became the most acclaimed actress in Hollywood after winning back to back Best Actress Oscars for her performances in *The Great Ziegfeld* and *The Good Earth*. Gran was so impressed by her. Because of Luise Rainer, Gran recalled *Dramatic School*

With Virginia Grey, Jean Chatburn, Paulette Goddard, Ann Rutherford (standing), Alan Marshal, and Luise Rainer (seated).

more fondly than did Mother, who remembered Luise not as a fan but as one who had worked with her. She thought Rainer behaved very badly on the set. Actually, the intense actress was extremely unhappy in Hollywood and *Dramatic School* turned out to be her final film at the studio. But it was Paulette Goddard who impressed Mother because she thought she was so beautiful.

This was Mervyn LeRoy's first film with Mother under the MGM banner. He produced. Robert Sinclair directed. There was not a whole lot for Mother to do except be part of the chorus, chiming in along with the other young actresses as they practiced fencing, recited Shakespeare and, most of all, gossiped.

LeRoy had a difficult time getting *Dramatic School* passed by the censors. It was deemed to violate the production code because of the "explicit and suggested details of illicit sex relationships" shown in the story. Script revisions earned the movie a seal of approval, though specific territories could always remove scenes they found objectionable after the movie's release. For instance, the censors in Holland cut a scene of Mother's in which she, Paulette Goddard, and Virginia Grey have Hans Conreid judge who has the best legs.

Calling Dr. Kildare (1939)

Plot Points: Jimmy Kildare (Lew Ayres), a medical intern, is turned out of Blair General Hospital by his cantankerous mentor, Dr. Gillespie (Lionel Barrymore), after one disagreement too many. Actually, Gillespie's plan is to test how his young protégé handles himself on his own, though he does keep close tabs on Kildare by way of Nurse Mary Lamont (Laraine Day). Soon Mary must report some unusual activity to Gillespie after Jimmy becomes involved with a mysterious blonde named Rosalie (LT) in a murder cover-up.

Mother celebrated her eighteenth birthday right before making *Calling Dr. Kildare*. Now "of age," she played a very sultry character for the first time, almost a femme fatale as she seduces the young doctor for her own reasons and gets him into plenty of trouble. It took a concentrated effort to make Mother look older for *Calling Dr. Kildare*. After several makeup and costume tests, there was still concern that she looked too young.

"Looking too young" for her role in a costume test.

This was the second installment in Metro's *Dr. Kildare* series. Lew Ayres starred and Laraine Day made her debut as his romantic interest, Nurse Lamont. Lionel Barrymore supported them as the famous Dr. Gillespie, which spun off into its own series. Mother did not have specific memories about Barrymore except to say that whenever she saw him he was in his cups. But he was the grand old man by this time and whatever he did people loved. In her autobiography Mother says she and Laraine Day didn't get along then or when they made *Keep Your Powder Dry* six years later, but I know they were friends later on, when Laraine was married to baseball great Leo Durocher. He was a close friend of Frank Sinatra's and they were all in the same group of friends.

Mother's favorite *Calling Dr. Kildare* cast member at the time was probably Don Barry, who had a bit part as one of the hospital interns. They dated frequently before she became engaged to Greg Bautzer.

At the close of production in March 1939, a parchment scroll signed by the company was presented to director Harold S. Bucquet. The men signed as "Doctor," the girls as "Registered Nurse." Left to right are Lew Ayres, production manager Charles Stallings, Mom, Bucquet, and Laraine Day.

These Glamour Girls (1939)

Plot Points: It's time for the annual house parties at Kingsford prep school and any upper crust girl in Manhattan caught without an invitation from one of the college boys is automatically a social outcast. Dime-a-dance girl Jane Thomas (LT) wins her invite from Philip Griswold III (Lew Ayres) after some of the "glamour boys" drop into the Joy Lane for a spin around the dance floor. At Kingsford, Jane becomes the center of attention as the new girl with more personality and style than any of the others, but her endurance is put to the test in a melee of snobs over the most memorable weekend of house parties Kingsford has seen yet.

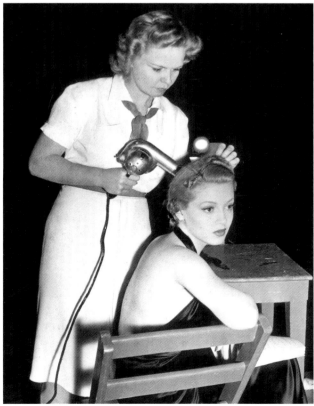

Behind the scenes photos snapped in June 1939.

As the girl from a dancehall thrust into a world of wealthy young snobs, Lana Turner took center stage for an entire film for the first time with *These Glamour Girls*. This was the first film that really focused on her. It gave Mother the courage to make her first demand, insisting on (and getting) her own dressing room. Her co-star was Lew Ayres for a third time and the movie featured her with another large cast of fresh faces. Starring as beautiful, fun-loving kids, they weren't required to do much more than play variations on themselves.

Cast members included Tom Brown, Richard Carlson, Jane Bryan, Marsha Hunt, Ann Rutherford, Mary Beth

With producer Sam Zimbalist and director S. Sylvan Simon.

It appears Mother and Tom Brown's on-the-set jam session . . .

Hughes, and Anita Louise. Most of them were in their teens or early twenties and had never been to college themselves. The boys played it blithely while the girls made their characters very catty, competing with each other for the best hairstyles, best dresses, and best boyfriends. Mother made friends with Tom Brown and dated him a few times. S. Sylvan Simon directed the film and he would go on to work with Mother twice more.

I know that Mom enjoyed *These Glamour Girls* because she got to dance a lot in the film. There is a party sequence that plays out through the night, Mother sheathed in form-fitting black satin, which was realistic for her in those

. . . inspired them to move on to the dance floor of the Trocadero.

days. Mother herself was a creature of the night, though she didn't like the dark. She kept a dim light in her room overnight. There was also something disquieting to her about twilight. As soon as the sun began to go down, all drapes were drawn and the lights went on to avoid the diffused light of dusk.

Dancing Co-Ed (1939)

Plot Points: As a publicity stunt in the search for a partner for dancing star Freddy Tobin (Lee Bowman), promoter Joe Drews (Roscoe Karns) decides to scour the nation's college campuses. But not just any "cluck" will do. Enter Patty Marlow (LT). To ensure that the girl who wins the contest can indeed dance, Drews has her enrolled at Midwestern College. They don't anticipate interference from Pug Braddock (Richard Carlson), a newspaper editor who senses something fishy about the contest and is bent on finding the "plant" right at Midwestern. To misdirect Pug, Patty joins the investigation.

Mother kept a photo memento of the first time she saw her name on a movie theater marquee. It was for *Dancing Co-Ed*. Beyond that, this was a memorable film for Mother because of Artie Shaw. His disdainful attitude toward the movies made him unattractive to her during production, but she adored his music and got to show off her dancing abilities to the terrific rhythm of his orchestra.

Though dancing was such a big part of her private self, this was the first time she was ever thought of as a dancer in her work. And she probably only got the opportunity because this was once planned as a project for one of the best dancers in Hollywood, Eleanor Powell. But then they decided to make it a showcase for Lana Turner instead. Patty was a slick part for Mother in those days, described by the

Neither one of them thought of as dancers, Mother and Lee Bowman displayed new talents in *Dancing Co-Ed*.

Recovering from dance rehearsals.

film's U.K. title, *Every Other Inch a Lady*. Her friend Ann Rutherford was on hand again. It was another happy film for her, one of her favorites.

Mom didn't let Artie's attitude bother her. She just waited it out. When production wrapped on August 22, 1939, she thought he would be gone forever, but it was never that cut and dried with Mother. She married him first, six months later. A second future husband was in the cast. Fred May, who was earning extra dollars by working as a movie extra at the time, was employed for the college scenes. When they were dating in 1959, Fred reminded Mother that they had met on the set of *Dancing Co-Ed*. She remembered that young extra, which isn't surprising. She never forgot faces or names.

With Richard Carlson, best known for sci-fi films of the '50s, like *Creature from the Black Lagoon*.

As dancing star Patty Marlow.

Tapping her feet to the music of the Artie Shaw Orchestra was very exciting.

Two Girls on Broadway (1940)

Plot Points: Dancers Molly (Joan Blondell) and Pat Mahoney (LT) come to New York when Molly's fiancé Eddie (George Murphy) gets them an audition at a nightclub. The result of the tryout is that Pat is hired to dance with Eddie, and Molly is consigned to selling cigarettes. The result of Pat and Eddie's successful pairing onstage is that they fall in love. Desperate to end the romance before it begins, Pat takes up with playboy Chat Chatsworth (Kent Taylor), who would love to make her his next bride. It's up to Eddie and Molly to save her from the fate of becoming the fifth Mrs. Chatsworth.

Two Girls on Broadway was the last of three consecutive films Mother made under the direction of S. Sylvan Simon. Simon was a producer and director who made several

Behind the scenes of *Two Girls on Broadway.*

first-rate comedies with Red Skelton, Lucille Ball, and Abbott and Costello. Mother enjoyed working with him on *These Glamour Girls*, *Dancing Co-Ed*, and *Two Girls on Broadway*. The story for their last movie together was almost as old as MGM. Released in 1929, *The Broadway Melody* was the studio's first talking film, earned a Best Picture Oscar, and inspired three follow-up *Broadway Melody* films with new stars and plotlines.

The remake of the 1929 film gave Mother another chance to display her dancing abilities in tap and ballroom numbers. Everyone was surprised by how well she did in those sequences. A number of critics, just getting over the breakup of the Fred Astaire-Ginger Rogers team, paid her the high compliment of comparing her favorably to Rogers in their reviews. She earned it, working hard on the numbers with dance directors Bobby Connelly and Eddie Larkin.

Mother also ice skated, played comedy with Joan Blondell, and even got to have fun with a drunk scene. Although she was acting with performers with at least a decade of experience behind them, when it was over she left no doubt as to who the star was. She took advantage of the opportunities afforded by the script and made *Two Girls on Broadway* her film.

On Mother's nineteenth birthday, the company presented her with a cake that read, "To the Sweater Girl. From the gang that make the yarn."

Mother sipped coffee between takes all day from her earliest films.

Dancing tap and ballroom fashion with George Murphy.

With director S. Sylvan Simon.

We Who Are Young (1940)

Plot Points: Newlyweds Margy (LT) and Bill Brooks (John Shelton) embark on married life with hope and visions of comfort and babies in their future, but a series of misfortunes shake their optimism to the core. When Margy becomes pregnant, joy is overshadowed by mounting bills, scowling collectors, and an insensitive boss. Discord seeps into Margy and Bill's relationship and Bill finds himself out of a job. At the darkest hour, help and generosity comes from unexpected sources, and the Brookses have a tiny new addition to the family to help them celebrate life.

We Who Are Young was a strange interlude between *Two Girls on Broadway* and *Ziegfeld Girl*. They put Mother in a serious role to offset her reputation as a Nightclub Queen who marries in haste. This campaign was helped by the fact that during production she was supposedly happily married to Artie Shaw and the publicity was playing up her domestic side. The film she was making accented that aspect of her as well. She had a baby for the first time in a film. In fact, she said it was supposed to be twins at first.

This was the first Hollywood film from veteran producer Seymour Nebenzal, whose collaborations with G. W. Pabst in German cinema produced *Pandora's Box* and *M*. The working title of the movie was *To Own the World*. It was a Depression-era story written by Dalton Trumbo. The none-too-subtle message seemed to be that we should beware of falling into debt.

With co-star
John Shelton.

We Who Are Young was completed on June 1, 1940. A lot was happening for Mother in that brief first half of the year. In January she started *Two Girls on Broadway*. In the middle of production she created a media stir with her surprise marriage to Artie Shaw. After the film's completion they took a trip to New York. The honeymoon ended before it began and Mother was taken to the hospital after becoming hysterical in the middle of one of their fights. She bounced back and went to work on *We Who Are Young* at the end of April. Her marriage neared its end as the movie was being made that spring. When it was over she was exhausted. Leaving arrangements for her divorce in the hands of Greg Bautzer, she set off on a vacation to Hawaii.

Outside of her dressing room. On the dressing table behind her sits a photo of Artie.

Some unique candids from the set.

Ziegfeld Girl (1941)

Plot Points: A new edition of Ziegfeld's *Follies* is opening, and filling out the beauteous façade are three new faces from different walks of life. There's Sandra (Hedy Lamarr), deeply in love with her violinist husband (Philip Dorn) and hoping to keep them afloat until his big break, but only bringing to the surface flaws in their relationship. Susan (Judy Garland) is a born-in-a-trunk entertainer soon to get her much-deserved chance. The third *Follies* newcomer is Sheila (LT), a Flatbush beauty plucked out of an elevator by Ziegfeld himself and put on a pedestal, where she'll learn if she can take advantage of the opportunities and still bypass the temptations set before her.

Ziegfeld Girl epitomizes the glamour of the studio era. The cast, costumes, settings, story, and music are superb down the line. Busby Berkeley staged the musical sequences. A team of MGM musical talents collaborated on the soundtrack. It was in planning stages in 1938 to follow up director Robert Z. Leonard's 1936 musical *The Great Ziegfeld*. At that time, Joan Crawford, Virginia Bruce, Eleanor Powell, Margaret Sullavan, and Walter Pidgeon were reportedly going to star, but there were so many delays during pre-production that by the fall of 1940, an entirely new cast was stepping before the cameras. The group was led by Mother, Judy Garland, Hedy Lamarr, and James Stewart. In this assemblage it was Mother who gave the breakthrough performance.

Sheila Regan was her first grown-up, dramatic role. When it landed in her lap she took it as a sign that the powers that be at MGM believed in her, which gave her confidence as well as the desire to prove her bosses right. She dedicated herself to giving a great performance through training with acting coach Lillian Burns. There were many built-in challenges. For one, Sheila becomes an alcoholic and Mother insisted that she had never been drunk in her life up to then. Her well-known proclivity for nightclubs in those days was about dancing and being out with friends, not drinking. She gleaned inspiration from watching Bette Davis play drunk in the film *Dangerous* several times.

Ultimately, Mother came to truly understand her character. "I knew Sheila's every thought, every movement. I didn't even have to practice her walk. I knew how she would walk, because I knew everything else about her." Reacting to the performance he saw in the daily rushes, director Robert Z. Leonard had her part expanded further. In an interview in 1948, before many of her later memorable roles but after *Postman* and *Green Dolphin Street*, Mother said, "Perhaps if I could be remembered for only one performance, I'd choose Sheila."

The clothes and jewels, the most elaborate she had seen up to the time she made this film, made a huge impression on Mother, as did the script. She had a red basket purse in the '50s embossed around the edges with a paraphrased line she says in the film: "All the things I really like are illegal, immoral, or fattening." The Production Code Administration was less enamored of the dialogue. They asked for many lines to be rewritten, so many that MGM got away with not making all of the changes. Dan Dailey still got to call Mother a tramp, while her opening line, "And how do you like your heels, mister—round?" was changed. Instead of saying "round," she does a hand motion.

Surrounded by the showgirls; she was enveloped in pink tulle with silver stars, sequins, and spangles.

With Judy Garland and Hedy Lamarr.

"I got the idea that perhaps there was talent to dig for, and put myself into the part heart and soul."

As Sheila, from wide-eyed to drowsy-eyed as the story plays.

"Chin up. Shoulders relaxed. Smile." A fragile Sheila attempts to descend the stairs with all the majesty of a *Ziegfeld pro*. As the refrain of her theme song swells, she starts. Midway she hesitates with a subtle motion of her hand to the banister. Reaching the newel post she falls limp, her body meeting the floor with balletic fluency.

Mom was rightly proud of her famous fall down the staircase at the end. As executed you think she's dead when she hits the floor. Does she or doesn't she die? They leave it up to the audience, but that was not the original intention. Sheila actually dies in the script, but early audiences didn't like that. With a simple snip of the celluloid in her death scene the problem was fixed. Cutting out right before she closes her eyes left Sheila's fate up to the viewer and produced an ending that most approved of, with the possible exception of the writers. My own favorite part is when she talks with James Stewart about the fuzzy little ducks. When I was little I used to ask her to "do the fuzzy little ducks." They became a code for us when Mother and I had a fight. Over the years, showing up with a fuzzy yellow duck could patch things up between us.

An outtake from filming the famous fall.

Sheila's death scene, with Hedy Lamarr and Philip Dorn.

On the set with co-star James Stewart.

Dr. Jekyll and Mr. Hyde (1941)

Plot Points: Can the evil in man be expelled from the body, leaving only good? This question motivates Dr. Jekyll's (Spencer Tracy) laboratory experiments, which scandalize his colleagues and friends. Jekyll's research intensifies when his fiancée Beatrix (LT) departs for the Continent. Consuming his own latest experiments leads to ever more horrific episodes of transformation. The purely evil alter ego known as Hyde delights in terrorizing Ivy (Ingrid Bergman), a barmaid in whom he had taken an interest as Jekyll. Before long it becomes apparent that Hyde is in control and Jekyll lives no more.

I have heard that the original casting of *Dr. Jekyll and Mr. Hyde* had Mother as the tart, Ivy, and Ingrid Bergman as the dulcet Beatrix. I don't see Mother in the role of Ivy, not in 1941. She had some growing up to do yet. It's contrary to what her own book says, but if she had been offered the role, I can't imagine her saying no to anything at this stage in her career. Production records show that Ingrid Bergman was slated for the part from the earliest days, with no suggestion that they wanted Mother to play Ivy. The records do, however, show that there was quite a bit of back and forth regarding the casting of Beatrix. Ruth Hussey and Maureen O'Hara were suggested, and then shortly before filming began, Mother's name showed up on the cast list.

Beatrix was a perfect role for her then and she made it more interesting than the character appears on the surface. Beatrix is sweet but spirited, playful but deeply perceptive and capable of profound love. Her connection to Jekyll is almost on a mystic plane. It doesn't alter her love for him, but she has instincts that tell her something is awry with her fiancé.

Visually exciting photographic techniques were employed throughout the film by Joseph Ruttenberg, whose work earned him an Oscar nomination. In the dream montages by Peter Ballbusch, menacing figures are juxtaposed against the lovely faces of Beatrix and Ivy, overlapping with images of erupting volcanoes, corkscrews, and test tubes. Originally, there were scenes of the women being struck by Hyde's whip, but in the face of objections from the censors, it was edited so that Hyde's maniacal frenzy remains, but the actual whipping wasn't shown. Clarence Bull continued the intriguing visuals in his still photography with unusual compositions and using cutouts and giant props as backgrounds for the actors.

The attention to special effects caught audiences by surprise, but the film had a lot to live up to following the acclaimed 1931 version of *Dr. Jekyll and Mr. Hyde* starring Fredric March. The earlier film showed advanced superficial makeup for Jekyll to become Hyde before viewers' eyes, but March's Hyde ultimately looked like an ape man, causing some unintentional laughter from the audience. Spencer Tracy's transformation was not as extreme. He still looked like a man, and he helped the less superficial makeup with changes in body language.

Mother was delighted to be working in a film with Tracy and Bergman. She used to say "I learned so much just watching Tracy." She was disappointed that she and Bergman were not in the same scenes, with the exception of the dream sequence, which was awkward and uncomfortable to film. Their director, Victor

With Ingrid Bergman in a nightmare sequence. Mom considered Bergman one of the greats.

Fleming, was among the best, two years after his work on *Gone With the Wind* and *The Wizard of Oz*. It was true he had a great track record with women's films, but he was known as a macho director who favored his male stars. He did nothing to alter that reputation with Mother. She encountered his temper during filming.

The unpleasant lapses didn't diminish Mom's pride in the completed film. A large portrait of her (as her own mother in the movie) makes one brief appearance onscreen. About fifteen minutes into the story, Dr. Jekyll and Beatrix put on a waltz tune and then the scene cuts to her father. As he raises his head, the camera tilts upward to reveal a glorious painting of his deceased wife. Mother had this portrait cut down to a much smaller oval and saved it as a memento from *Jekyll and Hyde*.

Clarence Bull's still photography evoked the visual style of the film, which earned Oscar nominations for its cinematography, editing, and music score. To keep the mystique of the film, no behind-the-scenes photos were taken.

If the picture had followed Robert Louis Stevenson's original novel, there wouldn't have been any speculation about what roles Mother and Ingrid were going to play. Their characters were not created by Stevenson but appeared in later adaptations.

Honky Tonk (1941)

Plot Points: Candy Johnson (Clark Gable), who has refined the con game into an art form, wins the trust of the citizens of Yellow Creek, while winning the heart of the judge's daughter, Elizabeth Cotton (LT). If Candy cheats the townspeople out of their money, that's fine with Judge Cotton (Frank Morgan), a conman himself, but he won't stand for it after he involves Elizabeth and the child she's carrying in his crooked schemes. The Judge rouses the citizens against Candy. Candy can talk the people into his good graces again, but a silver tongue can't save the judge or Elizabeth when they need him the most, leading Candy to rethink his way of life.

With visions of a dashing Rhett Butler in *Gone With the Wind* fresh in moviegoers' minds, a rising actress couldn't ask for any better than a co-starring role opposite the King, Clark Gable. In 1941 Gable was in top form and Lana Turner was on fire after *Ziegfeld Girl*. It was a match made in heaven, but Gable didn't think so at first. Three years earlier, he had obliged when the studio asked him to play opposite Mom

in a test. The scene was from his torrid 1932 hit with Jean Harlow, *Red Dust*. Mother didn't perform it very well. While making *Honky Tonk*, he noted her improvement by telling her, "Baby, you sure have learned a thing or two."

One lesson Mother had learned was to absorb all she could from the professionals in the cast and among the crew. The director was Jack Conway, who had directed comedies

Though she was just twenty, critics said Lana Turner made Gable's hottest screen partner since Jean Harlow in *Red Dust*.

with Myrna Loy, Carole Lombard, and Jean Harlow. The photography was by Harlow's former cinematographer (and husband), Harold Rosson. Rosson's handling of the camerawork contributed to the common belief that Mother was Gable's best partner since Harlow.

Mostly, however, it was the dynamics between Mother and Gable as they acted out the excitement, drama, and comedy set in an old western town. They looked happy with each other. As she drinks him under the table and into marriage and he breaks down a door to get into her bedroom, they may be right that trouble is waiting for them "sitting on the bedpost," but they seem only thrilled to see what form it will take. *Honky Tonk* became MGM's highest-grossing film of the year and Mother and Gable made the cover of *Life* magazine, which was a very big deal to her. She took great pride in it.

Mom and Gable had a cute movie meeting on a train, exchanging winks and sly banter.

Who's putting something over on whom? Elizabeth can drink Candy under the table.

Candy has strengths of his own, as he proves when she locks him out of their bedroom.

Mother behind the scenes of *Honky Tonk*.

While the film was made, Gable's wife, the glamorous comedienne Carole Lombard, was interested in the new sensation appearing with her husband. Playing her first love scene with Gable, Mother turned around and there was Lombard on the set. Mother said she just froze inside. She was so much in awe of them individually and as a couple that she couldn't perform and scurried off to her dressing room, where she stayed until Mrs. Gable was gone. Rumors flew that she had come to check up on her husband because there was something brewing between Mother and Gable, but it wasn't true. Gable was her Saturday matinee idol, later her favorite co-star and a friend, but never her lover off the screen.

She and Gable had a great working relationship and an on-screen chemistry that led to their pairing in three more films. He helped her through *Honky Tonk* and at the end, she helped him through his unease while making his last film for MGM, *Betrayed*. They were, as advertised in their third film, *Homecoming*, "The Team that Generates Steam."

This tight shot captures the activity of a movie set. Mother's makeup is touched up, she's fed new lines, and a crew member adjusts the lights.

Johnny Eager (1942)

Plot Points: Johnny Eager (Robert Taylor), a well-known racketeer, has gone straight after his release from jail—or so it would appear to anyone outside of his inner circle. Only District Attorney Farrell (Edward Arnold) stands in the way of his opening a dog racetrack. Farrell loathes Johnny for romancing his daughter, Lisbeth (LT). Lisbeth becomes traumatized by killing a man in Johnny's defense, unaware that she was used as a pawn to get a permit from Farrell to open the racetrack. Only Johnny can penetrate her mind. Her love is so great that it teaches Johnny the meaning of the word and they go to desperate measures to protect each other.

In quick succession, Mother went from onscreen romances with James Stewart, Spencer Tracy, Clark Gable, and Robert Taylor, the biggest male stars at MGM. The studio was pulling out the heavy artillery to promote her and showed care in arranging her schedule to allow this remarkable lineup of co-stars (with another Gable movie to come next.) They hoped this pairing would be the most explosive yet. "Taylor 'n Turner are T-N-T," was the advertising tagline.

"You'd better get out of here! I'll try to cover up for you!"

Mervyn LeRoy directed *Johnny Eager*, which was shot from September 2 to October 28, 1941. Mother always felt secure under LeRoy's wing, and every production brought new pals. Van Heflin was brilliant as Taylor's philosophical drunkard best friend and won the Academy Award as Best Supporting Actor. He became a great friend of the family.

His daughter, Vanna, was my age and we had many play dates arranged by our parents.

Johnny Eager was a favorite in our family and among her fans. It has fine acting and writing and is a beautiful film to look at with the striking couple of Taylor and Turner. It was a steamy drama and the censors protested about the killings, excessive drinking, a district attorney willing to break the law, the number of women with whom Taylor's character becomes involved, and "innumerable other details." Mother found it hilarious to hear the censors' very precise reactions to different aspects of her films that were considered offensive.

The movie also pushed the envelope with the censors in terms of how intimate love scenes could be played. Mom and Robert Taylor took these scenes so seriously that a co-star romance emerged. She described their relationship as a terrific attraction that led to some ardent kisses in the guise of being for the sake of art. She wouldn't let it go further and felt there was nothing too compromising between them until the day Taylor told her that he was in love with her and wanted to leave his wife, Barbara Stanwyck. This shook Mother to her senses. Whatever romantic

The leading players: Edward Arnold, Mother, Robert Taylor, Van Heflin, and Patricia Dane. Dane, whom we thought so effective as Taylor's jilted girlfriend, had been one of the showgirl extras of *Ziegfeld Girl*.

Mother and Robert Taylor's kisses fired up the screen, and the censors. Besides his exterior looks and charm, criminal Johnny's redeeming quality is the selfless love he finds himself capable of for Lisbeth.

involvement she and Taylor had ended there and the Taylors remained together.

Hollywood was a close-knit community in some respects. Mother and Stanwyck steered clear of each other, but never made their personal feelings public knowledge or caused scenes. There was a kind of code in Hollywood. Generally speaking, there was loyalty among those in the business in spite of any ill feelings. The sense of protection was not limited to the complicated crossings of romantic paths; even personal information in households where domestic violence, child abuse or drug addiction took place was not discussed.

Shots are fired by Lizbeth's hand, a man falls dead, and she goes into shock. Not even Johnny can snap her out of it.

Behind the scenes with Mervyn LeRoy.

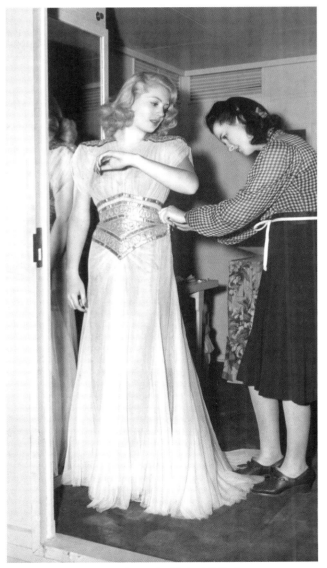

Her beautiful gowns were the work of Robert Kalloch.

Absorbed in the funny pages of the newspaper.

Somewhere I'll Find You (1942)

Plot Points: From overseas, foreign correspondents Jonny (Clark Gable) and Kirk Davis (Robert Sterling) see firsthand the inevitability of the U.S. entering the war on the eve of Pearl Harbor. When the Japanese attack, the boys are stateside pursuing fellow reporter Paula Lane (LT). Kirk wants to marry her, but Paula loves Jonny, who takes a dim view of her. Paula leaves both behind for a job in China, where she disappears from view while transporting children from the battlefields to safety. When Kirk and Jonny are sent to find her, Jonny discovers that Paula is no ordinary girl, but romance must take a back seat as war rages.

Mother and Gable's second co-starring vehicle proved to be another hit.

Paula's heroism in Indochina shows Jonny what a great woman she is.

Mother's second film with Clark Gable was her first to acknowledge the war, and it hit home in the most terrible way for the cast and crew of *Somewhere I'll Find You*. The bombing of Pearl Harbor had occurred about a month before production began, bringing America into what up to then many Americans saw as a European conflict—none of our business. Carole Lombard was among the first who rushed to raise money for the war effort by departing on a bond drive. On January 16, 1942, the plane which was taking Lombard home again crashed outside of Las Vegas. Lombard, her mother, and all aboard the plane were killed.

Back in Hollywood, the news reached MGM, where *Somewhere I'll Find You* had just begun filming. Gable was devastated. Production was closed down until the end of February. Mother went to New York and it was there she celebrated her twenty-first birthday during the break. She spent it fulfilling an engagement Lombard had to record a radio version of her film *Mr. and Mrs. Smith* with Errol Flynn. Rumors reached her that Lombard had been nervous about leaving her husband "alone with Lana Turner," and that she came back by plane instead of train to arrive home sooner. Mother was terribly hurt by this story.

Presenting the "Victory Bob".

Gable's professionalism allowed him to return to work after several weeks and see the movie through to completion with his usual charm and personality still evident onscreen for his fans to enjoy. The irony of the release title was unintentionally insensitive, but it was considered preferable to the working title, which had been *Red Light*. Upon completion of the film, Gable joined the Army Air Force and was absent from the screen for three years.

Mother joined the war effort in her own way soon after filming. She went on tour with the USO in the summer, selling bonds and even kisses. She entertained, visited hospitals, laughed with the boys and listened to their stories. Even her hair was patriotic. In *Somewhere I'll Find You* she debuted her "Victory Bob." That way female war workers could continue to emulate her without the threat of getting dangling locks caught in defense plant machinery. The worst hair offender in those days was Veronica Lake. The actress's trademark "Peekaboo" wave that fell over one eye was so widely copied that she famously endorsed an upturned hairstyle in the interest of national defense.

Robert Sterling was also in love with her in this film.

In the movie, Jonny pulls a weary Paula out of a swamp. These are candids of Gable and Mom during production.

Du Barry Was a Lady (1943)

Plot Points: Nightclub star May Daly (Lucille Ball) has marriage proposals from both hatcheck boy Louie Blore (Red Skelton) and dancer Alec Howe (Gene Kelly). Alec has her heart, but Irish Sweepstakes winner Louie takes the lead with money-minded May. A wild hallucination takes them all back to the time of King Louis XV. Louie becomes king, with May as his notorious mistress Madame Du Barry, and Alec reemerges as an upstart called the Black Arrow. The lavish royal court of eighteenth-century France becomes the perfect setting to sort out a swing-era love triangle.

Du Barry Was a Lady featured Mother in her Technicolor debut. Unfortunately, she only made a cameo appearance. It was a gag at the end of the "I Love an Esquire Girl" number. Her name is in the last line of the lyrics, and suddenly there she is, on the arm of her pal Red Skelton. The camera closes in and she gives a wink. The moment was filmed in September 1942. Mother soon became pregnant with me and this bit, as well as another cameo in *The Youngest Profession*, was shot just before completion of her next big film, *Slightly Dangerous*. Besides *Slightly Dangerous*, those two brief appearances were all the studio had to offer her public for many months.

With producer Arthur Freed and *Du Barry* stars Gene Kelly, Lucille Ball, and Red Skelton. Mother is in costume for *Slightly Dangerous*.

Modeling her gown from *Du Barry*. It can be seen on another actress when Mom dances the rumba in *Marriage Is a Private Affair*.

While on maternity leave, the studio would have made efforts to keep her name before the public. She, however, took care of that herself, thanks to my father and their trouble-plagued union. Meanwhile, her studio kept hoping she'd get back to work. They announced to the newspapers that she was going to act in various films. The star of *Du Barry Was a Lady*, Lucille Ball, replaced her in one of these projects, *Best Foot Forward*. In that movie Mother would have played herself again, in a story about a movie star who accepts an invitation to be the prom date of one of her most devoted teenaged fans.

The song lyrics "And if Lana Turner doesn't set you in a whirl . . . " prompt an appearance from the woman herself.

The Youngest Profession (1943)

Plot Points: Teenager Joan Lyons' (Virginia Weidler) mission in life is to collect as many celebrity autographs as humanly possible. She and her cohort, Patty (Jean Porter), can track down any movie star who sets foot in New York. If they miss meeting Greer Garson at Grand Central Station, they can find her at her hotel, just as they met Lana Turner at the Waldorf. Nothing can stop Joan when she's hot on the trail of an autograph, and once she has it, she isn't shy about involving stars to sort out her many personal crises.

Mother's cameo as herself in *The Youngest Profession* evinced the fan mania that was growing in response to her recent hit films and her news-making activities off screen. It's an odd little movie, all about professional autograph hounds. They show Mother reading and answering fan mail, an aspect of her job she took very seriously. All my life I remember there was a part of her day dedicated to autographing photos and responding to special pieces of fan mail that were brought to her attention.

Director Eddie Buzzell gives Mother a shoulder to lean on while signing an autograph for Virginia Weidler.

Slightly Dangerous (1943)

Plot Points: Peggy Evans (LT) can't stand another dull day manning the soda fountain at a drugstore in Hotchkiss Falls. She runs away, leaving behind what reads as a suicide note in answer to a fight with her boss, Bob Stuart (Robert Young). To clear his name, Bob embarks on a search for Peggy, who by then has reached New York. Faking amnesia, she has convinced the wealthy Cornelius Burden (Walter Brennan) that she's his long lost daughter. Just as she earns his love and debuts in society, Bob rears his head and takes her on a fateful road trip that shows that everything Peggy ever wanted may have been right in Hotchkiss Falls.

A lot was going on in Mother's life at the time *Slightly Dangerous* was filmed, but she remembered it with special fondness because she found out she was pregnant. Not showing yet, she was just slightly more curvaceous and possessed a certain maternal glow. Meanwhile she was incensed with my father. It was around this time the news broke that by an oversight regarding the divorce laws, she was not legally married to the man whose child she was carrying. Then she suffered fainting spells and went to the hospital a few times.

Mom was making headlines as new developments in her personal life constantly surfaced. The most suitable movie title for a star like her was disputed back and forth. *Careless Cinderella*, *Lawless*, and *Nothing Ventured* were working titles before they hit upon *Slightly Dangerous*. Whatever they called it, in spite of everything, she was inspired to give a delightful comic performance. The movie is full of fun moments, including when a can of

paint splatters all over her brand new suit. The director was Wesley Ruggles, with whom she was working for the second time in a row. Ruggles thought her energy and the "sparkle" in her acting was the nearest he ever encountered to '20s "It" Girl Clara Bow, whom he directed in *The Plastic Age*.

Co-star Robert Young was not of the stature of Gable, Tracy, or Taylor. This was the first time Mother was relied upon to carry a major production, with every bit of action revolving around her. Mother goes from brunette to blonde in *Slightly Dangerous*, her character spending the last penny to her name on a glamorous makeover. This is the first film in which I spot her wearing important pieces from her expanding jewelry collection. She wore her own amethyst ring in the scene where she and Young eat hamburgers while dancing.

A scene that was a joy to watch but a nightmare to film had her character, Peggy, saying that her job is so

As the pre-makeover Peggy Evans.

easy she could do it blindfolded, and then she proceeds to prove it by making a banana split with a handkerchief over her eyes. Mother truly could not see a thing behind that blindfold and it was a trial to get the correct portions of vanilla, chocolate, and strawberry ice cream, slice and arrange the banana, and top it with whipped cream, chocolate syrup, and a cherry. They had to shoot the scene over and over for a variety of reasons. The lights kept melting the ice cream. Then they would bring in new ice cream and have to wait because it was too hard for scooping. It was a long day but it paid off in the finished film.

A can of red paint falls on Peggy. This was a great comic scene for her.

This scene, in which she returns to the soda fountain at the end, was cut from the film.

From the look on Robert Young's face, her desserts don't turn out half as good when she's not blindfolded.

Perhaps a call from my father? They had married a few weeks before the film went into production. Walter Brennan is in the background.

Walter Brennan played papa, one surprised by the return of his long-lost "daughter."

Between takes with director Wesley Ruggles.

Plot Points: Theo Scofield (LT) has heard many marriage proposals. She isn't sure what makes Lt. Tom West (John Hodiak) different from any of the others, but he is sweet and she's willing to give married life a shot. She has seen four bad examples of marriage by her Mother (Natalie Schafer), and the sad reality of a "perfect couple," the Mortimers (Frances Gifford and Herbert Rudley). When her old flame, Capt. Miles Lancing (James Craig) hits town, Theo puts her marriage to the test to find out for herself if in spite of temptations and a poor family record, she loves Tom enough to make her marriage work.

Another ironic title based on events in Mother's life at the time. Excluding her two cameos, this was the third such title in succession. Mother's marriage was less a private affair than a public scandal and her MGM bosses knew it. But Mother had the unusual good fortune of having the publicity work to her advantage, making her an even bigger star.

Fan magazines said she was a girl with an impulsive nature and a heart of gold, both of which could lead to trouble. The public was sympathetic to her and showed their love through fan mail and box-office sales.

Mother had been very ill right after I was born. On *Marriage*, which was filmed between January and April 1944, she was back from maternity leave, still not feeling well, and thin. She dipped to 103 pounds. That was too low for her, but the weight loss gave her more defined cheekbones and less roundness in the face. Mother later described herself as not looking well in this period because

Irene designs for the film.

Mother had the know-how to maintain her own styles.

A moment with her director, "Pop" Leonard. Mother hadn't stepped before the cameras for over a year. She said she was "as jittery as when I appeared in my first picture."

of her anemia. Anyone looking at the movie would beg to differ. She's arguably at her most beautiful. A new makeup artist, Del Armstrong, worked with her for the first time on this movie. He was one of the greats of his profession. She trusted him with her face more than she trusted herself and she learned from him. He also became her best friend.

Mother is at her most experimental in this film. Her hair was long and lush and she could do anything with it, as evidenced by the myriad hairstyles on display. Seen in cascading waves, a coronet of braids, duet buns, knotted neatly at the back, and in ram's horn twirls above her forehead, the hairstyles were designed to harmonize with the fashions by Irene paraded through the two-hour length of the film. A wool bathing suit, housedresses, sports clothes, gowns, tailored suits, and finely detailed hats made up the trousseau of Mother's newlywed character and set fashion trends of the day. The standout was what Mother called her "rumba dress," worn for her first on-camera rumba. The black and white film didn't do justice to the striking satin panels of black and pink that matched the roses at the left side of the bodice.

Beyond the glamour, Lana the actress handled burping cloths, bottles, and baby bottoms, playing a mommy for the second time in her career. Playing Daddy was John Hodiak, who was a good choice for her leading man at the time. He was handsome and gaining respect as the classic film of his career, Alfred Hitchcock's *Lifeboat*, was opening in theaters across the country. Supporting actor James Craig was an up-and-comer as well. He could count Ginger Rogers, Lucille Ball, Hedy Lamarr, and Marlene Dietrich as his recent leading ladies.

Rehearsing with John Hodiak.

The censors were concerned about how little she had on under this apron.

They looked good together, but most of the time Mom and Hodiak worked together they were heard but not seen, on radio. They performed *Once Upon a Honeymoon*, *Honky Tonk*, *Marriage Is a Private Affair*, and *The Postman Always Rings Twice* over the airwaves.

In her dressing room.

Marriage Is a Private Affair had a history of conflict with the censors dating back to 1941, when a synopsis inspired by the Judith Kelly novel was submitted to the Production Code Administration. It was rejected for a long list of reasons. For starters, the heroine committed adultery, her mother was deemed immoral, and her married friends had affairs. There were also conversations about an abortion in the story to save Theo's life. Warners thought it was hopeless and sold the rights to MGM, who announced the film would be made with Robert Taylor and Myrna Loy, with director George Cukor at the helm. MGM writers went back and forth with the censors to produce a script that was finally approved in 1943 and then it became a showcase for Lana Turner. After it was released, many regional censorship boards made eliminations, the most popular being Theo's first words after childbirth: "I'm flat."

Keep Your Powder Dry (1945)

Plot Points: The only way for Valerie Parks (LT) to earn her inheritance is to prove to the trustees of her family estate that she's more than a playgirl. The best way to prove herself worthy, she decides, is to join the war effort by becoming a WAC. During training, Val clashes with a more serious daughter of the military, Leigh Rand (Laraine Day), and befriends the earnest Ann Darrison (Susan Peters) among a varied group of women. Her experiences in training begin to show Valerie there may be more to life than the hollow existence she'd been leading with her heedless, or rather, mindless, society friends.

With Laraine Day and Susan Peters. The film's premiere was made part of a WAC recruiting campaign.

WACS, WAVES, WASPS—the women's Army, Navy, and Airforce Service, respectively. Women were doing their part in World War II, so Mother lost the chiffon and lace of Irene and Adrian designs in favor of khaki to reflect the spirit of Rosie the Riveter in *Keep Your Powder Dry*. That title was given quite a bit of thought as they were calling it *A Woman's Army*, *Women in Uniform*, and *There Were Three of Us* in the trades before the final was reached. Joan Crawford was announced to star early on, but it became a vehicle for Mother instead.

Mom looked especially attractive in her early scenes, before the WAC uniforms come out and her long blonde hair is hidden under her Army-issue hat. Director Eddie Buzzell has her *revealed*, rolling over in bed, face into the camera. Besides her beauty, she is effective as Valerie Parks.

The mere thought of her waxing a floor, as she does in the film, was apparently hilarious.

It's interesting to watch her character's growth in the story from social butterfly, with little more on her mind than highballs and high heels, to a responsible woman. She becomes able to shed her self-interest and devote herself to a cause and to friendship with women very different from herself. As Valerie, Mother subtly progresses to that stage by degrees. She's as believable then as she is as the playgirl of early scenes.

The star puts her feet up between scenes.

There was no leading man for Mother in *Keep Your Powder Dry*. In fact, it was originally intended that the cast be all female, but several male members were added to the company as officers, soldiers, and Valerie's fair-weather friends as the start of production date neared in the late summer of 1944. All the major roles remained for ladies only.

Natalie Schafer, of *Gilligan's Island* television fame, was cast in a role not unlike her famous Lovey Howell character.

One could say that here she plays Lovey's catty, humorless cousin. Schafer often played this kind of part in the 1940s. In fact, she just had in *Marriage Is a Private Affair*. She kept on going in that mold in the '50s until finally she found a way to make that character loveable on *Gilligan*.

The main plot thrust centered on the relationship between three very different aspiring WACs. Laraine Day was convincingly stringent as Mother's rival. Susan Peters played the third lead. She was a lovely woman and an Academy Award-nominated actress whose life took a tragic turn when she was paralyzed in a hunting accident about a month after filming *Keep Your Powder Dry*. Mother felt great sympathy for her, as did the rest of her coworkers. She was very well-liked at MGM. Several years later Susan acted in one more film from a wheelchair, but she basically made her exit from the screen in this film as the meek girl who has strength to make peace between two headstrong women in uniform.

With Robert Stack.

A number of Mother's famous friends visited her on this set. Clockwise are Frank Sinatra, Gene Kelly (both in costume for *Anchors Aweigh*), and Lucille Ball (with director Eddie Buzzell).

Week-End at the Waldorf (1945)

Plot Points: Just another weekend at the plush Waldorf Hotel. Movie star Irene Malvern (Ginger Rogers) is in town, languishing in discontent. Chip Collyer (Walter Pidgeon), the hero of the newswire, has checked in for a rest, while Capt. James Hollis (Van Johnson) hopes to forget his illness by spending time with hotel stenographer Bunny Smith (LT). To Bunny, one of the perks of her job is that it puts her close to men like Martin Edley (Edward Arnold), a crooked businessman but a wealthy one. Bunny must decide whether to pursue her dream of marrying money or follow her heart to the side of Capt. Hollis.

As the ambitious stenographer Bunny Smith.

Production began on *Week-End at the Waldorf* on October 23, 1944. Mother's fabulous long mane of *Marriage Is a Private Affair* and *Keep Your Powder Dry* had been cut recently on the advice of her doctor, who actually told her that the long, heavy hair was draining her energy and should be cut. Mother didn't mind as she always enjoyed experimenting with new hairstyles. The cut permitted the styling of her V-shaped "Victory" hairdo. Named for the famous World War II call, "V for Victory," besides being patriotic, it also served as the artistic inspiration for "Toodles," the cartoon love interest for Tom Cat.

Mother had good memories of *Waldorf* and enjoyed watching it years later. It was a glossy remake of one of the biggest films in MGM history, *Grand Hotel*. The original, often identified as the first big-budget, all-star movie, was headlined by Greta Garbo, John Barrymore, Joan Crawford, Lionel Barrymore, and Wallace Beery. Set in a posh hotel in Weimar Berlin, it had a grandiose continental atmosphere to it such as most Americans could not imagine in the Depression era.

Waldorf made the original play by Vicki Baum, *Menchen im Hotel*, less of a fantasy than *Grand Hotel*. Made on a two-million-dollar budget, it brought the story stateside to that grand hotel of New York, at which Americans could hope to stay on a splurge, perhaps after wartime rationing. Of course, they could still only dream of arriving at a time it would be peopled by the cast lined up for the film by MGM: Ginger Rogers, Walter Pidgeon, Van Johnson, Edward Arnold, and Mother stepped into revamped versions of the roles once played by Garbo, John and Lionel Barrymore, Beery, and Crawford, respectively.

This was the first of Mother's sets that I visited. Director Robert Z. Leonard paid me a lot of attention.

Mother, Keenan Wynn, and Van Johnson turn the tables on Xavier Cugat's Orchestra. Cugat is the one with bow in hand.

Her boyfriend at the time, Turhan Bey, was on hand for her birthday celebration.

Ted Saucier (center), publicist for the Waldorf-Astoria and the film's technical advisor, acted as host to a party held on the studio-built reproduction of the hotel lobby. He's surrounded by director "Pop" Leonard, Mother, Ginger Rogers, and Walter Pidgeon.

The Postman Always Rings Twice (1946)

Plot Points: Frank Chambers (John Garfield) drifts into a roadside restaurant called Twin Oaks for a hamburger and takes a job as handyman at the first sight of proprietor Nick Smith's (Cecil Kellaway) wife, Cora (LT). Frank and Cora fall in love, but running away together won't do. Nick has to be murdered in order to ensure the comfort and security that will make their love last, so the two plot and carry out their deadly crime. Whether or not they can get away with killing Nick, aided by sly attorney Arthur Keats (Hume Cronyn), a combination of core-shaking fears, mistrust, love, and passion send them on a roller-coaster ride to the story's finish.

It took over a decade for MGM to get a script for *Postman* approved by the Breen Office, but in Europe two unauthorized films based on Cain's book had been made. *Le Dernier tournant* was released in France in 1939 and the Italian film *Ossessione* opened in 1943.

"Man Wanted" reads the sign outside of Twin Oaks. *The Postman Always Rings Twice* was very daring for its time, both for the story—a man and a woman, lovers, plotting to do away with the woman's husband—and for the smoldering way in which it was played out by two electric leads. Rumors to the contrary have persisted since 1946, but there was absolutely no off-screen tension between Mother and John Garfield during filming. What can be said is that the steaminess you see between them in the film did not exist in real life. She simply wasn't attracted to him romantically, but there was great affection between them until his death in 1952.

Mother was, in fact, very fond of all three of her male co-stars on *Postman*: Garfield, Cecil Kellaway, and Hume Cronyn.

When James M. Cain's book debuted it was considered very scandalous. Not surprisingly, *Postman* had a problematic history with the censorship board. What is less known is how far that history dates back. In 1933, a synopsis titled *Bar-B-Q* based on Cain's story was submitted for review to Joseph Breen of the Production Code Administration by RKO Pictures. That studio took the censors' advice not to proceed as it was too objectionable. The book wasn't published until the next year and at that time, Warner Bros., Columbia Pictures, and producer Lewis Milestone were all anxious to buy the screen rights, but the Breen Office dissuaded all takers. Then Eddie Mannix of MGM purchased the rights for $25,000 without seeking the advice of the censors.

MGM submitted their own synopsis in 1934, suggesting that Jean Harlow would be cast. Breen still found it "thoroughly objectionable," while the reader's reaction was that it was a terrific story, but too bad it would never make a suitable film. Cain's story made it to the Broadway stage in 1936, starring Mary Philips and Richard Barthelmess, but MGM didn't try to make use of their film rights again until 1944. The studio was encouraged by the success of Paramount's film adaptation of Cain's equally controversial *Double Indemnity*. A script for *The Postman Always Rings Twice* was finally approved by the censors in May 1945 and the film went into production three weeks later.

Three big films based on notorious Cain novels made it to theaters in a three-year succession. *Double Indemnity* in 1944, *Mildred Pierce* from Warner Bros. in 1945, and *Postman* in '46. The characters in them were in some ways abhorrent but in all ways absorbing. The films were landmarks in ushering in the *film noir* movement in Hollywood.

The Look

With Del Armstrong drafted into the Navy, Mother insisted on doing her own makeup. He had taught her to do her makeup down to the last stroke of the eyebrow pencil, so no other artist would replace Del in his absence. Del said he was proud to see what a great job she did without him.

The idea of Cora appearing almost exclusively in white costumes was an interesting concept, inspired by the censors' severity. Producer Carey Wilson and Garnett knew they had two major strikes against them putting together a star and story both loaded with sexual undertones. Dressing her in pure white was the solution they hit upon. The only other color she wears is black, on two occasions: in the kitchen when Cora toys with a knife, contemplating either murder or suicide, and late in the film when she wears mourning for her mother.

One of the two scenes in which Cora doesn't wear white. Lighting that forms a halo over the head of a killer creates an interesting motif in the film.

With John Garfield.

With Cecil Kellaway. Mother loved that Cora dressed primarily in white costumes by Marion Herwood Keyes under Irene's supervision.

Cast and crew went to Laguna Beach for location filming just as June gloom set in. Here they line up for lunch.

I visited Mommy during this interlude.

Foggy weather conditions disrupted shooting for weeks, which led to big trouble with the director.

A relaxed moment between Garnett and his stars, out of makeup and in their own clothes.

With Tay Garnett.

Cora

From the stunning opening shot of her in white, framed in the doorway, Mother set the screen on fire in *Postman*, and Cora Smith was her favorite role. What made the film so good was a combination of separate parts in front of and behind the camera: Mother at the peak of her appeal; John Garfield's earthy attractiveness; their chemistry together; and the wonderful Cecil Kellaway as the husband. The stars and a top MGM crew worked under director Tay Garnett, who was inspired, if not entirely dependable, throughout the making of *Postman*.

If she felt she was working with a good director, Mother depended on him (they were always men) to guide her performance. She and John Garfield thought Garnett was brilliant, but he was going through a torturous time personally and had fallen off the wagon. She and John came up with a scheme to take turns sitting up with Garnett at night, playing gin rummy, anything to keep him from drinking. They traded off until Garnett was set to finish the film. Mother wouldn't have done that in her first three years in movies. Dedication grew in her with each film she made.

Credit for Mother's performance must largely go to her growing dedication to her work since *Ziegfeld Girl*. There was tremendous maturity in her between the two movies, both as an actress and as a woman. As good as she is in *Ziegfeld*, progressing through being a drunk and the dramatics of the ending, she is a young girl. The grown woman appears in *Postman*.

Mother never saw the remake with Jessica Lange and Jack Nicholson, but she heard more about it than she ever wanted to hear. Cora was her role. Even James M. Cain said so. The relationship between Frank and Cora in the original is a thousand times more subtle and yet much more powerful. They sizzled without literally putting sex on the screen. Mother's reaction upon hearing about the love scenes in the remake was, "They did *what* on my kitchen table?"

These rarities are posed shots on the set of *Postman* before the movie was made. They were in line with the story, but not actual moments in the film.

After playing Cora, Mom loved Tay Garnett no matter what. This was at the wrap party.

Green Dolphin Street (1947)

Plot Points: Marianne (LT) and Marguerite Patourel (Donna Reed) love the same man, William Ozanne (Richard Hart). He prefers Marguerite, who loves him, shiftless though he is. Marianne loves the man she can make of him. She leads him into the Navy to grow up, but he winds up separated from his ship in New Zealand, where he goes to work for Timothy Haslam (Van Heflin), a man who has loved Marianne since childhood. A night of drinking leads William to send for Marianne to make his bride, not Marguerite—a mistake in a girl's name that steers the lives of all concerned onto unexpected paths.

Almost a year passed between the time Mother completed principal photography on *Postman* and the time she commenced *Green Dolphin Street*. Much had happened. She took me to Palm Springs; *Postman* met with an outstanding reception and elevated her to new heights of fame; she went on extensive promotional tours to New York, Miami, and throughout South America; and she entered into a relationship with her great passion, Tyrone Power.

A lot of early publicity for the film centered on the fact that its story had been the winner of a writing contest run

by MGM. The author who submitted the best novel to MGM would be paid $200,000 and have their book made into what was originally announced as a Technicolor production. A story by Elizabeth Goudge won and the book, published in 1944, became a national bestseller within

weeks. The novel was adapted for the screen by Samson Raphaelson, the adroit collaborator of Ernst Lubitsch. His script didn't have much trouble with the Breen Office. The censors focused on two primary concerns: the amount of drinking shown and the amount of Lana Turner's bosom shown in the costumes.

Her hair had grown in longer and been darkened several shades by the time she returned to the screen. Fast growing as her hair was, of course it hadn't grown in as long as that of the character of Marianne. She wore women's hairpieces called falls and nineteenth-century styles with hats, bonnets, and other accoutrements by Walter Plunkett. Plunkett was the best costume designer a period film could hope to have, his best known credit being *Gone With the Wind*.

Though Mother preferred modern settings, she was quite proud of *Green Dolphin Street*. Katharine Hepburn was originally set for the part of Marianne and Mother was thought of to play the sweet sister, Marguerite. Mother pushed to play Marianne, however, and she got her wish, while Donna Reed was assigned the role of Marguerite. Reed too had reservations about playing Marguerite because, beautiful as she was, she thought no one would believe

Mom played the dominant Patourel sister, Marianne, to Donna Reed's Marguerite. She said "it was such a challenge because it would be too easy to do Donna's part—and she did it beautifully, but mine was real gutsy and I had a chance to grow a little, you know, show a little muscle, make a characterization which was so different from the other roles that I had played."

Richard Hart would prefer her to Lana Turner. In the end, both actresses received favorable reviews. Marianne is an interesting character. She is everything Van Heflin wants and everything Richard Hart needs. Though she's the "wrong woman" to Hart, they become the right ones to make each other better people.

A contributing factor to Mother's special fondness for this film is that it was made during the height of her romance with Tyrone Power. Around the New Year and the approach of a long weekend, she decided to jaunt to Mexico to visit Tyrone, who was there making *Captain from Castile*. This rendezvous was unplanned, surprising even Tyrone,

and then the cast and crew who were back at Metro, when poor weather conditions prevented her from returning to the studio in time for her absence to go unnoticed. Suspecting trouble when she did make it back, she dressed herself in a serape, donned a sombrero, and clenched a rose between her teeth to take her medicine in Mexican style, but the *Green Dolphin Street* company, led by director Victor Saville, surprised her instead by greeting her in sombreros with a rendition of "South of the Border." She was docked two days' pay.

The making of *Green Dolphin Street* was not all fun and Mexican magic. The film was mostly shot on location at the

Klamath River in Oregon, where a village was built for the company of more than two hundred people. Mother talked about how physically grueling parts of the movie were. There were earthquake scenes that took a torturously long time to film and she was badly bruised in their efforts to make the sequence spectacular. The hard work did pay off when the special effects team on the film received an Academy Award.

The movie was also recognized with nominations for its editing, sound, and cinematography. The film deserved recognition for its score as well. The title song of this epic costume drama inspired one of the great jazz recordings of the '60s and '70s. The first to make the jazzified "Green Dolphin Street" famous was probably the version by Miles Davis. Mother had a 78 record of it which she played often.

At right is Linda Christian. She had a small role in the film, and in 1949 was the one to marry Tyrone Power instead of Mother. That's Del Armstrong on the left.

The filming of the earthquake scenes was physically grueling for Mother and Van Heflin. The epic film was the year's highest grossing for MGM.

This "candid" moment between producer Carey Wilson, director Victor Saville, and their star was actually a posed print advertisement for Warren's Mint Cocktail chewing gum.

Mother's practical joke with this Mexican getup was topped by the entire company.

On location with co-star Richard Hart. Even after finding her most famous look in the face and platinum locks of Cora Smith, she didn't mind appearing with brown hair.

Cass Timberlane (1947)

Plot Points: Judge Cass Timberlane's (Spencer Tracy) marriage to a girl from the wrong side of town, Virginia Marshland (LT), creates a stir in Grand Republic. Cass's society "friends" enjoy having a judge in their circle even if he is too honest to suit them. They sneer at Ginny, who becomes restless and anxious to get out of town. Eventually Cass has them give New York a try, even though Bradd Criley (Zachary Scott), a man with whom she'd nearly had an affair, has moved east as well. Cass soon learns where he belongs and returns home. Ginny is left to meet the temptations of New York life and find out who she loves.

With me on the set in November 1947.

In 1941 Mother made *Dr. Jekyll and Mr. Hyde* with Spencer Tracy. Their two films together are very dissimilar. *Cass Timberlane* placed them in a modern setting and their characters had an entirely different sort of relationship. Her character in the later film has more power. Mother herself had matured and there was another dynamic between her and Tracy. She was only twenty in 1941 and so in awe of him they didn't really get to know each other until they made *Cass Timberlane* in 1947.

The only complaint Mother had about the movie was that another of her co-stars was a cat. The film itself was a joy for a number of reasons. She was happy to be working

Preparing to go into a scene with Spencer Tracy. *Cass Timberlane* premiered as a special event benefiting the John Tracy Clinic for deaf children, an organization named after Spencer's son.

with Tracy and to be playing a complex part in a contemporary setting. She got to experiment with hairstyles again. It was cropped short and lightened up from *Green Dolphin Street*. She was given several lovely costumes, but she also had fun letting the tomboy in her come out by donning a baseball cap, blue jeans, and loafers and getting dirty sliding into home plate during a game of baseball.

Mother and Spencer were not the original actors intended to portray the characters in the Sinclair Lewis novel. After MGM acquired the film rights for $150,000, a number of possible stars were mentioned, including Walter Pidgeon, who instead made a cameo appearance, for the part of Cass, and Jennifer Jones or Vivien Leigh for the part of Ginny. Director George Sidney was known for musical comedies like *Anchors Aweigh*, but *Cass Timberlane* was his first major dramatic film. He was enthusiastic that Mother was ultimately cast in the female lead. Besides being a good friend, married to Mother's acting coach, Lillian Burns, he thought she had developed into "one of the finest actresses on the screen."

These may have been from Bob Topping, who began his courtship of Mother by sending roses and orchids to the set of this film.

Chatting with her co-star. The sight of Lana Turner in loafers was rare onscreen, but she used to wear them a lot in private life. She even had a pair in gold snakeskin.

Katharine Hepburn would come to visit Spencer.

Homecoming (1948)

Plot Points: Dr. Lee Johnson (Clark Gable) and his wife Penny (Anne Baxter) follow a settled, if insular, existence until the War. Lee jumps on the band-wagon and joins the fight as a surgeon on the front lines. There's an instant clash of personalities with his more enlightened nurse, "Snapshot" McCall (LT). Experiencing the war together, their relationship deepens into love more each day. Their parting moments before the war's end are in a hospital, where Snapshot lies dying. Lee then returns home. He's discovered that he never lived until he met Snapshot and will find out if there is life for him without her.

Heavy base makeup was a necessary evil for filming. It was required for the cameras under normal circumstances, but in *Homecoming* Mother was playing a war-weary nurse on the battlefields of Africa and Europe, so she got to wipe her face clean and was actually happy as can be. Getting to sleep in and skipping the five or six a.m. makeup call always remained a pleasant memory of *Homecoming* for her. Hair the same dark blonde shade it was in *Cass Timberlane*, she sported a freshly scrubbed look, shiny-nosed, with just a dab of lipstick and the necessary eyebrows. It made her look even younger than her twenty-six years. As bonuses she had Clark Gable beside her and Mervyn LeRoy as director for the first time since *Johnny Eager*.

Homecoming was Mother's third film with Gable. Though both were known for good looks, MGM decided to return them to the World War II battlefields, where audiences had left them at the close of their last movie, *Somewhere I'll Find You*. Again they didn't end in a great cinematic embrace. Mother's character this time must die. It could work either way as far as the story goes, but the tragic turn was largely influenced by the censors. This widowed mother and married man who fall into an extra-marital affair in the story could not be together at the fade out. Not if the censorship board had anything to say about it.

One story Mother liked to tell about Gable occurred while making *Homecoming*. She chewed gum regularly, especially to freshen her mouth for a love scene. She had a habit in those days of lodging the gum in the back of her mouth when the cameras rolled instead of taking it out. No one ever noticed until this particular day. Gable wore false teeth. That was widely known within the business. Mother's gum sneaked out of its hiding place during a kiss and when their lips parted, a sticky string stretched out between them. The gum had adhered itself to Gable's false teeth and he had a terrible time peeling it off. Mervyn LeRoy made sure Mother's mouth was empty before love scenes from then on. He'd put his hand under her chin and say, "Spit it out." After a few instances of sheepishly dropping the gum into his hand, she switched to mouthwash.

The company completed production on November 7, 1947. The working title for the movie was *The Homecoming of Ulysses* but it went into theaters with its shortened title the following spring. Advertised as "The Team that Generates Steam" this time around, Mother and Gable generated $3.7 million for MGM in domestic film rentals.

She found the non-glamorous part of "Snapshot" McCall a nice change of pace. She loved the shine on her nose.

With LeRoy and Tyrone Power.

Director Mervyn LeRoy in conference with Mother and Clark Gable.

Relaxing on the set.

The Three Musketeers (1948)

Plot Points: The daring D'Artagnan (Gene Kelly) arrives in Paris to become a Musketeer. With the current state of affairs, it isn't long before he becomes embroiled in court intrigue. Cardinal Richelieu (Vincent Price), an evil counselor to the king, is actually running the show, with the help of the wicked Lady de Winter (LT). Helping their cause is the Duke of Buckingham's (John Sutton) love for France's Queen Anne (Angela Lansbury), which could even lead to war with England. D'Artagnan and the Three Musketeers are the only ones who can save France and they have their work cut out for them.

Vincent Price became one of Mom's favorite people in the world. She had a ball playing scenes with him in this rousing, gently tongue-in-cheek version of Dumas's story. In their first moments together she realized that he was about to steal the scene right out from under her, inspiring Mother to step up her game and match him sin for sin. Playing off each other, they are as wicked as can be as Lady de Winter and Cardinal Richelieu. Hers was a stylized performance because of Vincent. Mother had turned down her role at first, but she was happy she came around and got to play the purely evil character. MGM was pleased as well when Mother's suspension could be cancelled, along with plans to employ actress Alida Valli as her last-minute replacement.

Walter Plunkett's costumes for Mother were enticing in his palette of greens, violet, coral, and turquoise, with colored jewel adornments to de-emphasize the low necklines. They were designed to flatter Mother in the Technicolor film. Her first appearance in color had been in *Du Barry Was*

The stars: Mother, Gene Kelly, Van Heflin, June Allyson, Angela Lansbury, Frank Morgan, and Keenan Wynn.

As the villainous Lady de Winter.

Praying for her life. From Dumas we know she must die, but the wicked grin on her face as she walks to the scaffold at the end of the film almost makes us believe she can escape execution.

a Lady, but that was only a cameo. To make her look even more eye popping in her feature-length color debut, her hair was lightened again and new experiments with makeup were in order. Makeup had to be done differently for color but she and Del Armstrong mastered the approach. They also played with "beauty marks" in the shape of hearts, circles, and moons and tried them out on different locations of her face. Meanwhile, director George Sidney worked out a beautiful way for the face to be *revealed*. In the first shot of her, she speaks from the shadows of the back of a carriage and the audience waits in anticipation for her to come into the colored light. When she did, she took people's breath away even as her harsh words revealed her wickedness.

Another of her best moments was done in the absence of makeup. She assumed an intensity in the eyes that co-star

A test shot of her as Lady de Winter.

An ultra-rare shot of Mom watching the action on the set.

June Allyson said frightened her to death during the filming of their big showdown in the jail cell. Everyone on the film seemed to put their all into it. When Gene Kelly had to throw Mother onto Lady de Winter's bed in a scene, he used such might that she lost her balance, hit the floor instead of the bed, and injured an arm. It had to be bandaged up, so they had Lady de Winter wear gauntlets in the story.

There have been many film versions of Alexandre Dumas's *The Three Musketeers*, but this is the most memorable of the studio era. Watching the rushes was very frightening for five-year-old me. At the end, Mother's villainess must keep her date with the scaffold. Staring at those intense eyes that were flickering and framed by an incredible Technicolor landscape, I was deeply affected. As far as I could see, my mommy was marching to her own beheading. Up there was "playacting," but Mommy here beside me was all right. It took a long time for me to accept that Mother could be "up there," but also "right here."

Tension for the cameras, laughter in the dressing room with her friend Gene Kelly.

Anxious to begin her next scene with Vincent Price.

A Life of Her Own (1950)

Plot Points: Lily James (LT) has no family or friends when she arrives in New York and only one interest—to become a model. With a combination of style, photogenic features, and a top agent (Tom Ewell), she soars to the top of the modeling world. There's no one to share her success with until Steve Harleigh (Ray Milland) enters her life. He's a great catch, but already caught. His wife is ill; he can't get a divorce. In love but unable to marry, Lily and Steve carry on their affair and Lily becomes a kept woman, but not without misgivings. As she has seen, defying social mores could have a tragic end.

After making *The Three Musketeers* in 1948, Mother went on suspension several times for turning down roles that were assigned to her. The public grew anxious with each press release from Metro that announced her return in this role or that. A steamy adaptation of Flaubert's *Madame Bovary* and a comedy called *The Reformer and the Redhead* (opposite Robert Taylor, no less) were planned and then recast without her because she stayed away on a long honeymoon with Bob Topping from mid-1948 into 1949. Then the time came when she had to return to life at home in Los Angeles and to work at MGM in a film called *A Life of Her Own*.

Numerous actors were considered to be Mother's new leading man, among them Cary Grant, Howard Keel, James Mason, and Robert Ryan. I would have voted for James Mason. Mother was embarrassed when she had to get his autograph for me. MGM didn't share my vision. Wendell Corey was finally borrowed from producer Hal Wallis, but he rubbed Mother the wrong way before any film was shot of them by making a remark to her about Barbara Stanwyck. Mother pulled a movie star maneuver and had MGM pay Corey off and hire Ray Milland.

A Life of Her Own had a problematic history long before Wendell Corey. It took fourteen years to get approval from the Production Code Administration. MGM's proposed adaptation of "The Abiding Vision," a story by Rebecca West, was first reviewed in 1936. It was rejected numerous times by the censors, primarily because it presented a sympathetic view of a couple having an extramarital affair, which the board felt condoned their actions. Moreover, there was "no satisfactory regeneration, and no proportionate punishment of the transgressors." Harsh reports back and forth continued. In 1949 the script was called "a shocking and highly

The intense staging of this photo with Ray Milland has little to do with the story.

Del Armstrong (right) applies her makeup.

The diet Mother went on for *A Life of Her Own* didn't include the dough-
nuts that were brought to the set every day.

With directorGeorge Cukor and co-star Barry Sullivan.

offensive story of adultery and commercialized prostitution, [which] carries no 'voice' for morality, and hardly a semblance of 'compensating moral values.'"

The writers did finally make the board come around, although they didn't change as much as one might expect. The ending written to appease the censors had Mother's character commit suicide, like the washed up model played by Ann Dvorak. Preview audiences disliked this conclusion so much that in the finished film she was allowed to survive, alone and weary, but still breathing. MGM got the censors' approval with the original ending and production got underway on the film in January 1950.

The first order of business for Mother to ready herself for *A Life of Her Own* was to lose the weight she put on from the time she began dating Bob Topping through the end of their honeymoon. They were on a merry round of events and nightclubbing, drinking and keeping late hours, but what did all of us in was the French chef. André had us on a strict diet of three rich meals a day. Our favorite for breakfast was his dish of shirred eggs and croissants. The eggs were cooked in cream and butter and then put under the broiler to brown on top—oh so good and oh so fattening. Mother, Bob, and I all got a bit round. Mother actually reached a good thirty pounds over her ideal weight of 110.

In *A Life of Her Own*, Mother would be playing a model, of all things, with a model's wardrobe to display. Once she was set for the film, she had six weeks to slim down before costume fittings. She turned for help to our family doctor, who put her on a strict diet of his own. When the reducing plan began, poor André was let go. We all dropped

After the film's completion, Grauman's Chinese Theater manager George Kane (left) and "Mr. Footprint," Jean Klossner, watched Mother leave her impressions in their forecourt.

Mother posed like the model she played in publicity shots.

weight with that move. Mother's diet cut out all but one cocktail per day. Her drink of choice at the time was a Scotch Old Fashioned and she waited for it all day. Her new breakfast consisted of a cup of coffee and a glass of orange juice. Salad for lunch; no dressing, just lemon. A plain broiled steak for dinner. She followed the diet and got herself in "camera-ready" condition once again.

Mr. Imperium (1951)

Plot Points: While performing in Italy, singer Frederica Brown (LT) falls in love with Mr. Imperium (Ezio Pinza), royalty of a small European nation. The couple is separated when he ascends to the throne and twelve years pass before they meet again. By then Frederica is Fredda Barlo, a Hollywood star, and the time may be right for Mr. Imperium to become a commoner. During a top secret weekend rendezvous they confirm that their love for each other hasn't changed, but neither has his people's need for their king. Mr. Imperium must either resume his role of real-life king or choose love and remain with Fredda.

Not doing a good job of hiding her discomfort with Ezio Pinza.

Ezio Pinza was the biggest hit on Broadway in 1950, having won a Tony for his work in *South Pacific*, so MGM signed him to make his film debut in hopes of capitalizing on his popularity in the theater—with Lana Turner beside him in case he should have less appeal to moviegoers. Her lofty station was supposed to elevate him. Instead, it worked the other way, with *Mr. Imperium* bringing her down a few notches.

Mother never had anything positive to say about the movie, instead describing her troubles so vividly that when I see a photo of Ezio Pinza, I can almost smell the Roquefort. They had a great romance in the movie and after a day of filming their love scenes, Mother used to come home sick to her stomach because he did adore his cheese pastries and what seemed to her gallons of espresso.

Bob Topping went with Mother on location and shot these photos.

Shot in the summer of 1950, much of the story was set in one of Mother's favorite locales, Palm Springs. Don Hartman directed and the movie was shot in beautiful Technicolor by George Folsey. Mother met young Debbie Reynolds during filming. That was the biggest of the few pluses regarding this movie, as they became friends.

Mr. Imperium (released in the U.K. as *You Belong to My Heart*) was Mother's first musical since *Two Girls on Broadway* in 1940 though she didn't get to dance and her singing here was dubbed by Trudy Irwin. This was one movie of Mother's that she simply could not force herself to watch. The public must have found it hard to take as well, because it was a box-office dud. Ironically, the movie later fell into the public domain and it became the most readily available of Mom's films for a long time, sold at supermarkets and drugstores.

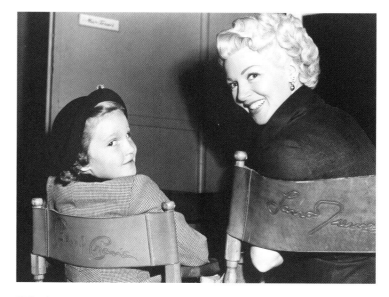

Sitting in our personalized chairs

A unique view between equipment as a scene is filmed.

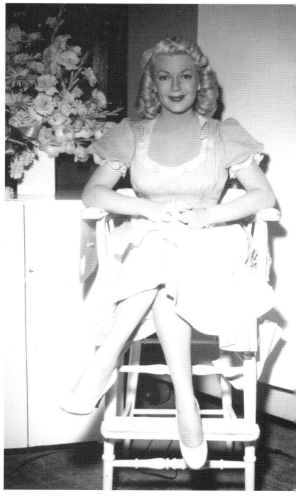

In costume as Frederica Brown.

The Merry Widow (1952)

Plot Points: Only Crystal Radek (LT), the widow of Marshovia's all-time wealthiest citizen, can save the realm from bankruptcy. The dashing Count Danilo (Fernando Lamas) is selected to woo her and bring the Radek millions back into Marshovia by marriage. Many a broken-down aristocrat is after her money and it disturbs the widow so much she has her maid, Kitty (Una Merkel), pose as her, while she pretends to be Fifi of Maxim's. Will Danilo follow his heart to "Fifi" or follow the money to Kitty? That's what the Widow would like to know and she's prepared to put her suitor to the test.

Bouncing back from the dark spell that followed her separation from Bob Topping, Mother fell into the spirit of the story and had a ball with *The Merry Widow*. There was so much for her to love about it. At the top of the list was, of course, her

new leading man, Fernando Lamas. But there were the most incredible dance sequences too, which even attracted a rare appearance by Gran to the set. Mother also loved the costumes by Helen Rose, even if it was a period film.

The music was glorious. Mother had a record of "The Merry Widow Waltz" that she played again and again. I visited the soundstage and heard her voice recorded for the song, so I was surprised to learn later that her rendition didn't make it into the finished film. She had a sweet, but thin singing voice and I suppose they wanted a more professional sound even if the character wasn't a professional singer. She did her turn on the dance floor, however, in the arms of Lamas. The "Waltz" musical sequence featured a chorus of beautiful dancers dashing about all in pink. It appears dance director Jack Cole looked back to his own work in these moments the following year in his choreography of Marilyn

Monroe's "Diamonds Are a Girl's Best Friend" number.

This was the third American film version of *The Merry Widow*. The first, a silent film released in 1925, featured Mae Murray and made a star out of John Gilbert. Ernst Lubitsch's cleverly risqué 1934 remake starred Maurice Chevalier and Jeannette MacDonald. Both of these versions, different though they were, were extremely successful. This third version, which also took a unique approach to an old story, came about once enough time had elapsed.

The censors didn't have much to object to in the script submitted by MGM. They expressed considerable concern, however, about the scene where the widow and Prince Danilo share a private room at Maxim's. The script indicated they would sit on a sofa in the room. The censors wanted it to be a love seat instead, or some other, smaller piece of furniture. They also asked that a table be included in this room, set for dinner, presumably to show that this was a room for eating, not a romantic assignation.

Besides being the first film of Mother's I viewed in its entirety, *The Merry Widow* is the first set I remember clear-

The romantic pairing of Mother and Fernando Lamas carried over into their personal lives.

ly, because in my earlier trips to the studio, I spent most of the time in her dressing room. I would play with toys, color, or read while she worked, or it would be arranged for me to come at lunchtime. I had not gone "on the set" all that often. When I was little, it could be terribly boring to watch actors run the same lines time after time, and get only bits and pieces of the story. Mother was careful in choosing appropriate scenes for me to see being filmed. Her choice of "The Merry Widow Waltz" ball sequence was ideal, and by no means boring.

Production wrapped on December 10, 1951. Mother signed a new long-term contract with Metro later that month. The film's producer, Joe Pasternak, a friend of Mother's, sent a message to Dore Schary: "If God and Lana are with us I'm sure we shall have something we'll be proud of. I gave GOD first billing—please don't tell Lana."

In her dressing room with Fernando.

With the terrific character actress Una Merkel.

A visit from Spencer Tracy.

Practicing the widow's waltz.

Her waltz gown, by Helen Rose, was black velvet and trimmed with Alençon lace.

The Bad and the Beautiful (1952)

Plot Points: Producer Jonathan Shields' (Kirk Douglas) track record for making great pictures is unparalleled and his record for making enemies is also one for the books. Those closest to Shields have felt the deepest hurt, most of all Georgia Lorrison (LT), the self-destructive extra he turned into a star, but whose love he couldn't handle. Director Fred Amiel (Barry Sullivan) and writer James Bartlow (Dick Powell) have also been manipulated and betrayed by the "Shields Touch." Now down-and-out, Shields hopes to interest Georgia, Fred, and James in collaborating on his great cinematic comeback.

Tribute to a Bad Man was the working title of Mother's second release of 1952—arguably the best movie about the movies. Her starring role influenced the decision to release it as *The Bad and the Beautiful*. It was based on stories by George Bradshaw when it wasn't borrowing from the lives of prominent filmmakers like David O. Selznick and Val Lewton.

Movies about Hollywood didn't have the best track record at the box office. This one succeeded, probably because the settings and the characters were so true to life and played by a great cast. In their honesty, each of the stories told in the film reached people outside of the business. It didn't hurt that they got away with a lot, right under the nose of the censorship board. Records show that scenes the censors insisted be changed were ultimately left unaltered, like the frank dialogue when Georgia thinks Jonathan is trying to get into her bed by offering her a screen test.

The film provided Mother with one of the most challenging roles of her acting career. Georgia Lorrison was a multifaceted character who goes from a drunk to an A-list actress and experiences all of the peaks and valleys in between. Her great dramatic scene takes place in a car when Georgia, betrayed by the man she is in love with, sets out into the stormy night, gets behind the wheel, and takes off

This scene with Kirk Douglas, as Georgia's director, rehearsing his actress at the balcony was one among many dramatically striking visual compositions by Vincente Minnelli.

Shields is determined to make Georgia a star, driven by the challenge of sobering her up, even if her heart is broken in the process.

Ready to perform her big dramatic scene.

Minnelli let her loose in this turbulent scene with no more direction than to do whatever she felt like doing.

Preparing for her closeup.

on a wild ride during which her emotions lead her to the brink of disaster. This scene was filmed some time after the rest of the movie because director Vincente Minnelli and his crew were still working out the mechanics of how they were going to shoot it. He wanted the camera tumbling, reflecting Georgia's hysterical state in the scene. It took so long to figure out Mother began worrying that in living her own life, she was getting too far removed from the character. But when it came time for her to go before the camera again it was as if there had been no break at all. Mother played it memorably, and she did it in a single take, with no cuts. Minnelli kept having her repeat the scene, however, and each time Mother got more and more upset as she drew from her own experiences. The uncontrollable sobbing in that scene was from the heart.

The artistic eye of Vincente Minnelli produced a movie filled with visually outstanding moments. He was a talented artist, but Mother found something a bit lacking in his ability to articulate what he was looking for of her as an actress, so she was left to rely on her own instincts in playing Georgia. Mother's performance was hailed as her best to date by critics. Oscar talk was in the air, but she was overlooked by the Academy. Why I will never understand because she is powerful and totally honest in it.

Fortunately, the movie, and others in the cast, fared better at awards time. Kirk Douglas was nominated. Gloria Grahame was named Best Supporting Actress. Awards also went out for the film's art direction, cinematography, costume design, and screenplay.

A very rare color shot with Kirk Douglas.

She loved that they had her in this costume for no reason in the middle of the movie (ostensibly Georgia was in costume for one of her movies).

In her dressing room. The image of ex-boyfriend Fernando Lamas lingers on her end table.

Latin Lovers (1953)

Plot Points: Businesswoman Nora Taylor (LT) has never been sure any man loved her for more than her money, even doubting her fiancé, Paul Chevron (John Lund). She goes to South America to think about Paul, but instead falls into a romance with the handsome Roberto Santos (Ricardo Montalban). Nora fears any self-respecting man would feel intimidated that she's the family breadwinner and leave her, so she keeps her wealth a secret. When it's ultimately revealed, Roberto's joy that she is rich is alarming. Perhaps she should give away her fortune, Nora wonders. Any maneuver will be tricky, but Nora is determined to learn if it's love or money Roberto's after.

Latin Lovers was originally intended to re-team the lovers of *The Merry Widow*, but after Mother's breakup with Fernando Lamas, it had to be recast with another Latin on the Metro roster, Ricardo Montalban. Ironically, Ricardo had been the original choice for *Merry Widow*. Having been with MGM for five years, he was a popular leading man to MGM ladies like Esther Williams and Jane Powell. He had been a Lana Turner fan ever since he saw her in *They Won't Forget* and was the very model of the kind of man that attracted

Swaying to the samba rhythms with Ricardo Montalban. He became a friend to the end.

Mother. It looked like love in the publicity photos, yet there was no romance between them. He was very Catholic and very devoted to his wife, Georgiana Young (Loretta's sister), and Mom respected that. Besides, her relationship with Lex Barker was just starting. She and Ricardo became good friends instead.

Latin Lovers started filming in December 1952. Mother knew it was not one of her better films. *The Bad and the Beautiful* was the last of her MGM movies that she really loved, but certain aspects of *Latin Lovers* made it a pleasant memory. She liked that it involved horseback riding, the South American setting, the samba music, and Ricardo. I was crazy about horses myself, so Mother would take me to the set to watch those scenes.

Close-up tests for her role of Nora.

Helen Rose's sketch and the completed silk taffeta gown.

At a horse ranch location with director Mervyn LeRoy (seated) and Ricardo (standing).

Behind the scenes with co-stars Ricardo Montalban and John Lund.

Flame and the Flesh (1954)

Plot Points: Madeline (LT) has no family, friends, or money to speak of, but since the age of thirteen she's known how to get by on her looks. In Naples she is taken in by a nice boy named Ciccio (Bonar Colleano), who wants to marry her. Ciccio's roommate, Nino (Carlos Thompson), disapproves, as Madeline ruins his own engagement to the virtuous Lisa (Pier Angeli). Nino and Madeline go away together, but Madeline is still interested in other men, driving them apart. Then the unexpected occurs. She falls in love—with Nino. What she does in reaction to this new emotion is the most astonishing part of all to Madeline.

To take advantage of the tax benefits of working in Europe for eighteen months, filming across the Atlantic became extremely attractive to Hollywood filmmakers and actors beginning in the late '40s. At the end of her marriage to Bob Topping, Mother's finances were so drained she joined the exodus and agreed to make a film in Italy. If taking off to work abroad wasn't enough of a shock to Mother's fans, her new haircut and dye job floored them.

I think every woman in the mid-'50s wished they could pull off the closely cropped "Italian look" of Gina Lollabrigida. A few were brave enough to try and Mother became one of them. The public wasn't too fond of her new look. She just didn't look like herself as a brunette. But then, being unrecognizable was part of the fun for her. With the new haircut, she discovered a sense of freedom. She said, "I could go into the shops and walk along the streets and have a ball and nobody knew me."

Mother's hair wasn't her only reason for creating headlines. There was a new man in her life, the movies'

Mother's "new look" debuted in 1953.

"King of the Jungle," Lex Barker. The *Tarzan* star was her companion during the trip, raising eyebrows because they weren't married. Lex escorted her to premieres and the Cannes film festival before work separated them. He went on to Italy and Mother flew to London to shoot interiors for *Flame and the Flesh*. Gran and I were sent for as soon as I could leave school for the summer.

We all remained in London until Mother had to leave for location work in Italy. When the time came, Gran stayed behind and Mother brought me to Italy to meet my future stepfather and his children. They were married a few weeks later, in September 1953.

Mother received guidance through *Flame and the Flesh* from Richard Brooks, who attempted to recreate the style of the era's Italian neo-realists. He had already made a name for himself, as a writer of films including *Key Largo* and *Crossfire* mainly, but he had also directed several movies. Mom thought Brooks was "wonderful" and he extracted a playful bad girl performance from her.

Mother's character was unusual. She acts feminine and sexy, but Madeline's sensibilities and outlook on relationships would have been seen as completely male in those days. Though she hasn't even a place to call home, finding security by getting married is the last thought in her mind. Madeline picks her partners by the challenge they pose. The Nino character that she leads astray is no longer a playboy but a choirboy in her presence.

It's since been difficult to find a good copy of *Flame and the Flesh*, as we wait for the studio to restore a print for DVD, but the picture's original Technicolor photography was superb. At the time of this writing, the film isn't even shown on television due to a legal question that begs to be resolved in order to make an airing on the Turner Classic Movies network possible.

"It's not a Lana Turner role at all. It's one of the few times I've had a chance to really act."

With co-star Carlos Thompson.

Mother's character was like one of the children of Naples herself.

Director Richard Brooks and Mother welcome Ava Gardner to their set.

Other actresses spoke of difficulties with Brooks, but Mother always spoke highly of him.

Betrayed (1954)

Plot Points: When the identity of Col. Pieter Deventer (Clark Gable) of Dutch Intelligence is discovered by the Nazis, a new liaison between the British and Dutch resistance is needed, and Carla Van Oven (LT) is recruited for the job. A team led by a charismatic freedom fighter called "The Scarf" (Victor Mature) has caused significant trouble for the Nazis and Carla proves herself up to the demands of her mission amid constant danger, but the resistance is being lethally undermined from within. Carla, Deventer, and The Scarf, having formed close ties, must find out which one of them is a double agent.

When *Betrayed* was about to go into production in September 1953, I had been in Europe for months and my summer vacation was over. Mother's plan was to transfer me to a French school while she and Lex worked in Europe for

at least another year. I didn't want to stay there with Lex, I didn't want to switch schools, and I didn't want to be separated from Gran. Mother and I had a big fight and ultimately I left for home shortly before Mother went on to Holland to film *Betrayed*.

The team of Clark Gable and Lana Turner was back together for a fourth and final time in this film. It's unfortunate that for the third time in a row, it was a war picture and they were back in military fatigues for much of the time. Mother would have liked to do another kind of story with him, even another costume picture if it was like *Honky Tonk*, which included many slyly sexy scenes. But *Betrayed* was the project that came up at the right time and the right place for them to be re-teamed.

Gottfried Reinhardt, a German producer who had worked on Mother and Gable's previous film, *Homecoming*, was trying his hand at directing for the second time on *Betrayed*. *The True and the Brave* had been his working title for the project and it was once planned for the trio of stars to be Gregory Peck, Ava Gardner, and Richard Widmark. In the end it turned out to be Gable's last assignment for MGM after a twenty-three-year run at the studio. His contract wasn't going to be renewed and apparently it was getting

Lovers or not, everyone's a suspect in *Betrayed*.

Clark Gable was on his way out of MGM after twenty-three years under contract.

With Victor Mature.

to him. Mother remembered he wasn't himself during production. He seemed apprehensive and she did her best to put him at ease, as he had done twelve years earlier when they made *Honky Tonk*.

Though shot in Holland, re-dubbing for the film was done back at Metro. That was Gable's last day on the lot. It was the same for "The King" as it was for Mother and every other great star that made millions for the studio—no words of "Farewell and thank you" from the bosses. Gable and others just packed their belongings and drove out with only a goodbye from an old friend, Ken Hollywood, who had watched them grow up over the years as the man at the studio gate.

Mother later looked back on this entire period in Europe with Lex as a mistake. Mistakes in career choices, in men, and in the fights with me and Gran. Upon completion of *Betrayed*, she decided to abandon her plan to continue working abroad and come home. It would soon be Christmastime. The studio would welcome her back too. The tone of the period echoed in the title of her next film, *The Prodigal*.

In conference with director Gottfried Reinhardt.

Saying hello to children in the village of Valendam.

The Prodigal (1955)

Plot Points: Micah (Edmund Purdom), a prominent young Hebrew, betrays his family, fiancée, and faith after coming in contact with Samarra (LT), the high priestess of a pagan goddess, Astarte. Samarra welcomes Micah into her world to collect tribute, while her male counterpart, Nahreeb (Louis Calhern), exacts cruel punishment on the "infidel" Micah. Samarra begins to love Micah against her teaching, though she remains faithful to Astarte, even as her followers turn into a vicious mob against her. After colliding with sin and near-death encounters, Micah the Prodigal returns home to his waiting family.

The intricacy of Mother's hair and costuming as Samarra was remarkable.

Samarra, high priestess of the goddess Astarte, was Mother's role in the movie that returned her to studio filming in August 1954. Unlike her previous two productions, *The Prodigal* was going to be over-the-top lavish, filmed in EastmanColor and CinemaScope on a $5,000,000 budget. MGM was gearing up for a big promotional campaign for the film, but it was an assignment that she absolutely did not want. Other projects she wanted to do in this period, with Lex Barker, with Ava Gardner, and with Norman Krasna, didn't pan out for various reasons. She had to get back to work, but she thought this whole production was ludicrous. In her first scene, when she walks with a candle in each hand, from the look on her face I can guarantee she was trying to stop herself from laughing.

With Sandra Descher, her protégée in the film.

"If they're going to make me do this, I'm going to do it naked," were her words to Del Armstrong. Well, she went as far as she could with the costumes, anyway. She had never been one to wear very revealing clothes in private or public life, but tearing up the costumes on *The Prodigal* became an emotional and artistic release for her. Her costumes were all beaded and bejeweled creations held together with strings and metal plates covering the nether regions. She had all of the flesh-colored netting ripped out so that there was actual flesh on display. The revamped costumes worked on the screen, but they were censorable in publicity and advertisements, where additional material was added in retouching stages.

Mother remembered being very uncomfortable much of the time on *The Prodigal*. Besides the heavy costumes weighted down by metal and beads, she was covered in thick body makeup, which she abhorred, for the sections where skin showed. Once she got into the role she found more not to like. She didn't get along with Edmund Purdom, her leading man, which was rare for her. At least Louis Calhern was on hand, who was funny, always telling jokes.

I, on the other hand, loved Mom's new movie. It made me more enthusiastic about going to the studio than I had ever been. It was like being in history with the guards and slaves and everyone in costume. I was awestruck by the massive set with pillars and a great fire pit. Mother's day to fall into the pit was terrifying for me in spite of the huge mattress I knew was waiting to catch her. At the critical moment of her fall I let out an audible gasp. Horror of horrors! One of my very first lessons growing up was to never, *never*

That statue, in life, with its snake, spikes, and horns, was the most astounding thing my eyes had yet seen.

The scene of seduction.

make a sound on a set after the director yelled "Roll 'em!" For a few horrible moments I thought I would be thrown into the pit next, but blessedly no one had heard my gasp.

In particular I also remember her stoning scene having to be tested over and over again. It was a technical issue of what to hurl at Mother. Sponge stones didn't have enough heft to them. Mother retreated to her dressing room, but I stayed and watched her stand-in do her job of filling in until the prop men figured it out. Back in Mother's dressing room I would watch the magic between her and Helen Young as they created these magnificent Samarra hairstyles. They went back and forth between bangs and no bangs. They decorated with jewels and came up with endless variations.

It was all fun and games for me on the set until I saw Mother act with Sandra Descher. She played her child protégée in the film. Watching them felt so strange to me because the little girl looked so much like Mother. To me she was what Mother's daughter was supposed to look like. By the age of eleven, I always had a feeling that I didn't look like Mother at all, but this was the first time it was ever pointed out in such a startling way.

With co-star Louis Calhern, whose costume was even wilder than hers.

Inspecting color transparencies with cinematographer Joseph Ruttenberg, hairdresser June Roberts, makeup man Del Armstrong, and wardrobe assistant Kitty Mager.

Co-star Edmund Purdom watches Mother paint her nails. He was making a name for himself in costume films. Before playing the prodigal son of Luke's gospel, his most important part was the title role in Fox's epic *The Egyptian*.

The Sea Chase (1955)

Plot Points: Capt. Karl Ehrlich (John Wayne), commander of the German freighter *Ergenstrasse*, is on a mission from Australia to the South American port of Valparaiso. His secondary duty is to transport to safety Elsa Keller (LT), a woman whose shady past is all too familiar to Ehrlich. En route they must elude the British against impossible odds. The courage and skill of *Ergenstrasse*'s captain and crew capture the attention of a world at war. Reaching Valparaiso is only half of their miraculous story. As the adventure continues, Erlich and Elsa come to treasure each other's company, unsure how long it will last.

Director John Farrow said, "She doesn't need coaching or preparation. . . . There is nothing like a top old pro." With John Wayne co-starring, Farrow had two old pros.

Warner Bros. paid $10,000 for the film rights to Andrew Geer's *Sea Chase* in 1951. It became a vehicle for John Wayne and they began searching for a leading lady, the only female role in the film besides extras. Among the many considered for the role of Elsa Keller were Susan Hayward, Lauren Bacall, Yvonne DiCarlo, Deborah Kerr, Gene Tierney, Arlene Dahl, Grace Kelly, Maureen O'Hara, and Joan Crawford. Hedda Hopper made the announcement that Lana Turner had been signed for the role in September 1954.

The first film Mother made for any studio but MGM since 1938, *The Sea Chase* took her back to her career beginnings, at Warner Bros. After the $300,000 Warners paid MGM in the loan-out deal for her services, much of the remaining budget went toward filming on location in Hawaii. Del Armstrong was brought over at her request after she agreed to pay part of his salary. They did splurge on one beautiful champagne-colored dress by Moss Mabry. The rest of the clothes, jewelry, and furs she wears were from her own wardrobe.

Part of the publicity for the film centered on Mother's latest hair change. It was dyed "coralescent blonde." Myrl Stoltz, who invented the shade, says her inspiration was "a coral reef shimmering in a phosphorescent sea." It seemed to inspire her makeup choices because this is the first movie in which

A publicity portrait for *The Sea Chase*.

With director John Farrow and John Wayne.

Making faces for an on-set photographer.

I notice her wearing her favorite coral lipstick color instead of the red that had been the fashion prior to the mid-'50s.

Mother liked this movie because making it took her to Hawaii in the fall of 1954. Lex Barker joined her for the last four weeks and they rented a house near the village of Kailua, but for the company, all was not as idyllic as the setting. John Farrow, the director, could be difficult at times and there was tension caused by disputes between Wayne and his wife, Pilar. It didn't help that Wayne had developed an ear infection before filming began. There were days it was so painful that he couldn't work and they had to shoot around him. Mother, too, became ill. Additional delays were caused by uncooperative weather conditions. It all proved worth the trouble as far as Warner Bros. was concerned, however, because the movie attracted large audiences and major profits.

Doused with water in preparation for a scene.

Diane (1956)

Plot Points: Diane de Poitiers (LT) appeals to King Francis (Pedro Armendáriz) to save the life of her husband, Count de Breze (Torin Thatcher). Her wish is granted and in return, the king asks her to train his son, Prince Henri (Roger Moore), in the social graces befitting a royal in preparation for his marriage to Catherine de Medici (Marisa Pavan). Over the course of his instruction, Diane and Henri fall in love. She remains at court after the arrival of Catherine and Henri's ascension to the throne, all the while gaining renown as Henri's mistress and the enmity of Catherine, whose position she threatens as Queen of France.

A movie like *Diane* gets its audience caught up in the story and stimulates interest in the period. It got me interested in studying the history of the Borgias, King Henry II, etc. I visited this set as often as I could. What most impressed me were the sixteenth-century garments by Walter Plunkett, which were breathtaking, though Mother complained they were terribly uncomfortable. She never made another costume picture.

Mother worked particularly hard on this movie. She had to learn to ride side-saddle, so we went out to the stables in Culver City and learned together. We were horseback riders, adept at English and Western, yet we found that riding side-saddle was not so easy. Our backs would get sore from being twisted, but we had great laughs. I was going on twelve at the time, Mother was thirty-four, but it was as though we were girls together learning a new game. Fencing was another skill she had to acquire. She learned it easily because of her rhythm and dancing abilities. She was proud that she was able to do all the fencing in the film and no doubles were needed.

Marisa Pavan, the twin sister of Mother's *Flame and the Flesh* co-star Pier Angeli, had the supporting role of Catherine de Medici. I had met her in Italy two years earlier. In that time she had grown considerably both in talent and beauty, I thought, as I watched her and Mother film a confrontation scene in which Catherine subtly warns Diane that she can be a deadly force if her marriage is threatened. It involves this business between them with an apple, Marisa with a knife and Mother taking a slice. It was all understated but persuasively played.

With Marisa Pavan. Catherine de Medici offers apple slices between thinly veiled threats to Diane.

Studying the action from the sidelines.

With Roger Moore.

I consider *Diane* a very well done film, telling a story of great interest. Mother's own feelings about it were complicated, but this had more to do with what was going on behind the scenes. She had been unhappy at MGM under the management of Dore Schary and complained about the roles she was given. She was still an MGM artist when she made her next film, *The Rains of Ranchipur*, on loan to Fox in the fall of 1955. *Diane*, however, was to be the last picture she made as a contract player at her home studio.

We had a great time learning to ride side-saddle for her role in *Diane*.

Riding side-saddle was not the only new trick Mother learned for *Diane*. She also took up fencing. Here we see a rehearsal with Roger Moore alongside a scene from the finished film.

The Rains of Ranchipur (1955)

Plot Points: Lady Edwina Esketh (LT) arrives in exotic Ranchipur with her long-suffering husband (Michael Rennie). Living in the Indian province is a long-extinguished flame of hers, Tom Ransome (Fred MacMurray), who finds her to be as cynical as ever, until she encounters Dr. Safti (Richard Burton). With Safti, lust grows into a love unlike any she has known, as Tom is likewise startled by his growing love for the daughter of local missionaries, Fern Simon (Joan Caufield). Fierce emotions reach their pinnacle as the world crumbles around them through a sky that rains destruction on Ranchipur.

A slip in a bathtub nearly prevented Mother from making *The Rains of Ranchipur*. The accident occurred in her suite at the Villa Vera hotel during a vacation in Acapulco after filming *Diane*. She was knocked out cold and woke up in the hospital just as her new film went into production at Twentieth Century-Fox in mid-August 1955. The company shot everything they could without her for the first two weeks and then finally had to close down, unable to shoot around her any longer.

For the second and last time in her career at Metro, Mother was loaned to another studio. *The Sea Chase* had been shot at a location, so *The Rains of Ranchipur* was her first experience making a movie in its entirety at another Hollywood studio. Nothing was like MGM. It wasn't "her" team behind the scenes, but she always got along with the crew. They tried to make Mom feel at home while cinematographer Milton Krasner photographed her and the film beautifully in Technicolor and CinemaScope.

The Rains of Ranchipur was a remake of Fox's great 1939 film *The Rains Came*, and based on the novel by Louis Bromfield. The original was a more interesting treatment of Bromfield's story. It had starred Myrna Loy and Mother's great love, Tyrone Power. Tyrone made a much more honest and likeable Dr. Safti than Richard Burton in the remake. Loy had been flawless in the role Mother assumed. Like Loy, Mother's interpretation was sensitive, aloofness giving way to passion when called for, but always restrained.

The 1939 film benefited from the onscreen chemistry between Tyrone and Myrna Loy, which was somewhat lacking in the relationship between Mother and Burton.

With Fred MacMurray, Richard Burton, June Haver (Mrs. MacMurray), and Lex Barker.

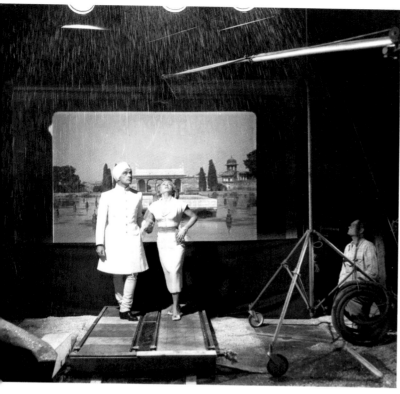

A revealing look at the filming of an "outdoor" rain scene.

Showing off a Helen Rose design.

In her book Mother says that they didn't hit it off during production because she found Burton stuffy and egotistical. I never heard anything like this from her myself. What I do know is that they were very friendly a few years after *The Rains of Ranchipur* was made, during his marriage to Elizabeth Taylor. Whether or not she included Burton in the group at the time, there were a number of people in the cast who made things as easy as possible for her, as she still experienced pain from her fall throughout filming: Michael Rennie, Joan Caufield, and one of my idols—a model father, Fred MacMurray. She adored her director, Jean Negulesco, who was a true artist. He painted the most beautiful portrait of her as Lady Esketh.

I visited this set a number of times. My strongest memory is meeting Eugenie Leontovitch, the actress who played the Maharani. She fascinated me. When she walked she glided, ramrod straight, like she was floating. She was a stage actress who made only a handful of films.

Helen Rose designed Mother's wardrobe. The gowns were lovely, but for one particular scene, jarringly inappropriate. Mom said at the time, "The gown was divine, but I didn't think that even the fabulously rich girl I'm playing would wear a blonde chiffon cocktail dress and pearl embroidered sweater on a tiger hunt. . . . I wore some black gabardine slacks of my own instead and turned down a sweater they suggested in favor of a blouse. I've been identified so much with sweaters." That captures Mother's sense of humor. Director Jean Negulesco contended that Lady Esketh had overdressed in chiffon because while the men were hunting tigers, she was on the prowl for Dr. Safti, but Mother won producer Frank Ross to her side and got to wear her slacks and blouse.

With Mother at her most professional and a supportive company operating as an antidote through her severe headaches, they completed principal photography in October, only five days behind schedule. An eighteen-month break in Mother's filming calendar followed. *The Rains of Ranchipur* opened in December 1955. Two months later, nearly eighteen years of service to MGM ended for Mother when they mutually agreed to terminate her contract.

A costume test for a Helen Rose gown.

With Fred MacMurray, a friend whom we both adored.

Lunch with Fred MacMurray.

A hairstyle test shot.

The Lady Takes a Flyer (1958)

Plot Points: When flyers Maggie Colby (LT) and Mike Dandridge (Jeff Chandler) are wed, the airplane ferrying service they run allows them to enjoy a globetrotting start to married life. The time comes when Maggie is ready to settle down on solid ground, but even after giving birth to their daughter, she can't keep Mike from taking off for weeks at a stretch, and spending time with Nikki Taylor (Andra Martin), a flirtatious new flyer. Maggie decides to turn the tables on Mike, taking jobs and leaving Mike with the baby. Finally, he gets the picture, but not before the baby has racked up a number of flying hours herself.

The Lady Takes a Flyer was released after, but made prior to, *Peyton Place*, so this was Mother's first movie independent of Metro. Universal hoped to cash in on the notoriety of the explosive *Peyton Place*. That's why it was released when it was. *The Lady Takes a Flyer* seemed to come and go in our lives with little notice. Right after it was made I had a riding accident and broke my back, so we spent my fourteenth birthday in a hospital. When I recovered we got so caught up in *Peyton Place* that this movie passed in a blur. By grace of the enduring power of movies we have a filmed record of it, for which I am grateful. Mother looks lovely and natural in a lighter role. I thought it was very cool that she was playing a lady pilot.

Aviatrixes were not a common sight in the first half of the twentieth century, but they made interesting characters,

with Amelia Earhart at the front of the line, so they were seen with some regularity in films of the 1930s and '40s. There was Katharine Hepburn in *Christopher Strong*; Kay Francis in *Women in the Wind*; Loretta Young in *Ladies Courageous*; and Rosalind Russell in a fictionalized treatment of Earhart's life, *Flight for Freedom*. The lead characters in Mother's film were fashioned from real-life husband and wife Mary and Jack Ford, pilots who established a successful ferrying service specifically for airplanes.

The director was Jack Arnold, famous for directing some of the classic sci-fi films of the '50s, among them *Creature from the Black Lagoon* and *The Incredible Shrinking Man*. This comedy-drama starring Mother was certainly a change of pace for him. Perhaps that's why they had so much trouble making up their minds about what to call it. At various times it was known as *A Game Called Love*, *Wild and Wonderful*, and *Lion in the Sky*.

One memory I have of this period is answering the phone one day and taking a message for Mother, who wasn't home. "May I tell her who's calling?" I asked. It was Mother's co-star, Jeff Chandler. I nearly dropped the phone. I was just starting to get starstruck. Growing up, I had no idea who the people milling around the house were outside of being Mom's buddies. Van Johnson, Judy Garland, Fred MacMurray, Joan Bennett, Cesar Romero, and Elizabeth Taylor were just family friends who spent a lot of time at the house.

Listening intently to co-star Jeff Chandler.

On the set with director Jack Arnold and producer William Alland.

They were probably never as glamorous as Mother and Jeff Chandler, but actual husband-and-wife pilots Mary and Jack Ford served as a vague inspiration for the plot of *The Lady Takes a Flyer*.

Peyton Place (1957)

Plot Points: As an adult, Allison MacKenzie (Diane Varsi) looks back on her last year in Peyton Place. Her mother, Constance (LT), was an emotionally repressed woman struggling with dormant emotions aroused by the new the high school principal, Michael Rossi (Lee Philips). Allison's best friend, Selena Cross (Hope Lange), faced sexual abuse at the hands of her stepfather that ended in his death. It was 1941. When Allison left town in the fall, Pearl Harbor was not far off. In that year marked by suicide, abuse, family revelations, and burgeoning love, Allison, the town and indeed the country, came of age.

The most notorious book in the nation was going to be made into a film and my mother was going to play the lead role. I was blown away by the news. I couldn't wait to get my hands on *Peyton Place*, the book that was talked about, read, avoided, or banned by seemingly every person on the planet. The scandalous novel by Grace Metalious contained seduction, abortion, incest, rape, and murder, all set in small town America. I was as riveted by it as everyone else.

How the story was ever going to get a seal of approval from the censors was the question on everyone's minds. The Production Code Administration had become less stringent in their efforts to retain power by proving to studios that they could adjust to changing times. In *Peyton Place* a lot had to be left out or toned down, but they were permitted to get away with more than anyone thought would be permissible. Thanks to the skill of screenwriter John Michael Hayes, it was all very tastefully done and the movie holds up well fifty years later.

Mother was recently out of the MGM nest and in need of a good role. When the part of Constance MacKenzie in *Peyton Place* was first offered to her by Twentieth Century Fox producer Jerry Wald, it didn't seem to her like the godsend it was. Mother had serious trepidations about playing a mother for the first time, to a daughter who was

With Diane Varsi and Hope Lange. Her character was unique in her day. She was a single, working parent—like Mother herself.

practically an adult—older than her own daughter. At thirty-six, Mother was actually too young. She would have to play older, unglamorous, with darker hair and subdued costumes. I gave her my own professional counsel: "Mom, you've *gotta* do this!" It was a film that was generating excitement far beyond Hollywood. Mother realized she couldn't afford to say no, so she bit the bullet and told her agent, Paul Kohner, to accept the role. Wald was offering $125,000, but in fact, the part was priceless.

Mother tried to hold back on the de-glamorization process early on, until Wald became aware of what was happening after looking at the makeup tests. He sent a memo to her hairdresser stating, "She looks as though she has just come off the Metro lot . . . I see no reason why Lana shouldn't have a slight feeling of being a woman who doesn't primp and spend all her time in front of the mirror." He insisted that they move toward a darker and less coiffed look.

Glamour was a crutch for Mother onscreen. If she had that then she was comfortable that at least something, whether it be clothes or makeup, was perfect. Without it she felt vulnerable. I can't say that she went all that far in *Peyton Place*, but it is considerably less glamorous than was customary for Mother. Eventually she came to terms and enjoyed herself.

A New England autumn cannot be recreated in California, even on a movie set. Fortunately, Fox was willing to put the financing behind this production to do it right. Originally they were going to film exteriors in Woodstock, Vermont, but a controversy erupted in the local newspapers and the town couldn't decide whether they wanted *Peyton Place* filmed there or not. The White River Junction chamber of commerce then extended an invitation to use their town, but Fox opted to film in Camden, Maine, instead. I found it fascinating to discover that Wald once wanted to shoot the film in black and white. In a memo to a Fox executive, he thought, however briefly, that "color will distract" from the story. Fortunately, he changed his mind because the location looks incredible in the color photography.

I didn't go to Maine with the company in the summer of 1957, but I was on the set frequently for the scenes shot at Fox—perhaps too much. As during *The Prodigal*, I was fascinated to see Mom interacting with her "daughter," Diane Varsi. This time I was looking at Mother as an actress. As I watched her say things and give looks to Diane that I had experienced with her in real mother-daughter

situations, those words and expressions suddenly lost their power with me. She was bringing her natural characteristics into her performance, but I then began to look at her at-home behavior as "acting." That was a turning point in my development and how I reacted to Mother. It was not the best way for us to move into a more mature relationship, but that's how our lives evolved.

When *Peyton Place* premiered, Mother was in Europe making *Another Time, Another Place*. My father took me and Gran to the premiere in December 1957. David Nelson, who played Ted Carter in the movie, was my escort to the after party at Romanoff's. It was my first grownup event and a terribly exciting night. As a family, we were representing Mom in her absence. Watching her performance that night we were very proud. She did a hell of a job. *Peyton Place* became the year's highest-grossing film, owing both to the phenomenon that the book was and the headlines of Good Friday 1958, after which there was a thirty-two percent jump in ticket sales.

All the town's secrets were revealed in court. Even the censorship board took pride in *Peyton Place*. The board cited the film as proof that it was possible to produce an exciting and realistic picture "and still operate within the basic tenets of taste and decency urged by the Code."

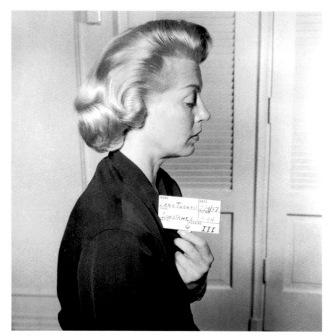

One of her first hairstyle tests. It was still too blonde.

This darker shade was better suited to the role.

When the news went out that they were going to film *Peyton Place*, it was the talk of all age groups. Even at my school we were placing bets on who was going to play whom. Terry Moore was perfect in everyone's estimation as the lusty Betty Anderson, but we were no more certain about who should play the other characters than the people making the movie. The center of the hot debate was Jerry Wald's headquarters at Fox rather than my classroom. Following are some among the long list of contenders mentioned for each role:

Constance MacKenzie:

Almost every major actress in Hollywood was considered for this coveted role, including Ginger Rogers, Barbara Stanwyck, Dorothy McGuire, Irene Dunne, Audrey Meadows, Ann Sheridan, Betty Hutton, Virginia Mayo, Deborah Kerr, Rita Hayworth, Olivia de Havilland, and Joan Fontaine. For Wald, Susan Hayward was the most serious contender for a time and he prepared a formal offer to her in March 1957. From his records, it is unclear whether he extended it to Hayward. Then suddenly he switched preference to Mother and six weeks later it was officially announced that she would play Constance.

Michael Rossi:

Mother would have liked a stronger leading man than Lee Philips opposite her. That was Wald's original vision too, as evidenced by some of the actors he considered for the male lead: Robert Mitchum, Richard Burton, Errol Flynn, Van Heflin, Tyrone Power, Gregory Peck, James Stewart, Rock Hudson and Robert Ryan. The majority of Mother's leading men after MGM were not of her star magnitude. Besides Lee Philips, there was John Gavin, Cliff Robertson, and Sean Connery and Efrem Zimbalist, Jr. before their careers hit their stride.

Allison MacKenzie: In the crucial role of Allison they envisioned Joanne Woodward, Susan Strasberg, Eva Marie Saint, Julie Harris, Elizabeth Montgomery, and Natalie Wood before settling on the unknown Diane Varsi, who was perfect in the part. Afterwards, Varsi had absolutely no interest in continuing movie work and left Hollywood.

Selena Cross: Carroll Baker, Natalie Wood, Debbie Reynolds, Joan Collins, Carol Lindley. Hope Lange, who had made her big screen debut a year earlier in Marilyn Monroe's *Bus Stop*, led the list.

Norman Page: There was no long list for the part of Norman, but Barry Coe was mentioned. Coe ended up as Betty Anderson's boyfriend, Rodney Harrington. Meanwhile, Jerry Wald surprised everyone by selecting Russ Tamblyn, who was known as a dancer from *Seven Brides for Seven Brothers*, to play the troubled Norman.

Mother was surrounded by a great company and she had only kind words to say of them.

With Lee Philips.

With Hope Lange.

With Diane Varsi. Mom was believable as the mother of a college-aged girl, even though at thirty-six she was a little too young.

Mother received an Academy Award nomination as Best Actress for *Peyton Place*. Oddly enough, I think she was more proud of her performance before she got the nomination. She felt she had done better work, like in *Postman* or *Bad and the Beautiful*, that the Academy didn't feel merited a nomination, so why now? Just because she had played a mother, she wondered? When Mom looked back on it, she thought of the nomination as a back-handed compliment. At the time, before she thought about it too much, she was overjoyed to be among the nominees and thrilled it came so soon after her split with MGM.

When the nominations were announced, a few months after *Peyton Place* opened, Mother was in Mexico. At the end of her trip, Gran and I picked her up at the airport, an event well recorded by the press, ostensibly because of the Oscar nod, but also to photograph Mother with her boyfriend, Johnny Stompanato.

Mother was in high spirits that day, when she announced to Gran and me that we were going to be her dates to the Awards ceremony. I was going to have a brand new dress made in whatever color I wanted. My choice was the lurid green of Prell shampoo, with matching shoes called spring-a-lators. These very popular shoes had spike heels, no backs, no sides, and required a lot of walking practice.

The night of the thirtieth annual Academy Awards was pure magic in an art deco movie palace setting. Mae West performed "Baby It's Cold Outside" onstage with Rock Hudson. Mother was a nervous wreck before and during the show. Her shoe slipped off her foot and she couldn't find it. I offered her a spring-a-lator, which she declined. She got her own shoe back, thanks to James Stewart. Mine would have been laughable with her "fishtail" gown of white lace over nude silk. Mother was tanned from Mexico, accentuating her silver-blonde hair and diamond necklace. She made quite a statement when she took the stage to present Red Buttons with his award for *Sayonara*.

Mother's competition in the category of Best Actress was Deborah Kerr (*Heaven Knows, Mr. Allison*), Anna Magnani (*Wild Is the Wind*), Elizabeth Taylor (*Raintree County*), and Joanne Woodward, the star of *The Three Faces of Eve* whose performance everyone was buzzing about. We all knew that

Wearing comfortable slacks and flats during rehearsals for the big show. Actress Janet Leigh is at left.

Mother adored Red Buttons, to whom she presented the Best Supporting Actor Oscar for his performance in *Sayonara*.

Woodward would get it, but I held a glimmer of hope. My heart sank when Woodward's name was called. Mother was the only one of the other Best Actress nominees who had made it to the ceremony, so just as many eyes were on her as the name was announced as were on Woodward. Mother beamed. She had voted for Woodward herself. She felt she truly deserved it for playing three roles within a single character. *Peyton Place* was a bridesmaid all around, a nominee for nine awards, including Best Picture, but no wins.

The evening was young yet after the ceremony. We waited and waited outside the Pantages Theater for our limousine to come to take us to the after party. The car had gotten a flat tire, so finally we hopped into a cab. We dropped Gran off at her apartment and Mother and I continued to the Beverly Hilton Hotel. The *River Kwai* march was played as waiters came in to serve the food. Mother was seated like a queen at our table. I danced with

Sean Connery, Mother's last co-star, whom I had met in England during the making of *Another Time, Another Place* a few months earlier. Cary Grant came and sat with us. It was some night for a fourteen-year-old. I can still close my eyes and recall the sights, sounds, smells, and emotions of the Academy Awards, 1958. There were so many feelings that night, good and bad, that it's all indelible.

Cary Grant stopped by to pay his respects at the after party.

Another Time, Another Place (1958)

Plot Points: Sara Scott (LT), an American reporter in World War II England, finds love with a celebrated BBC journalist, Mark Trevor (Sean Connery). It's an affair marred when Mark reveals that he has a wife and child. Sara loves him so deeply, however, that when he is killed she is unable to let go and is compelled to go to his home in St. Giles. Sara is welcomed by his wife, Kay (Glynis Johns), because she says she is there to write an article on Mark. Talking with Kay and their son (Martin Stephens) brings Mark back for all of them, but it turns out to be more damaging a process than Sara knows.

Mother flew to England right after completing *Peyton Place* in order to begin work on *Another Time, Another Place*. I went over at the start of my Christmas vacation from school, traveling from Los Angeles to London on Pan American's inaugural flight over the pole. That trip was a nightmare. We had an emergency landing in Canada, where we were socked in for over three days in the middle of a blizzard. Mother was frantically calling the airlines demanding that her daughter be delivered to her, but she had to wait it out with the families of other passengers.

With her co-star, a very young Sean Connery.

After that horrendous trip, Mother and I had a truly wonderful time during my three-week stay, both on and off the set. We both thought highly of the completed film, though it has the feel of a television movie more than a major motion picture. Mother was proud because it was her first Lanturn production. Lanturn was a company she had just formed in order to take ownership of her film projects by being involved in their development and sharing in the profits. For the first time she had a say in lighting, casting, costuming, everything.

Playing a war correspondent in Europe, she had an unglamorous wardrobe of suits, sweaters, and skirts. No furs or evening gowns. Young Sean Connery would be her romantic interest and remained a friend after he became a major star. I met Glynis Johns, who played the second female lead, at Polperro, the fishing village where some of her scenes were filmed. Joanne Dru was the first choice for that role, but she was replaced by an English actress due to union rules.

I wasn't Mother's only guest in England. John Stompanato had been around before my arrival, causing endless trouble. It affected me too when Mother and I were scheduled to be presented at court. An etiquette teacher came to the house to teach us the proper curtsy. Then Scotland Yard intervened when they investigated Mother's male traveling companion and our meeting with the queen was canceled. Some of the jewelry Mom wears in *Another Time, Another Place* was later thrown down the garbage chute because she associated the pieces with John.

While in England, Stompanato grew jealous of Sean Connery and stormed onto the set brandishing a gun. An undisturbed Connery reacted by casually walking over and knocking him out with a strong right jab. John became more difficult to handle than ever and got even by knocking Mother around. Her swollen face and bruises were impossible to hide, least of all from Del, her makeup man. He called a friend of his at Scotland Yard and set the wheels in motion to have Stompanato deported from England.

John was soon back in Mother's life, however. After the movie was finished, Mother vacationed in Acapulco. Stompanato was with her and the events leading up to April 4, 1958, were set in motion. Paramount, the distribution company of *Another Time, Another Place*, rushed the movie into release to cash in on the headlines. It premiered less than a month after his death.

Polperro was a picturesque village. Mom added leopard-print shoes to the scenery.

Playing with children at the location.

With Sean Connery.

Imitation of Life (1959)

Plot Points: Actress Lora Meredith (LT) and Annie Johnson (Juanita Moore), both single mothers, raise their daughters practically as sisters, but they face very different problems. Annie's Sarah Jane (Susan Kohner) struggles with shame and frustration in a prejudiced world as a black woman who can pass for white. Lora has been so busy becoming a star, her daughter Susie (Sandra Dee) has felt neglected. Lora resolves to devote herself to Susie and her fiancé, Steve Archer (John Gavin), but life is only complicated further as Susie falls in love with Steve and Sarah Jane sets out on her own.

Ross Hunter deserved an award for sheer tenacity in bringing Mother out of the self-imposed jail she locked herself into after Stompanato. When the producer began contacting her by phone, telegram, through her agent and friends, to make *Imitation of Life*, she was a wreck, afraid to leave the four walls of the little rented house that she was living in with a maid. Ross courted her with flowers, gifts, and fruit baskets until finally he was invited to come to the house and

Day One of filming, with supporting player Sandra Gould and Ross Hunter. Mom looks a little apprehensive in many of the photos of her first day back before the cameras.

tell her about the project. At that point it was his duty to talk her into returning to work at all. Only then could he begin convincing her on the story.

The famous novel by Fannie Hurst had been adapted for the screen in 1934 with Claudette Colbert and Louise Beavers. Mother said she didn't want to do a remake, but in updating the story it was going to be very different from the original. Gone was the queen of instant pancakes that Claudette Colbert played and in came the role of a Broadway star in an extravagant world of gloss and enough melodrama to soak four hankies with tears. These were Ross Hunter's signature ingredients and the astute director Douglas Sirk knew how to make them rise above sheer melodrama and how to use the music, sets, his actors, and even a series of fabulous Jean Louis costumes, to make a comment on contemporary values and social injustice.

Ross won Mother over with a number of conditions that made *Imitation of Life* impossible to refuse. She would have approval of her co-star, Sirk as director, and all the glamour Ross could muster. In lieu of about half her normal salary, she would get a fifty percent share of the profits in a deal negotiated by her agent, Paul Kohner (father of Susan Kohner, who played Sarah Jane). To Mother, money signaled her importance in the business, so it meant a lot that the money she earned for this movie added up to more than any actress's salary for a single film up to then.

Once the barrier came down, Mother was excited about *Imitation of Life*. Jean Louis piqued the passion for costume design that had been in her since childhood. The entire movie was a showcase for his beautiful work. Mother also adored Douglas Sirk. He was gentle and didn't tell her exactly what to do. He would take her aside and ask questions that would influence her and then they would part and start filming. This method proved very effective.

Production began in August 1958. When I visited the set, again I was engrossed watching Mom interact with her onscreen daughter. This time it was Sandra Dee, a sixteen-year-old actress who looked more like Mother than Mother. She was the image of what Lana Turner's child should look like. The parallels between the mother-daughter issues faced in the movie and our real life relationship were too obvious not to upset me. Then they filmed scenes at my school, Town and Country, which made it all the more surreal. It was like watching my own life in many ways. I don't think I ever voiced my resentment to Mother but I did to Gran, who said, "Oh, don't be silly. Your life isn't anything like that."

Years later Sandy and I had a long talk about *Imitation* and *Portrait in Black* and the significance of these films in her life. The daughter of a true stage mother, Sandy said she gravitated to my mom, in whom she saw a gentleness that her own mother didn't possess. Sandy was very young and nervous about working with Lana Turner. Mother put her at ease and throughout the production they would run lines

Mother's leading man, John Gavin, later served as U.S. Ambassador to Mexico. Gavin and his future wife, Constance Towers, were friends of hers.

Douglas Sirk runs through a dramatic scene with Mother, Karin Dicker, and Juanita Moore.

Mom became so emotionally involved in Annie's death scene that her tears continued long after Sirk called "cut."

Lora embraces the role of mother to Susie as well as Sarah Jane after Annie dies.

together and hold their own rehearsals before going on the set. I grew very jealous of Sandy, but we later became friends.

The other mother-daughter pair in *Imitation of Life*, Juanita Moore and Susan Kohner, was incredible. They were heartbreaking while earning their Oscar nominations. I cry just looking at Juanita Moore. She was a very sweet lady. Juanita and Mother were very good friends up until the end of Mom's life. Mother had a breakthrough on the set during the filming of their big scene together. When Juanita is on her deathbed and Mother breaks down and cries, the dam

within Mother burst. Inconsolable, she cried and cried out all of her tears of the past few months. It was therapeutic. Afterwards she dried her eyes and felt better.

Mother's entire career was riding on whether this movie succeeded and the town watched the outcome closely. The film enjoyed a blockbuster theatrical run, surpassing any Universal release to date. *Imitation of Life* was a star showcase for Mother as completely as it was a dramatic challenge for her as an actress. It combines the two sides of the professional Lana Turner like no other film.

A break during filming of the Coney Island scenes.

With co-star Juanita Moore.

With producer Ross Hunter and designer Jean Louis. According to publicity, Mother wore a $78,000 wardrobe and jewels valued at over a million dollars.

This costume, intended to show Lora in her days as a struggling actress, was not used.

The Premiere

I was Mother's date to the gala premiere of *Imitation of Life* on February 19, 1959. Fred May and Gran attended too, but they stayed in the background to give the spotlight to Mother and me at a glittering event that was to show Lana Turner and daughter well again. At the house before the event, Fred was relaxed, happy to be taking out his three girls. Mother followed her usual pattern of locking herself in the bathroom, intensely nervous, saying she had a stomachache. This, in turn, made Gran anxious about how late it was. She tried in vain to speed up Mother as a limousine waited to deliver us to the theater.

We were working at it, but the wounds of 1958 were still fresh, though Mother never let it show in public. I was nervous but proud that I looked presentable for the cameras for the first time in a long while. I wore a lavender taffeta and organdy dress embroidered with flowers that off-set the violets pinned in my hair. It was my first up-do and my first time out with *things* in my hair, as Mother always had. I was afraid to move my head. Instead of the impossible Prell "spring-a-lators" from the 1958 Academy Awards, this time I wore satin pumps dyed to match my dress and an ermine fur that had been refashioned from a coat Mother gave me when I was three years old. Mother wore a chiffon dress trimmed with ostrich feathers. Emeralds encircled her neck and I borrowed her double strand pearls.

After our big entrance, Mother, Gran, Fred, and I sat at the back of the theater. Sobs could be heard throughout the film. At the end, a stampede of women lined up for their turn in the ladies room to repair their makeup. It was even worse at the *Madame X* premiere seven years later.

I wore a gown made by Mother's dressmaker, Wilma, to the premiere. I made use of it again at my sixteenth birthday party later that year.

We sat in the back of the theater, as usual. Gran and Fred May are sitting to the left of Mother.

Portrait in Black (1960)

Plot Points: Sheila Cabot (LT), the long-suffering wife of shipping magnate Matthew Cabot (Lloyd Nolan) has entered into a passionate affair with the one man keeping her husband alive, Dr. David Rivera (Anthony Quinn). Sheila and David carry out Cabot's murder, but it isn't the perfect crime they thought, for besides sympathy cards, Sheila's mail brings threatening notes. Fear and anxiety overcome Sheila as they await word from the blackmailer, who could be one of the eccentric household servants, Cabot's partner Howard Mason (Richard Basehart), or even Sheila's stepdaughter, Cathy (Sandra Dee).

A scene with Anthony Quinn.

Director Michael Gordon (far left) oversees rehearsal of a scene with Mother and Sandra Dee.

To follow-up the success of *Imitation of Life*, Ross Hunter lined up a lavish melodrama for Mother. Like *Imitation*, it would be photographed in color by Russell Metty, feature the music of Frank Skinner, and she would be dressed by Jean Louis. For the role of director, Hunter recruited Michael Gordon, who had recently completed work for Hunter on a Doris Day-Rock Hudson romantic comedy, *Pillow Talk*.

I wasn't present for any of this filming. It was done on location in San Francisco. We knew the owners of the beautiful house in Pacific Heights that was used in the movie. They were a wealthy society couple who rented their house out to Hunter's production company. Besides the San Francisco setting and Anthony Quinn as Mother's lover, title designer Wayne Fitzgerald made the opening memorable. The titles incorporate photos of all of the stars and flipped from positive to negative prints and color to black and white.

As a play by Ivan Goff and Ben Roberts, *Portrait in Black* had run for a short time on Broadway in 1947. It is pure soap opera, but gripping and well constructed. It has suspenseful scenes that are best captured on a big screen in a darkened theater. The way the story plays out, Mother's performance is most appreciated upon a second viewing.

As the wealthy Sheila Cabot, her wardrobe is as elegant as anything from Jean Louis would be. Her hair went darker and she and Helen Young created a flattering new style that is particular to this movie. After this, Mother and Helen reached a hairstyle that she maintained, with few variations, pretty much for the rest of her life. From then on, most of her color and style changes were more subtle than in the past.

Mother and Ross Hunter's good friend Virginia Grey had a small role. She was Ross's "good luck charm." Mother also enjoyed working with Sandra Dee again, and the profit participation she was now receiving. The movie paid well. It was a big hit at the box office, thanks to Mother's popularity and an exhaustive publicity campaign.

Portrait in Black inspired a beautiful and dramatic series of photos of Mother alone and with Anthony Quinn.

By Love Possessed (1961)

Plot Points: Frustration reigns supreme in the Penrose home. The wheelchair-bound and cold Julius (Jason Robards) drives his wife Marjorie (LT) to drink, telling her to seek the passion he can no longer give her with another man but refusing divorce. Before his accident, she thought there was more to their relationship than sex. Now she falls into an affair with the husband of a friend and Julius's law partner, Arthur Winner (Efrem Zimbalist, Jr.). The Winners, along with the rest of their friends, have unsuspected troubles of their own, with an alleged rape, suicide, and embezzlement only scratching the surface.

A story of scandal in New England with shades of *Peyton Place* fixed *By Love Possessed*, a novel by James Gould Cozzens, on bestseller lists for over thirty weeks after its publication in 1957. The book was rather loosely adapted for the screen by *The Bad and the Beautiful* scriptwriter Charles Schnee, who used the pseudonym John Dennis after required script changes altered his vision for the story. It seemed to be a continuation of Mother's Ross Hunter melodrama mold, though it wasn't Ross but Walter Mirisch

As Marjorie Penrose.

"Movie star" shots from the set.

who gave *By Love Possessed* its glossy production values.

Mother plays practically the opposite of her character in *Peyton Place*. Marjorie Penrose in *By Love Possessed* drinks to excess and falls into an affair with a friend's husband after her own husband sends her out to find a lover. Mother doesn't give way to the dramatics of the story but plays it coolly and sympathetically. She had a fine director in John Sturges, who was known for dramas like *Bad Day at Black Rock* and *The Old Man and the Sea*.

The movie runs nearly two hours in which it alternates between several different stories enacted by a strong cast. The male leads were Efrem Zimbalist, Jr. as Mother's lover, Jason Robards as her husband and, as Efrem's son, George Hamilton, with whom Mother went on to do *The Survivors*. Efrem replaced Robert Taylor, who was unavailable, which was fortunate in that the Zimbalists became close friends of ours. Barbara Bel Geddes and Susan Kohner were the female co-stars. After *Imitation of Life*, I thought Susan would go on to a great film career, but instead she married and happily retired from the screen by 1964.

Shortly after making *By Love Possessed*, Mother married Fred May, whom she had been dating since late 1958. In the early-'60s she was taking longer breaks in between films and she and Fred used to go down to Cabo San Lucas for deep-sea fishing. There, natural with Fred as she was with no other man, they would have a great time.

By Love Possessed opened in New York in July 1961, but it had another debut of sorts later that year, when TWA used it for the launch of the first regularly scheduled in-flight movie program.

The opposite of *Portrait in Black*, here the stars (Mother and Efrem Zimbalist, Jr. and Jason Robards) couldn't keep a straight face during photo shoots intended to reflect the melodrama of the story.

They did manage to keep serious for a few shots.

Susan Kohner and Mother get hair and makeup touch-ups.

Bachelor in Paradise (1961)

Plot Points: Best-selling author A. J. Niles (Bob Hope) is the leading expert on the love lives of the Italians, Greeks, and Spaniards. Forced to return to the U.S. for tax reasons, he decides to find out how the Americans do it for his next book in the suburban housing development called Paradise. The wives are all a bit fascinated by the bachelor in their midst and he takes an interest in their mode of living, but his eyes are focused squarely on his favorite real estate agent, Rosemary (LT). She helps him out of constant troubles with the husbands of Paradise and with her help, *How the Americans Live* promises to be his best book yet.

"Paradise" was a suburban housing development for Mother and Bob Hope when they filmed *Bachelor in Paradise* in 1961. Among the other women who populate Hope's bachelor pad in the movie are Virginia Grey, Janice Paige, and Paula Prentiss. They worked from a clever script by Hal Kanter and Valentine Davies that was based on a story by Vera Caspary, the author of *Laura*. The movie had a musical score by Henry Mancini and featured an Oscar-nominated title song.

Bachelor in Paradise is a cute film that took Mother back to MGM. It offered her a definite change of pace as her first comedy since *The Lady Takes a Flyer*, made four years earlier. She and Bob Hope played off each other well and their performances received excellent reviews. Mother and Bob had been friends since the '40s. A year after *Bachelor in Paradise*, she and co-star Janice Paige joined him for a series of Christmas shows for the troops at military camps in the Far East.

Cinematographer Joseph Ruttenberg gets a birthday cake on the set . . .

. . . so does Bob Hope.

Having been in the real estate business for thirty years, I enjoy seeing her play a real estate agent in *Bachelor in Paradise*. Mother was a platinum blonde again and sported a perfectly coiffed style, fitting to the role she plays. The character of Rosemary is very starched and reserved until she warms up to Bob. Then she dances the hula at a nightclub while she gets tipsy and shows the fun side lurking below her surface.

Another great moment for me is when they have Mom shopping in a supermarket because I know what she was like when she got inside of one. Mother actually never went to the supermarket by herself, but when I took her she would go overboard, buying everything that called out to her, especially in the condiment aisle and frozen dinner section. She had never seen "TV dinners" before and was fascinated.

At a party for the *Bachelor in Paradise* company.

Director Jack Arnold and a script girl rehearse Bob Hope and Mother on the porch of one of the actual San Fernando Valley homes used in the film.

Who's Got the Action? (1962)

Plot Points: Melanie Flood's (LT) only thought was to discourage her husband Steve's (Dean Martin) gambling when she became a bookie. Her scheme was to take all his bets without him knowing the identity of his bookie. After a time, she would present Steve with the cash he thought he'd squandered. But Melanie underestimated his ability to pick winning horses. Her friend Saturday Knight (Nita Talbot) helps Melanie raise the money she owes Steve. Saturday's boyfriend, gambling czar Tony Gagouts (Walter Matthau), however, is determined to put a stop to the unknown bookie who's stealing the action.

"The Most Ridiculous Bedtime Story in Years" was the tagline for *Who's Got the Action?* Mother stuck to comedy as a follow-up to the successful *Bachelor in Paradise.* Edith Head designed her wardrobe for the movie. She kept it simple, except for a costly negligee custom dyed to match Mother's skin tone. Helen Young was still with Mom to attend her hair, and finally getting onscreen credit for her work. Sadly, it was the last time, as Helen retired after this movie to move to Santa Barbara with her husband.

Mom played an unlikely bookie in *Who's Got the Action?*

Del was taking care of her face. She had a good director in Daniel Mann, though his proven talent up to then was seen in the dramas he directed, among them *Come Back, Little Sheba* and *I'll Cry Tomorrow.* He was very good with big leading ladies.

A cast of first-rate comedians surrounded Mother. Walter Matthau was a hoot as the gangster. Eddie Albert was the put-upon best friend of the stars, Mother and Dean Martin. Mother had known Dean for years through Frank Sinatra. She frequented his Sunset Strip restaurant, Dino's, but this was their first time working together. The story for their film was based on *Four Horse Players Are Missing,* a novel by Alexander Rose.

The new title for the film was very apropos. Everyone on the set had the action. Both Dean Martin and Mother were card game fiends. Cast and crew joined in. Their game was poker—high stakes. There was more card-playing than moviemaking on the set, with director Daniel Mann trying to rein them in. There was nothing he could do about Dean, who also enjoyed two or three hour lunches with drinks flowing in his bungalow. There was more celebrating on the set on the occasion of Mother's forty-first birthday. That party actually ended with the birthday girl fainting. Mother hadn't been feeling well. She said she was lightheaded and the birthday toast apparently had a bad effect on her.

Otherwise, Mother had fond memories of this movie. She remembered lots of laughs. It involved horse racing, a passion of hers and of Fred May's. As for her part in the film itself, it wasn't a demanding role, which freed her up to simply have fun with it and play with bits of business, like using reading glasses as the aspiring playwright pens her masterpiece. She's at her best playing the comedy scenes with Eddie Albert, and with Margo, who played a wacky maid.

With Dean Martin, Eddie Albert, Paul Ford, John McGiver, Nita Talbot, and Walter Matthau

At $750, Edith Head claimed this was the most expensive negligee she had ever designed for a movie. It was made from embroidered Alençon lace and custom colored to compliment Mother's skin tone.

With Dean Martin.

Cinematographer Joseph Ruttenberg invites the star to peek through his camera.

Enjoying free rides around the Paramount lot.

Love Has Many Faces (1965)

Plot Points: The body of beach boy Billy Andrews washes ashore in Acapulco, his wrist bearing a bracelet that marks him as one of the former lovers of the wealthy Kit Jordan (LT). Kit idles her days away hosting parties or on the beach with her husband Pete (Cliff Robertson) in tow. A sullen Pete enters into a relationship with Carol Lambert (Stefanie Powers), a girlfriend of Billy's who has come to investigate his death. Beach boy Hank Walker (Hugh O'Brien) tries to tempt Kit as well, but funnily enough, she loves Pete. Pete has a similar choice to make between Kit and Carol.

There was little better enticement in 1964 to get Mother to do a film than the lure of Acapulco, which was the setting of Columbia's *Love Has Many Faces*. They made use of actual homes for the sets. I didn't go down to the location, but Gran visited. I liked that in this movie her hair is softer, less sculpted. That was the Mexican climate, which also gave her a deep bronze glow.

Harkening back to the women's pictures of the '40s, the story of *Love Has Many Faces* was interesting. It centered on beach boys at a vacation spot and the rich, slightly aging women on whom they prey. It's full of metaphors and high drama, like Mother being gored by a bull. Meanwhile, Mother was enjoying as many bullfights as she could. If you were a fan of bullfighting (which I was not), it was a terrific time to be in Mexico. Many greats were fighting in the capital in this period, among them Luis Miguel Dominguin, El Cordobes, and Jaime Bravo, who got a part in the movie. Mother became friends with them all and racked up an unparalleled number of dedications from the bullfighters.

The male leads were Hugh O'Brien and Cliff Robertson. Virginia Grey played one of the women attracted to the beach boys. But I was most excited by my friend Stefanie Powers, who went on to fame in TV's *Hart to Hart*, being given one of her first big roles in the movie. Mother never warmed up to Stefanie, which baffled me at the time. In retrospect I see it stemmed less from anything Stephanie did than Mother's insecurities about the new generation of screen beauties—and the fact that they both had their eye on Jaime Bravo.

With Hugh O'Brien.

Edith Head's costumes for Mother took on a life of their own. Billed as her "Million-Dollar Wardrobe," the clothes were given more attention in the ad campaign than her co-stars.

Madame X (1966)

Plot Points: Holly Anderson (LT) is the wife of a rising politician whose career keeps him away from home. She spends more time with a friend, Phil Benton (Ricardo Montalban), who is killed in an accident while Holly is present. Her mother-in-law (Constance Bennett) arranges a cover up, but forces Holly to give up her son and husband. She drifts for years, becoming addicted to drugs, but Holly will do anything, even kill a man (Burgess Meredith), to protect her grown son (Keir Dullea) from finding out what became of his mother. In a twist of fate, Holly's son, a prominent attorney, is assigned to defend her in court, and neither one is aware of their connection.

After two moderately successful films in four years, *Madame X* brought Mother back with a bang. The tear-jerking tale originally told in a French play by Alexandre Bisson had already been brought to the screen several times before, both in the U.S. and abroad, the most well-known versions starring Ruth Chatterton in 1929 and Gladys George in 1937. Playing a drunk, and the haggard and aged look required for certain scenes terrified Mother, but she hand-picked this property for herself and she trusted producer Ross Hunter, the man who had rescued her career once before. They first acquired the rights in 1962, but three years passed before they had a script suitable to put the film into production. It would be a joint venture between Mother's small company for her own films, Eltee Productions, Ross Hunter, and Universal.

The opening scene of *Madame X* was filmed down the street from our old house on Mapleton Drive, at the *Playboy* Mansion before it was the *Playboy* Mansion. The film crew was permitted to use the front of the house and the driveway to the mailbox, but not any of the rest of the grounds or the interior. I had been fascinated with the property since I was little and I used to try trick-or-treating there at Halloween

to catch a glimpse of the house. It didn't work then, but during filming, I finally got in. That was was my only day on the *Madame X* set.

One reason I wasn't at the filming of *Madame X* was that Mother asked that no one come when she had to wear the "ugly" makeup. Mother cried when she looked in the mirror and saw the old and weary woman the makeup had created. She would go from her dressing room to the set with a dark veil over her head. In her mind the makeup was ten times worse than it was. She did get to look her best in early scenes and even play younger. In the older makeup she

Holly's apparently charmed life is only a façade.

There was extensive testing done to capture the appropriate hair and makeup for the various stages of Holly Anderson and *Madame X*.

had the eyebrows with no arch, hair brushed back, and dark circles around the eyes. Mother seriously feared that this was going to ruin her career. Gran and I would try to boost her confidence, telling her that it was a great role.

There was one bit of vanity Mother retained to comfort herself. In later scenes at the jail, this desolate character has perfectly manicured nails. I found it very jarring when I saw the film. When I talked to her about it, she brushed it off. She said it happened because the film was shot out of sequence and she may have needed youthful hands for a scene they shot later. According to her, it was an unintentional oversight. Once the movie was done, Mom never regretted going through with the "ugly" makeup and hair. Knowing what a trial this was for her, when I watch *Madame X*, I see what made her performance a personal triumph. She did a fine job through the touching scenes with her son and going from society wife to a disintegration into alcoholism and drug abuse.

The eight-week shooting schedule was intense. They would sometimes work long into the night and there was some friction between Mother and Ross. One argument ended with him storming out of Mother's trailer into her full-length three-way mirror and shouting "How do I get out of here?" He missed the comedy of his misstep in the heat of the moment. Mother sent him an epergne of lemons at the end of filming that restored peace between producer and star.

Burgess Meredith was appropriately hateful as the scumbag she meets in Mexico. Here they break up the tension between scenes.

Director David Lowell Rich helps his actors through their scenes. Mother won the David di Donatello Award, the Italian equivalent of an Academy Award, for her performance.

John Forsyth, Ricardo Montalban, and Burgess Meredith were her co-stars, along with Virginia Grey again. Then there was Constance Bennett as her mother-in-law. Ross originally wanted Kay Francis for the part, but the actress wasn't available. Mother was a friend and former neighbor of Bennett's sister, Joan, but Mother and Constance didn't get along. Constance had been one of the most popular stars of the 1930s. Each jockeying for position, neither Mother nor Bennett was going to give an inch in a scene. In costuming too they competed like mad, each wanting at least to match the other in style. It only helped the believability of their onscreen conflict. *Madame X*

Holly on her way to becoming *Madame X*.

With Constance Bennett. Ross Hunter had coaxed Bennett into accepting her first film role since *As Young As You Feel*, a light comedy from 1951 remembered for featuring a young Marilyn Monroe.

turned out to be Bennett's final film. She passed away at the age of sixty before the movie opened.

Right before the premiere, Mother had Gran and me come to the studio and arranged for us to preview *Madame X*. She said, "I know you're going to cry, so come see it now and get it all out." It didn't quite work out that way. At the premiere, the whole audience was wringing their hankies and Gran and I, and even Mother, joined in. Like every other woman in attendance, we came out with mascara-streaked faces. There was quite a lineup of celebrities standing outside of the ladies room waiting to repair their makeup. Photographers outside the theater had to be held at bay while the women they were waiting to snap pictures of made themselves camera-ready.

The banister, which figures prominently in the drama of the film, was a toy between scenes.

Bob Eaton, Gran, and I attended the press preview of *Madame X*.

Mother followed the lead of a teary audience and that perfect eye makeup was no longer in place when the film was over.

The Big Cube (1967)

Plot Points: Broadway star Adriana Roman (LT) marries the wealthy Charles Winthrop (Dan O'Herlihy). His daughter Lisa (Karin Mossberg) disapproves of Adriana, though her own partner, Johnny (George Chakiris), gets his kicks out of spiking sugar cubes with LSD and supplying them to friends. When Winthrop dies, his will puts the family money in Adriana's control and she prevents Lisa from touching her inheritance because she distrusts Johnny. He tries to drive Adriana out of her mind with LSD. Lisa tries to call it off, but Johnny is now in control. It's up to Lisa and Adriana's friends to put a stop to him.

It must have been the location shoot in Acapulco that persuaded Mother to make *The Big Cube* in May and June of 1968. Director Tito Davison and his writing partner, Edmundo Báez, were actually highly regarded in Mexico. The title refers to sugar cubes laced with LSD—and then, exploiting a big name, given to Lana Turner. Minus the LSD, the basics of the story—stepmother facing contentious stepdaughter—was not unlike some of her earlier films. In other respects I can't believe my eyes.

Released in 1969, the movie was supposed to reflect my generation and the nightlife we lived. It's an exaggerated version of youth culture in that time. They tried so hard to make the dialogue "hip," using streams of slang, that it doesn't ring true. The costumes aren't quite right either. Only the hair is perfectly accurate. I can understand the view being intentionally distorted in line with the LSD theme, but it doesn't make it any easier to watch.

Viewing scenes from *The Big Cube* recently, it still worried me to see that the fall, or hair extension, Mother wears, is not a correct color match for the rest of her hair. She was so meticulous I don't understand her not fixing that. She isn't serious for a moment. She played it as the campy role that it was. On a positive note, she does look beautiful in her Travilla gowns.

Adriana's world under the LSD influence.

Adriana is feted after a stage triumph.

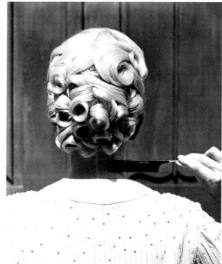

Some of the hairstyles were as wild as the story.

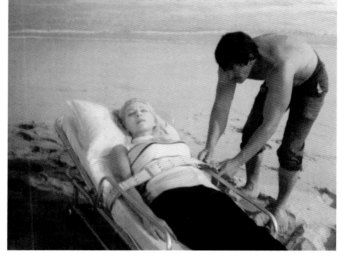

A bucket of water is poured over Mom in preparation for the scene at right.

Mother's favorite aspect of this film: the Mexican location. She is shown in these photos around town and with co-star Karin Mossberg, dressed in the spirit of '69.

Persecution (1974)

Plot Points: David Masters (Ralph Bates) never felt loved by his mother, Carrie (LT). As a boy desperate for attention, he drowned her Persian cat in a bowl of milk and ever since he has felt the wrath of Sheba avenged through Carrie. Years later the terror persists with the arrival of David's wife, Janie (Suzan Farmer), and their child. The baby is smothered to death by a new Sheba. Carrie wants Janie out too. When Janie becomes ill, a sexy nurse, Monique (Olga Georges-Picot), is hired not to care for Janie but to seduce David. Monique, however, may have power all her own that threatens Carrie, and David is building up to retribution.

Ralph Bates turns the tables on a wicked woman.

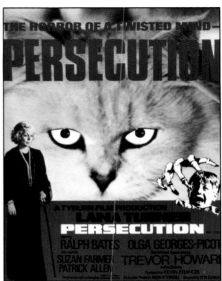

Mother had been famous for her walk. Here they have Mother do a lot of walking, emphasizing the cane. Her character is twisted from the inside out.

Once it was done Mother said she should have known better than to make a movie for which she would have to go to England, because the weather always upset her mood. *Persecution, Purrsecution, Sheba, The Seven Lives of Sheba, The Graveyard*—this film has had many titles. The script actually was decent if it had been a small horror movie. Starring Lana Turner, it was the kind of exploitation horror featuring star ladies they called "grand dame guignol."

Mother thought the world of director Don Chaffey, and the script she signed on for changed during production. They went to London in mid-October 1973 and Mother didn't return until two days before Christmas. At least co-star and friend Trevor Howard brought a ray of sunshine to the damp location for her. The base for the company was Pinewood Studios, but they filmed at an old rented mansion. They would work long hours and because the mansion was far from the studio, Mother wasn't seeing any footage they shot until filming was completed.

"I think I'm retired, but no one has given me my watch yet."

After a horrific opening, there really is nothing to redeem *Persecution*, though it actually did bring Mother an award from a Spanish festival of horror films. Many of the big actresses of the old guard, like Bette Davis, Joan Crawford, and Barbara Stanwyck, were getting into this horror genre, but I didn't want to see Mom follow that pattern. Unless they could find a good character role, there were scarcely any decent parts available to these actresses. That's why there were long breaks in between Mother's last four movies. She turned to other mediums for better roles and gave great performances in television and live theater in her later career.

A scene with Trevor Howard.

With producer Kevin Francis.

Bittersweet Love (1976)

Plot Points: Michael (Scott Hylands) and Patricia (Meredith Baxter) have a cute meeting followed by an equally idyllic courtship and marriage. When Patricia takes Michael home to meet his in-laws, her mother, Claire (LT), realizes that she had an affair with Michael's father (Robert Alda) many years ago. Michael is her son and Patricia, who is carrying his child, is Michael's sister. The truth is revealed to the couple and they are warned that their baby could be born with health defects. Abortion is suggested and dismissed, but Michael and Patricia's relationship deteriorates under the weight of unbearable anxiety.

Meredith Baxter, one of the stars of *Bittersweet Love*, was also the stepdaughter of Mother's agent, Jac Fields. Mother was pointed in the direction of this movie and she went. It reunited her with *Diane* director David Miller and a good cast

was gathered for a tired story. She was always looking for a good film role. There were piles of scripts at her house—piles bound for the "circular file" (Mom's term for trash can) and piles she was considering. A script she liked in the beginning wasn't necessarily the one that ended up being filmed.

Mother had been in the dream factory since she was fifteen years old and never seriously cultivated any interests that exercised her creativity as much as films did. I don't fault her for having made her last movies, but *Madame X* should have been Mom's screen capstone. We both came to think of her film period as ending on that high note in 1966. Fortunately, that is largely true in that her final movies were poorly distributed in their time, and afterward she was remembered for the films worth remembering.

As Claire Peterson, a Mother with a deep dark secret.

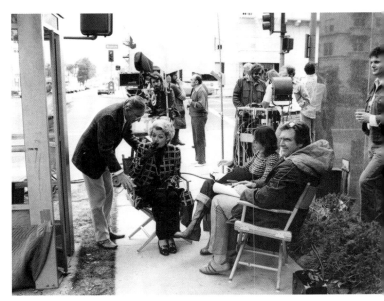

On location.

Witches' Brew (1980)

Plot Points: Vivian Cross (LT), a society woman with strange supernatural powers, talks Margaret Lightman (Teri Garr), the wife of a university professor (Richard Benjamin), into using witchcraft to further her husband's career. Vivian secretly hopes to transfer her spirit into the young woman's body, but Margaret is unaware of her dark ulterior motives and sets about trying to cast a few spells. Margaret's friends, Susan (Kathryn Lee Scott) and Linda (Kelly Jean Peters), join the act in a series of amateur witchcraft experiments with disastrous results.

Weird Woman was the working title for this crazy little movie, Mother's last. It was a remake of an old Universal horror film that starred Lon Chaney, Jr. Another movie that was based on the novel *Conjure Wife* by Fritz Leiber was produced in the U.K. in 1962 under the title *Night of the Eagle* (known in the U.S. as *Burn, Witch, Burn!*), though these sources are not listed in the credits of *Witches' Brew*.

The script came to Mother by way of producer Jack Bean, the husband of Mitzi Gaynor, who on a tight budget rounded up a good cast. She respected his reputation and liked the idea of playing the head of a witches' coven. The fact that she was a rich witch gave Mother an excuse to wear her own $40,000 sable coat as well as her own jewelry, which added about a million dollars to the look of the finished film.

Witches' Brew was shot in 1978 by first-time writer-director Richard Shorr, then it turned into a mess in the editing room and additional scenes were filmed a year later by director Herbert Strock. The picture never had a theatrical release due to legal battles between Bean and Shorr. It finally premiered on television in 1985 and was made available on home video.

Josh and I once watched *Witches' Brew* with Mother at her home. She could laugh at herself and she certainly did that day, providing a very funny running commentary. When I later talked to co-star Teri Garr, I found she shared Mother's oh-it's-so-bad-it's-funny view of *Witches' Brew*.

As Vivian, she works her magic.

With co-star Teri Garr.

Short Subjects

Mom appeared in a handful of the shorts that were shown as part of the movie-going experience in the old days. In the studio era, audiences could enjoy a cartoon, a newsreel, a double feature, and short subjects. Shorts usually ran ten to twenty minutes long, could show drama or musical comedy, and be as realistic as a documentary or as nonsensical as *The Three Stooges*. Shorts could provide young actors with dramatic experience when they had plots or, in the case of Mother, simply show film personalities at work and play.

Vitaphone Pictorial Revue, No. 6 (1937): In this Warner Bros. Vitaphone short, Mother appears in a segment titled "Horseplay." She and other contractees sit on the sidelines and watch such talented horses parade by as the stallion that performs rescuing missions. They show Mother close up, laughing with Kenny Baker. At the end of the segment, a chariot race is staged and Mother is shown waving the starting flag.

With Warner contract players on the ranch location of the Vitaphone short filmed in 1937. From left to right are Vicki Lester, Kenny Baker, Anna Johns, Dick Foran, Mother, Ronald Reagan, and Marie Wilson.

Chester Morris and Mother in *Rumba Rhythm*.

Rumba Rhythm (1939): In this one-reel short, two starstruck girls (Sally Payne and Mary Twain) enter a rumba contest held at in Hollywood's La Conga nightclub, affording them many star sightings. It was filmed in sepia, so Mother was shown in a warm glow enjoying the show with Chester Morris at her side.

Meet the Stars: Stars at Play (1941): In the early '40s, Harriet Parsons, the daughter of columnist Louella Parsons, produced a series of short subjects under the title *Meet the Stars*, released by Republic Pictures. With voiceover commentary by Harriet Parsons, they sustained an air of informality as they introduced film personalities in their off-screen lives. "Stars at Play" is the sixth installment, and in its ten-minute running time presents thirty-eight screen personalities. In early segments Rita Hayworth is shown supervising construction of her new home and Cesar Romero plays backgammon with Patricia Morison. Then Parsons moves on to Santa Anita racetrack where Mother, with date Tony Martin, and Lucille Ball and Desi Arnaz are among a star-studded assemblage in the stands.

The March of Time: Show Business at War (1943): The war effort, Hollywood style, was on parade in this two-reel short released as part of the *March of Time* series. Mother turns up selling defense stamps (with kisses) to an enthusiastic crowd at the Los Angeles Victory House. Dozens of other members of the motion picture industry and stars of stage and radio appear, helping the cause in various capacities.

Screen Snapshots No. 8: Looking Back (1946): "Looking Back" was a special twenty-fifth anniversary edition of the popular *Screen Snapshots* series. It offered a rare look at dozens of top stars in off-guard footage shot early in their careers. There are interesting glimpses of Mom as a teenaged starlet attending industry functions, along with candid clips of Bette Davis, Tyrone Power, James Stewart, David Niven, Fred MacMurray, Cary Grant, and others.

Million-Dollar Wardrobe (1965): The *Love Has Many Faces* wardrobe created for Mother by Edith Head was so spectacular that it warranted its own featurette for airing on television as well as in theaters. It was just five minutes long, but filmed in color. Mother played model while Edith described the costumes she wore in her narration. My friend and Mother's co-star, Stefanie Powers, got to do a turn as well.

Television

It may have been the arch nemesis of movies at first, but Mother was a television fanatic as early as the late 1940s. There was a set in almost every room of her house. At Mapleton we had six, including a portable to take out by the pool. She would have gone into TV much sooner if she had been allowed to by MGM, but in those days they didn't want their stars appearing on the small screen. It was considered beneath them. Mother's agent in the late '50s and '60s was Paul Kohner. He started encouraging her to do TV guest spots in addition to movies. They were popular appearances and she had fun with them.

Mother was an MGM-trained movie star and in reality not the best candidate for regular television work. Deluxe guest appearances were better suited to her. She never got used to the fast pace of TV. Furthermore, the conditions and quality of accoutrements she required were expensive. Most budgets couldn't carry a $100,000 wardrobe for a single character.

Richard Anderson, Edmund Purdom, John Erickson, and Steve Forrest played Gentlemen of the Press who come to interview the Great Star regarding her next picture.

Ed Sullivan's Toast of the Town (February 14, 1954):

I remember watching Mother's television debut at Paul Kohner's house. MGM was having its thirtieth anniversary celebration on *Ed Sullivan's Toast of the Town*. Among the stars in attendance were Ann Miller, Fred Astaire, Lucille Ball, Desi Arnaz, Howard Keel, and Jane Powell, but Mother was presented last at every opportunity as the studio's most exalted representative. She was just back from Europe after the close of production on *Betrayed*, and this was her last filmed appearance as a brunette. They

Backstage of *Ed Sullivan's Toast of the Town*, 1954.

wanted her to hurry up and go back to blonde but then decided the dark-haired appearance would promote her latest movie. She performed the "Madame Crematante" number by Roger Edens and Kay Thompson that Judy Garland had made famous in the 1946 film *Ziegfeld Follies*.

The 26th Annual Academy Awards (March 25, 1954):

In the second national telecast of the Academy Awards ceremony, which was held at the Pantages Theater, Mother and Lex Barker took the stage together to present awards in the category of cinematography. Burnett Guffey was honored for his work in black and white on *From Here to Eternity*, and a second Oscar statuette was bestowed upon Loyal Griggs for color cinematography on *Shane*.

Colgate Variety Hour (November 27, 1955):

In Mother's third TV appearance, *Modern Screen* presented her with an award to officially inform her that she was "the star who has appeared on the most fan magazine covers."

The 28th Annual Academy Awards Nominations Show (February 18, 1956):

This was an NBC ninety-minute special in which the year's Academy Award nominees were announced. It was done with a starry lineup that included Mother. This was the year that Ernest Borgnine and a little film he starred in called *Marty* stole the show.

Climax! (February 29, 1956):

Mother and Lex Barker appeared briefly, along with a slew of other stars, in a biographical episode of this CBS series titled "The Louella Parsons Story." Teresa Wright portrayed the famous Tinseltown columnist and a young John Frankenheimer directed.

The Bob Hope Chevy Show (March 10, 1957):

This TV appearance was Mother's best yet. She did a skit called "Playhouse 180" (a play on the popular *Playhouse 90* drama series) with Bob Hope and Wally Cox. It was like the old Cary Grant film, *My Favorite Wife*. Mother played a woman whose long-lost husband (Bob) returns on the very day she has married another man (Wally). Old Bob has been missed terribly; even his wedding breakfast has been kept waiting for him for seven years. At the end of the live show, Mother did another routine with Bob. She sang (not dubbed) and danced a funny number about what a star like her demands for a television appearance, including Clare Booth Luce to write the script and Fred Astaire instead of Bob as her dancing partner.

On TV with Bob Hope, 1957.

The 30th Annual Academy Awards (**March 26, 1958**)**:** Mother's big Academy Awards night, when she was nominated for *Peyton Place*, was recorded for posterity by NBC. Television audiences watched her present Red Buttons with an Oscar for his supporting performance in *Sayonara*.

What's My Line? (**March 22, 1959**)**:** Playing "mystery guest" on one of her favorite shows was a lot of fun for Mother, besides which it afforded her an opportunity to promote *Imitation of Life*. Mel Ferrer was a guest as well.

The Dinah Shore Chevy Show (**April 19, 1959**)**:** Host Dinah Shore and her guests, Mother and Kay Starr, sang and danced their way through this popular hour-long variety show. The best was a series of routines in which the three ladies recreated well-known sister acts.

Sunday Showcase (**October 11, 1959**)**:** Milton Berle's show, part of NBC's *Sunday Showcase* anthology series, brought Mother together with her former boyfriend, Peter Lawford, for the only time onscreen. They performed a duet to "You'll Never Get Away," from *Gypsy*, and did a comedy skit with Berle and Danny Thomas. Mother did solo turns as well, singing "Turn Me Loose on Broadway" and "Taking a Chance on Love."

The Bob Hope Christmas Show (**January 16, 1963**)**:** Bob Hope's holiday specials were already a standard by 1963. This one showed scenes from the tour in which Mother, Bob, Jerry Colonna, Janis Paige, and others entertained troops in Korea and Japan. Again, Mom got to perform comedy and sing. She also danced with Bob Hope again, this time the bossa nova.

What's My Line? (**February 27, 1966**)**:** A second visit to the CBS hit *What's My Line?* was in order when Mother was promoting *Madame X*. She and the Supremes, featured in their own segments, were mystery guests. Mother's assumed voice kept the panelists guessing. They thought she was Jayne Mansfield and Betty Grable before coming around to Lana Turner.

The 38th Annual Academy Awards (**April 18, 1966**)**:** It was fitting for Mother to present the awards for excellence in costume design in 1966. The winner that year for color was Julie Harris for *Darling*; for black and white, Phyllis Dalton for *Doctor Zhivago*.

The Smothers Brothers Comedy Hour (**March 15, 1967**)**:** One of Mother's favorite television appearances was on this show, which she attempted to watch every week. She performed skits with her series hosts. For one with Tom Smothers, she donned a wig and an enormous period cos-

Hiding a lover behind door number one? This is one of her *Smothers Brothers* skits.

The Carol Burnett Show, 1968.

tume to play an eighteenth-century Italian "Madame X," who is courted in her boudoir by Casanova. The Smothers brothers and the show producers seriously worried Mother wouldn't go through with it after the studio audience poured in. They found her almost paralyzed with fear about appearing on the live show, but she rose to the occasion when the cameras rolled.

The Carol Burnett Show (January 6, 1968):

When Carol Burnett, Mother's neighbor two houses down in Malibu colony, asked her to appear on her show during its first season, Mother didn't hesitate to accept.

The Academy of Professional Sports Awards Show (February 14, 1968): NBC televised the

presentations of awards honoring athletes who excelled in a wide range of sports. Mother, who enjoyed owning, breeding, and betting on racehorses, presented the award for Jockey of the Year to Willie Shoemaker. Mother had great admiration for him. Many years later he was paralyzed after a terrible accident and she donated heavily to the benefit for him.

The Survivors (1969)

Sometime in the fall of 1964, I snuck into the Fox Theater in Beverly Hills with a friend after the lights were down, praying to go unnoticed. I slumped down as low as possible in my seat and endured a screening of *Where Love Has Gone*. There before me were Bette Davis and Susan Hayward, bringing from the printed page to the big screen a novel by Harold Robbins that was inspired by Mother, Johnny Stompanato, and me. I cringed for nearly two hours before slipping out of the theater. As far as I know, Mother never saw the movie, but we both read the book and we were both furious to be exploited by this man.

When, four years later, Mother told me that she was going to be in a television miniseries for Harold Robbins,

George Hamilton and Kevin McCarthy portrayed her brother and husband, respectively, in *The Survivors*.

With her onscreen son, Jan-Michael Vincent.

With Ralph Bellamy, who portrayed her father.

With Rosanno Brazzi, who played the father of her illegitimate son.

With Louis Hayward, part of her onscreen family.

I couldn't believe my ears. I had been keeping my distance since her marriage to Bob Eaton. They would soon separate, but they were still married during the long period of planning *The Survivors*. She had turned it down at first because she said she would never work for Harold Robbins. Eaton talked her into it, though she would never admit he had. His ambition was to be a producer and he told Mother that Robbins promised to give him a chance if he could get her to do *The Survivors*, so she went along with it.

With that background, *The Survivors* was jinxed from the start. After Robbins sold the show to Universal, a parade of writers, producers, and directors were in and out, fired or leaving of their own choice and causing no end of confusion. In spite of this turmoil, the company headed for the south of France for six weeks of location work. There trouble began immediately as Mother got into a confrontation with one of the producers, William Frye. She slapped him, he slapped back, and another producer was called in to replace him. Luis Estevez, the costume designer, walked out. His departure opened the door to Nolan Miller, who became one of Mother's favorite designers. Back in California all of the ruckus was being reported in the newspapers, to my shock. Most of what was filmed in Europe had to be scrapped amid constant rewrites and changing ideas. The company came back to shoot at Universal.

The story of a family of jet-setters who live their intrigues, loves, and hates on a grand scale, they spent all the money necessary to show the luxurious surroundings in which the family lived. Mother enjoyed playing Tracy Carlisle Hastings, the daughter of banking tycoon Ralph Bellamy, mother of Jan-Michael Vincent, and sister of George Hamilton. The show was lush and absolutely beautiful, but it was just too expensive. $100,000 was expended on Mother's wardrobe alone. Only fifteen of a planned twenty-six hour-long episodes of the miniseries were made. The first evening soap, *The Survivors* debuted in the fall of 1969 opposite formidable competition from *Rowan and Martin's Laugh-In*.

The Last of the Powerseekers (1971): *The Survivors* was visible again in a truncated form on television in 1971 when ABC attempted to recoup some of its losses after the cancellation of the expensive show. An hour and forty minutes of *Survivors* scenes were strung together and titled *The Last of the Powerseekers*. It was disjointed and the final fadeout left an awkward unresolved ending to the story, but it allowed them to make use of the some of the Riviera footage shot years earlier.

The Tim Conway Comedy Hour (September 20, 1970): This show, which attempted to launch Tim Conway on a solo career, ran for only thirteen weeks. Mother made it on in time to perform comedy skits with Conway and guest Dan Rowan.

The Johnny Carson Show (May 17, 1972): Mickey Rooney and Vicki Carr joined Mom as guests on the night she made her late-night talk show debut, chatting about her current happenings with Johnny Carson.

The David Frost Show (May 18, 1972): A day after Johnny Carson, Mother sat down for an in-depth interview with David Frost. She spoke candidly about her life and career in Hollywood throughout the ninety-minute segment, which also included clips from some of her best films.

The Mike Douglas Show (July 12, 1972): Daytime talk show host Mike Douglas welcomed Mother to his studio in Philadelphia for an interview. Comedian Marty Allen was another guest and Shirley Eder, one of Mother's favorite columnists, was on hand as well.

The Mike Douglas Show (May 7, 1975): A second sit-down with Mike Douglas came on the heels of the big Tribute to Lana Turner done at Town Hall in New York. John Springer, who conducted the tribute, was also present.

The Russell Harty Show (September 5, 1975): Mother went to London to participate in this

extensive program covering her career. London was never a favorite place to be for her, but she enjoyed herself with Russell Harty.

Peyton Place Revisited (September 26, 1975): This was a special show all about Grace Metalious's novel that spawned such controversy and the film and television series that followed its publication. Mother participated in voice only, discussing a scene between her and Diane Varsi.

Dinah! (October 29, 1976): Dinah Shore, in her new afternoon talk-show format, discussed Mother's new film, *Bittersweet Love*, in this interview.

Today (September 6–10, 1982): Bryant Gumbel interviewed Mom for an unprecedented five consecutive days on the NBC morning show. The segments were taped at Gumbel's home in Calabassas and she talked on many subjects, including past co-stars, husbands, and lovers. This appearance, along with the next four entries, were done in connection with the publication of her autobiography.

The Phil Donahue Show (September 20, 1982): Phil Donahue and members of his audience led Mother into discussions about Tyrone Power, her marriages, and her movies. Donahue was her favorite talk-show host.

Live at Five (September 21, 1982): Our good friend, columnist Liz Smith, conducted this interview with Mother.

Hour Magazine (September 27–28, 1982): Mom promoted her autobiography in this two-part interview with Gary Collins.

Tonight (September 28, 1982): Guest hostess Joan Rivers, subbing for Johnny Carson, talked to Mother about her new book.

Mother found Joan Rivers hilarious.

Falcon Crest (1982–83)

Mother experienced a resurgence of fan recognition when she did *Falcon Crest*, even though her guest spots were sporadic. I recall when she visited me and Josh in Hawaii, fans who spotted her on the beach would call out, "Hey, Jacqueline!" Her much-publicized first appearance was the highest-rated show in the popular nighttime soap's history. Thereafter, ratings shot up every time she appeared. A well-known feud sprung up between her and series star Jane Wyman that was believed by the public, and our family, to have led to the unfortunate demise of the popular

As time went on there was no love lost between her and *Falcon Crest* star Jane Wyman.

David Selby and Susan Sullivan give Mother a laugh on the set. Mel Ferrer eyes her in the background.

Jacqueline Perrault. It wasn't easy on either one of them. Mother was commanding the spotlight on Wyman's show. Wyman had a lot of small screen experience. Mom wasn't used to the rigid schedule and frequent changes that were normal in television. In spite of public denials, there was tension between the two actresses.

The 1982–83 season of the show ended with a cliffhanger episode in which someone is killed at a wedding reception and there is a funeral, but no one knows who's in the coffin. It was a secret to the members of the cast as well as the audience. No faces were shown at the funeral so that they could decide later who was getting buried. Mother spent that summer with us in Hawaii. One day we were talking about the show and she commented on the fact that she hadn't been sent a shooting schedule for the upcoming season. Kidding, Josh said, "Maybe it's you in the coffin." We laughed and Mother said, "Oh, *never.*" It turned out to be true.

Entertainment Tonight (September 14, 1983): This was part of another round of interviews that was called for to plug the paperback edition of her autobiography.

Thicke of the Night (September 15, 1983): Mother was one of Alan Thicke's first guests during his unsuccessful bid to compete with Johnny Carson as a late-night talk show host.

Good Morning America (September 16, 1983): A third day in a row of talk show duties for Mother to promote her book was led by interviewer David Hartman.

Entertainment This Week (October 30, 1983): Leonard Maltin, Mother's favorite film critic and historian, did a segment on the subject of romance in the movies in which Mother talked briefly about love in the films of her day in a pre-recorded interview.

"That's a real star!" yelled a voice from the crowd at *Night of 100 Stars*.

With Olivia de Havilland, Robert DeNiro, Laurence Olivier, Dustin Hoffman, and Sidney Poitier.

Entertainment Tonight (November 3, 1983):

Mother and one-time co-stars Terry Moore and Russ Tamblyn were shown reminiscing, in individual taped interviews, about *Peyton Place*. Tony Randall hosted.

The Most Beautiful Girl in the World (January 30, 1984):

While Mother was on vacation visiting me in Hawaii, a friend of ours, Richard Weiner, asked me if I thought she would be interested in participating in his program. I told Mother about it and she agreed to take part in the CBS special as one of a panel of judges who selected a winner from an international field of twenty-one contestants. She was broadcast throughout the nation live from the Blaisedale Center in Honolulu.

Lifestyles of the Rich and Famous (September 23, 1984):

Mother said she felt she'd gone back to her roots when she visited Cairo, certain she had been there before. This episode of *Lifestyles* followed her on a trot through the Egyptian capital by camel. There was also an interview with host Robin Leach. She came back home with many good luck scarabs and a deep interest in Egyptology.

Night of 100 Stars II (March 10, 1985):

Over three hundred celebrities from the entertainment, sports, and fashion industries gathered at Radio City Music Hall in New York to benefit the Actors Fund of America. The elaborate shindig cost $5.5 million to mount and the taping before a capacity audience ran some six hours, though the telecast was trimmed to three. In a segment titled "Salute to the Superstars," Mother shared the spotlight with Dustin Hoffman, Lillian Gish, Sidney Poitier, and Robert DeNiro. The biggest thrill of all to Mother was meeting Sir Laurence Olivier, though the audience seemed most appreciative of her. As she left the stage, a voice called out from the balcony, "That's a real star!"

Lifestyles of the Rich and Famous Salutes the World's Best (March 25, 1985):

A special edition of *Lifestyles* featured the Royal Princess cruise ship. The luxurious ship had been the setting for the episode of *The Love*

Boat in which Mother appeared and she and other members of the cast who were aboard talked for the *Lifestyles* cameras.

The Love Boat (May 4, 1985):

In this special two-hour trip aboard *The Love Boat*, Mother was billed as the show's 1000th guest star. Hers was a charming story among several in the episode. Playing an amorous lady in hot pursuit of Stewart Granger, she ends up a wife in a shipboard wedding and honorary grandmother to five fellow guest stars, the pop group Menudo. It's only regrettable that this thrust of the show isn't drawn out more. The fact is, Mother had difficulty keeping up with the fast pace of TV. If she was unprepared they would rework the script, giving extra bits of dialogue to Anne Baxter, who was more experienced in the medium.

Circus of the Stars (December 8, 1985):

Bea Arthur, Dick Clark, and Merv Griffin served as ringmasters in this celebrity-studded circus taped at Caesar's Palace in Las Vegas. Mother performed a magic act that was surprisingly adept. She never thought she could pull off the trick.

Happy Birthday Hollywood (May 18, 1987):

In a three-hour extravaganza, this ABC special spotlighted, for a few moments each, eighteen "Heroines of the Silver Screen." Mother didn't feel like a star when she had to share the limelight, and a single dressing room, with so many other actresses. She felt they were treated like cattle gathered in one room backstage. The gala celebration benefited the Motion Picture and Television Country Home.

A shipboard romance with Stewart Granger culminates in a shipboard wedding.

Mother stands at the gazebo rail in *Happy Birthday Hollywood*.

With *Lifestyles* host Robin Leach.

Lifestyles of the Rich and Famous (November 13, 1994):

Mother's final television show followed her on her trip to the San Sebastián Film Festival to accept a Lifetime Achievement Award.

Stage

The director of a play was never going to yell, "Cut! Let's do it again" in the middle of a performance. That fact made Mother have all the respect in the world for stage actors. She never thought she had it in her to do theater. Once Mother had been eased into it by John Bowab, a director and great friend, she didn't have Broadway ambitions. She liked dinner theaters, with smaller, more intimate audiences. She preferred a proscenium setting, but so much of her theater work was in-the-round that she got used to the entrances from ramps above and being surrounded by the audience and liked that, too.

Making live appearances was torturously nerve-wracking for Mother, but once she was on the stage all was well. For almost ten years, playing sell-out tours and getting standing ovations became her career. She was well paid, earning $25,000 a week, and could stop trying to find the diamond in the rough amid the stacks of bad movie scripts she had at the house.

Forty Carats

The only time I knew Mother was so petrified that she thought she wouldn't be able to meet her obligation as an actress was when she was going to take the stage in *Forty Carats*. As far I know, she never thought of going into theater before her agent, Stan Kamen, brought her this play from producers Lee Guber and Shelley Gross. She was on the fence about doing it for a long time until she got John Bowab as her director. Bowab had been the associate producer of the Broadway hits *Mame* and *Sweet Charity*. He was recommended to Mom by Dorothy Lamour and he delivered. Unlike film, you only get one chance to get a line right on stage and it scared her. Bowab helped get her through her stage debut, in theater-in-the-round no less, which is even more difficult for an actor coming from films.

With director John Bowab.

The play was a comedy by Pierre Barillet and Jean-Pierre Gredy, the authors of *Cactus Flower*. Jay Allen adapted *Forty Carats* for the American stage. It was about a divorcée of forty who falls into a romance with a twenty-two-year-old actor. It had been a hit in New York for nearly two years starring Julie Harris.

Mother's ten-week tour of *Forty Carats* began in June 1971 and played on the East coast. The "in-the-round" format took a lot of getting used to. Ramp entrances in the dark and the many quick costume changes were difficult for a novice. Having to constantly move around was possibly her greatest trial, and she couldn't help always feeling sorry for the people in the audience to whom her back was turned.

With *Forty Carats* co-stars Robert Kaye, Kathleen Coyne, Peter Coffield, and Wallace Engelhardt.

The Pleasure of His Company

Back in 1959 there had been talk of Mother and Louis Jourdan co-starring in a film called *The Streets of Montmartre*. Mother was disappointed when the project fell through. Now was her chance to work with the handsome and debonair Frenchman. *The Pleasure of His Company* had already been a play and a film. The play opened on Broadway in 1958 to great acclaim before it became a film starring Fred Astaire and Debbie Reynolds in 1961. Mother played a mother-of-the-bride who must try to maintain sanity when her long absentee first husband lends his disruptive presence to her home life as the wedding of their daughter approaches. John Bowab directed Mother again and their tour opened at the Arlington Park Theater near Chicago on November 14, 1975. It was well received and the tour was extended to meet the demand for tickets.

Bell, Book and Candle

In the late '70s, Mother's fans could watch her on the stage again in *Bell, Book and Candle*, another play that had been successful on stage and screen before Mother took a crack at it in a traveling company. This time she would play on a proscenium stage, which felt more natural to her than

The stars of *Bell, Book and Candle* take their bows.

"I am trying to remember my lines, trying to keep the cat from jumping out of my arms, trying to pretend I'm not scared of her."

"The tha'tre, so to speak, is not in my blood."

in-the-round because she thought of the audience as the camera. She knew how to perform and turn (or not turn) in front of a camera.

Lilli Palmer and Rex Harrison had starred in the show on Broadway in the early '50s. Seven years later the John Van Druten play was made into a film with Kim Novak as a beauty who uses magic and a mesmerizing cat named Pyewacket to hold her fiancé (played by James Stewart) when he breaks off their engagement upon learning that she's a modern-day witch. Cats recurred in Mother's work on stage and screen to test her fear. "I had a death grip on

Standing beside an ad for her next stage performance.

his hind legs," Mother told me. Luckily, it was a good-natured cat. Meanwhile, her leading man, Patrick Horgan, was allergic to the cat and if its hair got too near, his chin would break out. The things actors do for a good part.

The company's director was Harold J. Kennedy. They used to do rounds of summer stock, with stops at theaters in Detroit, Cape Cod, New Jersey, Denver, Maine, New Hampshire, Pennsylvania, and upstate New York. When I saw Mother in Denver, I was blown away by her performance.

Divorce Me, Darling

Appropriately titled for Mother, meowed some catty critics, *Divorce Me, Darling* took her to the the Drury Lane East theater in Chicago in the winter of 1978. In this comedy by Alex Gottlieb she played a San Francisco attorney who finds out on her fifteenth wedding anniversary that her husband (Ben Rawnsley) is leaving her for a fortune-hunting redhead.

Murder Among Friends

Mom purchased the rights to perform Bob Barry's *Murder Among Friends* in summer stock in the early '80s. She did series of this tour both in proscenium and in-the-round. The director was Ron Nash, who was taking a break from his Broadway work in the hit *Oh! Calcutta!* Mother had worked with him before on some advance work for *Bell, Book and Candle*. Don Marston had played Mother's second husband in *The Pleasure of His Company* back in 1975. They co-starred as Angela and Palmer Forrester in *Murder Among Friends*, a comic mystery about husbands, wives, and lovers plotting murder most foul on New Year's Eve.

Unrealized Projects

There are certain films I remember Mother being scheduled to do that for one reason or another were never made. Producers or directors would call and there would be pre-production talk. When there was something new that Mother particularly liked, whether it was a movie, a friend, or a home, she would go into a romantic trance and talk of nothing else. She was sure it was going to be the best—best trip, best dress, whatever—it was going to top everything that had come before. If a film project she wanted fell through, I would ask her what happened and she'd respond shortly, "Oh, it didn't work out." She didn't dwell on it. Following is a sampling of just some of the more interesting projects that never came about.

Idiot's Delight was to have put Mother in a film with Clark Gable three years before *Honky Tonk*.

Idiot's Delight: My redheaded Mother was prepared to begin bleaching as early as fall 1938 in order to be included as one of "Les Blondes," a troupe of showgirls being led through Europe by manager Clark Gable in *Idiot's Delight*. Instead of appearing in the film, Mother went into the hospital for a procedure that attempted to remedy the excruciating pain she suffered during menstruation. This would not be the last operation she had for what turned out to be endometriosis. The press reported that she was in for an appendectomy, but she'd had her appendix out when she was fourteen.

Gone With the Wind: In September 1938, producer David O. Selznick looked at the roster of MGM contract players to consider casting in his epic production. He sent his reaction to casting director Max Arnow. Regarding Mother he stated, "The only other likely youngster was Lana Turner who, although she screens very well, is yet too inexperienced to assay any of the principal roles in *Gone With the Wind*. However, she might be suitable for one of the smaller parts."

In spite of Selznick's assessment, six weeks later Mother made screen tests with Melvyn Douglas for the most coveted female film role of the twentieth century. She played two scenes for director George Cukor: one in which she first tells Ashley that she loves him in the library of the Wilkes plantation; the other a scene at Tara, in which she almost makes him, and herself, forget their obligations to their families and consider running away together. Mother was not up to playing Scarlett, as the tests show. Mom knew and she was mortified by the frequent replaying of the tests in documentaries on the film.

Mother's screen test for *Gone With the Wind*, with Melvyn Douglas as Ashley Wilkes.

She couldn't possibly star in everything planned for her in 1942. This is publicity for a film she did make that year, *Slightly Dangerous*.

The Rains Came: Lana Turner and Tyrone Power, co-stars in 1939? Well, not exactly. It was the supporting role of Fern Simon, eventually played by Brenda Joyce, that Mother was considered for. Might a romance have sparked between them then? Probably not. At the time, Mom was engaged to Greg Bautzer and Tyrone was in love with Annabella, the French actress he married during production of *The Rains Came*.

Best Foot Forward: The studio announced that Mother would appear in this musical based on the hit Broadway show in July 1942. It was said that Mervyn LeRoy would direct and Gene Kelly would be in it as well, though in what part is unclear because the male lead in the story is a teenager. Lucille Ball replaced her in the role of a movie star after Mother discovered she was pregnant.

Easy to Wed: This was another film MGM said would pair Mother and Gene Kelly. When the film went into production, a year after that announcement, Esther Williams and Van Johnson assumed the roles planned for Mother and Kelly. Lucille Ball also co-starred. They were really making an effort to get Lana Turner and Gene Kelly together while they were both the new sensations at the studio. Kelly was also reported as her possible leading man in both *Slightly Dangerous* and *Marriage Is a Private Affair* before Robert Young and John Hodiak, respectively, were cast.

Lady in the Lake: A project that would have brought Mother together with a favorite actor, Robert Montgomery, and a favorite novel of hers by Raymond Chandler, MGM announced that Mother was scheduled to play the co-starring role in December 1945. Audrey Totter, who had just acted a brief but impressive role in *The Postman Always Rings Twice*, got the part instead.

Forever: No book ever affected Mother as much as *Forever* by Mildred Cram. It's the book she wanted to make into a movie more than any other in the world, co-starring Tyrone Power. It would have been no small miracle if a loan-out for either of these two stars to rival studios could have been arranged. Short but powerful, *Forever* is an ethereal story about a love longer than life and stronger than death by the author of the story upon which *An Affair to Remember* was based.

In the story, Julie and Colin meet in some otherworldly land before they are born but in their adult forms. They fall in love and vow to reunite in the next world, in exactly twenty-seven years. Memories of this magic time before they are called to life are wiped from Julie and Colin's minds upon birth and they grow up leading very different lives; she growing up and marrying well in Philadelphia; he living a quiet life in England, going to war, and then returning to his fiancée. Drawn together by some mysterious force, Julie and Colin's paths converge on a fateful trip to the French Alps where love, tragedy, and a haunting recollection alter the course of their lives.

The short story was at one time planned as a vehicle for Janet Gaynor, but the idea never got off the ground. Years later, Mother held the option on it for a long time, well after

With Tyrone Power in 1947.

MGM wanted Mother back before the movie cameras in 1949. She started her return slowly, posing for this portrait session at the end of the year.

A number of films Mom wanted to make in 1954 fell through and she ended up making a religious epic, *The Prodigal*.

Tyrone was married to Linda Christian. She didn't want anyone else to make it. The story contains a physical description of the leads that is almost scary in its resemblance to Mother and Tyrone. It was a beautiful dream of hers to film this story with the man she loved best.

The Reformer and the Redhead: A comedy about a politician and an animal lover who helps her father run a zoo and keeps a pet lion was to reunite Mother with

Robert Taylor onscreen, according to news items printed in January and February 1949.

The Cobweb: I remember a great deal of talk about Mother making *The Cobweb* with Robert Taylor and Grace Kelly. The option on the story ultimately went to Fox and the three lead characters in this unusual drama set in a psychiatric rest home were played by Richard Widmark, Lauren Bacall, and Gloria Grahame.

With pal Ava Gardner, planned co-star of *My Most Intimate Friend*.

The Great Fall: This was a romantic melodrama Mother and Lex Barker bought to make together when they came back from Europe after *Betrayed*. It was about an ex-Army officer who has trouble putting his life back together in peacetime and ends up employed by Murder Inc.

The Ambassador's Daughter: In a 1954 interview with Hedda Hopper, Mother talked about wishing MGM would loan her out to appear in Norman Krasna's *The Ambassador's Daughter*. They didn't, and Olivia de Havilland was cast in this comedy of errors opposite John Forsyth.

My Most Intimate Friend: In the same article, Mother discussed MGM's plan to cast her and Ava Gardner in *My Most Intimate Friend*, in which they were to have played rival news reporters. They would have been great together at this time.

Return to Peyton Place: When Jerry Wald asked her to appear in *Return to Peyton Place*, she passed on the offer, as her plan then was to make *Anatomy of a Murder* for Otto Preminger. Eleanor Parker played Connie in *Return to Peyton Place*. Dorothy Malone went on to play Mother's original role in the television series *Peyton Place*, which ran from 1964 to 1969, and in a later made-for-TV feature called *Murder in Peyton Place*. Bettye Ackerman played her in a *Return to Peyton Place* daytime soap that debuted in 1972. There was still further life for the story in the television movie *Peyton Place: The Next Generation*, which brought back Dorothy Malone.

Anatomy of a Murder: Mother first told me about the possibility of her making this film with James Stewart when we came back to the Bel-Air Hotel after the Academy Awards in 1958, the year she was nominated for *Peyton Place*. She was excited about it because her role reminded her of the man killer she had played in *Postman*. I read the script and thought it was terrific, so I was terribly disappointed when the project fell through for her. Trouble began during discussions over wardrobe. She wouldn't stand for an "off-the-rack" suit for a film and wanted her dressmaker to recreate the suit, customized for her. Preminger was livid when his assistant relayed the message and he proceeded to phone and scream expletives at Mother. She, in turn, phoned her agent, Paul Kohner, insisting that he get her out of the picture. As successful as the movie was, she didn't regret losing it for a moment because of Preminger. "God forbid my family should ever be so hungry that I have to work for him," was her comment.

As Lora in *Imitation of Life*. That film's director, Douglas Sirk, was slated to lead her through *Streets of Montmartre*.

Streets of Montmartre:
Following the release of *Imitation of Life*, Mother's career was in high gear again and a number interesting projects came her way, one of which was all about the great artists of Montmartre in the late nineteenth and early twentieth centuries. Mother was looking forward to starring in this as Suzanne Valadon with Louis Jourdan. They were to film in Europe. She started studying up on Utrillo and so did I. In fact, it got us both very interested in the Impressionists and the entire era. Douglas Sirk, who was to have directed the film, fell ill and backed out, shelving the project. Actually, Sirk never made another film in America.

The Chalk Garden:
In the time between *Who's Got the Action?* and *Love Has Many Faces*, *The Chalk Garden* would have given Mom a demanding role of a woman hired as a nanny who attempts to win the love of a manipulative and deceitful teenager. The play by Enid Bagnold had been a success on Broadway in the '50s. In the end, Ross Hunter cast Deborah Kerr and Hayley Mills in the film.

North to Brindisi:
Mom thought *La Dolce Vita* was fabulous, and so began her love for the work of Federico Fellini. In 1966, director and star discussed teaming up in a co-production called *North to Brindisi*, but announcing the news to the press was as far as they got.

Shocking!:
One particularly memorable project of the grand guignol variety that first reared its head in the late '60s intended to cast Mother and Ava Gardner (and later Mother and Rita Hayworth) as homicidal siblings trying to do away with each other. Mercifully, these actresses resisted the temptation to try to capitalize on Bette Davis and Joan Crawford's success in *Whatever Happened to Baby Jane?* by making this "shocker."

About the time *Shocking!* came along, Mom was at work on a much more glamorous project, *The Survivors*.

"I would like to think that in some small way I have helped preserve the glamour and beauty and mystery of the movie industry."

The Hollywood Ending

As an ending for my mother, ultimately an optimist and a dreamer, it seems fitting to go back to what I believe, from the way she talked, was the happiest night of her life. Whether it was just that Tyrone Power was the one that got away or she would have felt the same if he hadn't slipped from her grasp, the result was the same. Well after she was no longer interested in dating, the memory of her love for Tyrone was profound. She had no ill feelings toward him in spite of the way they ended, but neither did she pine away. Her face glowed when she spoke of him. He was the love of her life.

A few months into their relationship, in December 1946, Mother was making *Green Dolphin Street* while Tyrone filmed *Captain from Castile* in the Mexican village of Morelia. When the long New Year's weekend arrived, Mom saw her chance to sneak away from the studio unnoticed and fly to Mexico for a surprise visit to Tyrone. They had been parted at Christmas, so to make up for it she came loaded down with gifts.

On New Year's Eve they were having a late supper in a small restaurant when midnight arrived. Bells from a nearby church began to chime the hour. "Without a word, we leaped from our chairs and ran across the tiny town square, racing for the church, determined to make it up the steps and onto the steeple balcony before the bells finished chiming. . . . I really can't remember why. Maybe we thought it would mean good luck for us both, maybe it was inspired by wine, but we just did it, like a pair of kids. Tyrone held my hand as we ran, and I struggled not to fall in my long dress and high heels. Eight, nine, ten—and we made it! Laughing, we reached the church balcony just as the last two peals of midnight sounded. . . . " They turned to each other, made their silent New Year's wishes, and closed the moment with an embrace. At the end of their kiss they clasped hands and walked down from the steeple, into the town alive with music.

She in white gown and jewels and Tyrone the personification of tall, dark, and handsome, their beauty then was literally entrancing. The trumpet player of the band playing in the square couldn't take his eyes off of them. He leaned so far over to see them walk past that he tumbled down from the bandstand. When he got up, unharmed and still entranced, Mother and Tyrone blew kisses to him and he blew them back. Then the rest of the band joined in the love fest. Mother laughed and cried at the wonder of that unreal moment. She and Tyrone went off into the night to join the New Year's revels.

Sights, sounds, smells, beauty, a helping of comic relief, and then the fade out. This magic memory embodied her quixotic notion of love. If the reality of that New Year's night in Mexico was like a dream, then it's perfect for my mother, Lana, the beautiful, laughing romantic.

Mom said, "He was a beautiful person, possessing not just outer beauty but sensitivity and gentleness."

Appendix

Radio Chronology

The Chase and Sanborn Program (April 6, 1941, NBC)

Lux Radio Theatre (June 2, 1941, CBS)

Salute of Champions (September 22, 1941, NBC)

Phillip Morris Playhouse (November 14, 1941, CBS)

Night of Stars (November 26, 1941, multi-network)

The Chase and Sanborn Program (December 14, 1941, NBC)

New Year's Eve Dancing Party (December 31, 1941, NBC)

Lux Radio Theatre (January 19, 1942, CBS)

Screen Guild Players (February 8, 1942, CBS)

Hollywood All-Star USO Rally (May 30, 1942, NBC)

Portland Oregon Rose Festival (June 10, 1942)

Command Performance (October 9, 1942, CBS)

Lux Radio Theatre (March 29, 1943, CBS)

Night Clubs for Victory (September 29, 1943, CBS)

Phillip Morris Playhouse (October 1, 1943, CBS)

Radio Reader's Digest (October 19, 1943, CBS)

Lux Radio Theatre (October 25, 1943 CBS)

Abbott and Costello Show (November 4, 1943, NBC)

Command Performance (November 13, 1943, CBS)

The Burns and Allen Show (May 2, 1944, CBS)

The Star and the Story (May 7, 1944, CBS)

The Frank Sinatra Show (June 14, 1944, CBS)

The Orson Welles Show (July 5, 1944, CBS)

Democratic National Committee Program (November 6, 1944, multi-network)

Screen Guild Players (November 20, 1944, CBS)

Dick Haymes' Everything for the Boys (November 28, 1944, CBS)

Take It or Leave It (March 4, 1945, CBS)

Suspense (May 3, 1945, CBS)

Lux Radio Theatre (April 11, 1946, CBS)

The Year One (April 25, 1946, CBS)

Kate Smith Sings (May 3, 1946, CBS)

Screen Guild Players (June 17, 1946, CBS)

Academy Award Theatre (August 14, 1946, CBS)

The Victor Borge Show (September 9, 1946, NBC)

The 19th Annual Academy Awards (March 13, 1947, ABC)

Screen Guild Players (June 23, 1947, CBS)

The Louella Parsons Show (October 5, 1947, ABC)

The Edgar Bergen-Charlie McCarthy Show (November 16, 1947, NBC)

This is New York (December 10, 1947, CBS)

Broadway and Vine with Radie Harris (December 11, 1947, CBS)

The Bob Hope Show (April 13, 1948, NBC)

Broadway and Vine with Radie Harris (December 10, 1948, CBS)

Lux Radio Theatre (September 19, 1949, CBS)

Screen Guild Players (October 5, 1949, CBS)

Suspense (December 15, 1949, CBS)

Screen Guild Players (February 8, 1951, ABC)

The Louella Parsons Show (November 11, 1951, ABC)

Monitor (March 20, 1966, NBC)

Filmography

A Star Is *Not* Born

Mother disclaimed any connection whatsoever with the 1937 version of *A Star Is Born*, in which she is said to have worked as an extra. She insisted she was never an extra. That statement covers like credits that are often cited in modern souces, including *Topper* and *Four's a Crowd*. The chronology is impossible. *A Star Is Born* was filmed between October 31 and December 28, 1936. Mom arrived in Los Angeles around October, entered Hollywood High, and then was discovered by Billy Wilkerson in January 1937. She was in school during that brief interim, not out looking for work as an extra.

What she said about it was all I knew for years, but daily production reports of these films, which list the names of extras day by day, have been examined and the name of Lana, Judy, or Julia Jean Turner is not listed. In the case of *Four's a Crowd*, the only names that stand out among the extras are that of actress Carole Landis and a *Don* Turner, who played a chauffeur.

They Won't Forget

A First National Picture

A Warner Bros. Release

Cast: Claude Rains (Andy Griffin); Gloria Dickson (Sybil Hale); Edward Norris (Robert Hale); Otto Kruger (Gleason); Allyn Joslyn (Bill Brock); Lana Turner (Mary Clay)

Credits: Mervyn LeRoy (producer and director); Robert Rossen and Aben Kandel (screenplay), from novel by Ward Greene; Arthur Edeson (photography); Thomas Richards (editor)

Run time: 95 minutes

The Great Garrick

A Warner Bros. Picture

Cast: Brian Aherne (David Garrick); Olivia de Havilland (Germaine); Edward Everett Horton (Tubby); Melville Cooper (M. Picard); Lionel Atwill (Beaumarchais); Luis Alberni (Basset); Lana Turner (Auber)

Credits: Mervyn LeRoy (producer); James Whale (director); Ernst Vajda (screenplay and story); Ernest Haller (photography); Milo Anderson (costumes); Warren Low (editor)

Run time: 89 minutes

The Adventures of Marco Polo

A Samuel Goldwyn Picture

A United Artists Release

Cast: Gary Cooper (Marco Polo); Sigrid Gurie (Princess Kukachin); Basil Rathbone (Ahmed); George Barbier (Kublai Khan); Ernest Truex (Binguccio); Binnie Barnes (Nazama); Alan Hale (Kaidu); Lana Turner (Nazama's Maid)

Credits: Samuel Goldwyn (producer); Archie Mayo (director); George Haight (associate producer); Robert E. Sherwood (screenplay); N. A. Pogson (story); Rudolph Mate and Archie Stout (photography); Omar Kiam (costumes); Fred Allen (editor)

Run time: 104 minutes

Love Finds Andy Hardy

A Metro-Goldwyn-Mayer Picture

Cast: Mickey Rooney (Andy Hardy); Louis Stone (Judge James Hardy); Cecilia Parker (Marian Hardy); Fay Holden (Emily Hardy); Judy Garland (Betsy Booth); Lana Turner (Cynthia Potter); Ann Rutherford (Polly Benedict)

Credits: Carey Wilson (producer); George B. Seitz (director); William Ludwig (screenplay); Vivien R. Bretherton (story), based on characters created by Aurania Rouverol; Lester White (photography); Ben Lewis (editor)

Run time: 91 minutes

The Chaser

A Metro-Goldwyn-Mayer Picture

Cast: Dennis O'Keefe (Thomas Brandon); Ann Morriss (Dorothy Mason); Lewis Stone (Dr. Prescott); Nat Pendleton ("Floppy" Phil); Henry O'Neill (Calhoun); Lana Turner (Miss Rutherford)

Credits: Frank Davis (producer); Edwin L. Marin (director); Everett Freeman, Harry Ruskin, and Bella and Samuel Spewack (screenplay); Chandler Sprague and Howard Emmett Rogers (story); Charles Lawton, Jr. (photography); George Boemler (editor)

Run time: 75 minutes

Rich Man, Poor Girl

A Metro-Goldwyn-Mayer Picture

Cast: Robert Young (Bill Harrison); Lew Ayres (Henry Thayer); Ruth Hussey (Joan Thayer); Lana Turner (Helen Thayer); Guy Kibbee (Pa Thayer); Sarah Padden (Ma Thayer); Gordon Jones (Tom Grogan); Virginia Grey (Selma)

Credits: Edwin Chodorov (producer); Reinhold Schunzel (director); Joseph A. Fields and Jerome Chodorov (screenplay), from play by Edith Ellis; Edgar Franklin (story); Ray June (photography); Frank E. Hull (editor)

Run time: 72 minutes

Dramatic School

A Metro-Goldwyn-Mayer Picture

Cast: Luise Rainer (Louise Mauban); Paulette Goddard (Nana); Alan Marshal (Andre D'Abbencourt); Lana Turner (Mado); Genevieve Tobin (Gina Bertier); John Hubbard (Fleury); Gale Sondergaard (Madame Therese Charlot); Virginia Grey (Simone)

Credits: Mervyn LeRoy (producer); Robert B. Sinclair (director); Ernst Vajda and Mary McCall, Jr. (screenplay), from play by Hans Szekely and Zoltan Egyed; William Daniels (photography); Adrian (gowns); Frederick Y. Smith (editor)

Run time: 80 minutes

Calling Dr. Kildare

A Metro-Goldwyn-Mayer Picture

Cast: Lew Ayres (Dr. James Kildare); Lionel Barrymore (Dr. Leonard Gillespie); Laraine Day (Mary Lamont); Nat Pendleton (Wayman); Lana Turner (Rosalie); Samuel S. Hinds (Dr. Stephen Kildare); Emma Dunn (Mrs. Martha Kildare)

Credits: Lou Ostrow (producer); Harold S. Buquet (director); Harry Ruskin and Willis Goldbeck (screenplay); Max Brand (story); Alfred Giks and Lester White (photography); Robert J. Kern (editor)

Run time: 86 minutes

These Glamour Girls

A Metro-Goldwyn-Mayer Picture

Cast: Lew Ayres (Philip Griswold); Lana Turner (Jane Thomas); Tom Brown (Homer Ten Eyck); Richard Carlson (Joe); Jane Bryan (Carol Christy); Anita Louise (Daphne Graves); Marsha Hunt (Betty Ainsbridge); Ann Rutherford (Mary Rose Wilston)

Credits: Sam Zimbalist (producer); S. Sylvan Simon (director); Jane Hall and Marion Parsonnet (screenplay), Jane Hall (story); Alfred Giks (photography); Dolly Tree (wardrobe);

Harold F. Kress (editor)

Run time: 79 minutes

Dancing Co-Ed

A Metro-Goldwyn-Mayer Picture

Cast: Lana Turner (Patty Marlow); Richard Carlson ("Pug" Braddock); Artie Shaw (himself); Ann Rutherford (Eve); Lee Bowman (Freddy Tobin); Leon Errol ("Pops" Marlow); Roscoe Karns (Joe Drews); Monty Woolley (Professor Lange)

Credits: Edgar Selwyn (producer); S. Sylvan Simon (director); Albert Mannheimer (screenplay); Albert Treynor (story); Alfred Giks (photography); George King (dance director); Dolly Tree (wardrobe); W. Donn Hayes (editor)

Song: "Jungle Drums" (Ernesto Lecuona, Carmen Lombardo, and Charles O'Flynn); Instrumentals: "Back Bay Shuffle," "At Sundown," "I'm Yours," "Nightmare," "Stealin' Apples," "Racket Rhythm" (Artie Shaw)

Run time: 84 minutes

Two Girls on Broadway

A Metro-Goldwyn-Mayer Picture

Cast: Lana Turner (Pat Mahoney); Joan Blondell (Molly Mahoney); George Murphy (Eddie Kerns); Kent Taylor ("Chat" Chatsworth); Richard Lane (Buddy Bartell); Wallace Ford (Jed Marlow)

Credits: Jack Cummings (producer); S. Sylvan Simon (director); Joseph Fields and Jerome Chodorov (screenplay); Edmund Goulding (story); George Folsey (photography); Bobby Connelly and Eddie Larkin (dance directors); Dolly Tree (wardrobe); Blanche Sewell (editor)

Songs: "My Wonderful One Let's Dance" (Nacio Herb Brown, Arthur Freed, and Roger Edens); "Broadway's Still Broadway" (Harry Revel and Ted Fetter)

Run time: 73 minutes

We Who Are Young

A Metro-Goldwyn-Mayer Picture

Cast: Lana Turner (Margy Brooks); John Shelton (William Brooks); Gene Lockhart (C. B. Beamis); Grant Mitchell (Jones); Henry Armetta (Tony); Jonathan Hale (Braddock); Charles Lane (Perkins)

Credits: Seymour Nebenzahl (producer); Harold S. Bucquet (director); Dalton Trumbo (screenplay); Karl Freund (photography); Howard O'Neill (editor)

Run time: 80 minutes

Ziegfeld Girl

A Metro-Goldwyn-Mayer Picture

Cast: James Stewart (Gilbert Young); Judy Garland (Susan Gallagher); Hedy Lamarr (Sandra Kolter); Lana Turner (Sheila Regan); Tony Martin (Frank Merton); Jackie Cooper (Jerry Regan); Ian Hunter (Geoffrey Collis); Charles Winninger ("Pop" Gallagher); Edward Everett Horton (Noble Sage)

Credits: Pandro S. Berman (producer); Robert Z. Leonard (director); Marguerite Roberts and Sonya Levien (screenplay); William Anthony McGuire (story); Ray June (photography); Herbert Stothart (musical score); Busby Berkeley (dance director); Adrian (costumes); Blanche Seweli (editor)

Songs: "Laugh? I Thought I'd Split My Sides" and "Minnie

from Trinidad" (Roger Edens); "You Stepped Out of a Dream" (Nacio Herb Brown and Gus Kahn); "Whispering" (John Schonberger, Richard Coburn, and Vincent Rose); "I'm Always Chasing Rainbows" (Harry Carroll and Joseph McCarthy); "Caribbean Love Song" (Ralph Freed and Edens); "The Kids from Seville" (Antonio and Rosario); "Mr. Gallagher and Mr. Shean" (Edward Gallagher and Al Shean); "You Gotta Pull Strings" (Harold Adamson and Walter Donaldson); "You Never Looked So Beautiful Before" (Donaldson)

Run time: 131 minutes

Dr. Jekyll and Mr. Hyde

A Metro-Goldwyn-Mayer Picture

Cast: Spencer Tracy (Dr. Harry Jekyll/Mr. Hyde); Ingrid Bergman (Ivy Peterson); Lana Turner (Beatrix Emery); Donald Crisp (Sir Charles Emery); Ian Hunter (Dr. John Lanyon); Barton MacLane (Sam Higgins); C. Aubrey Smith (The Bishop)

Credits: Victor Fleming (producer and director); John Lee Mahin (screenplay), from novel by Robert Louis Stevenson; Joseph Ruttenberg (photography); Franz Waxman (musical score); Adrian (gowns); Harold F. Kress (editor)

Run time: 127 minutes

Honky Tonk

A Metro-Goldwyn-Mayer Picture

Cast: Clark Gable ("Candy" Johnson); Lana Turner (Elizabeth Cotton); Frank Morgan (Judge Cotton); Claire Trevor ("Gold Dust" Nelson); Marjorie Main (Mrs. Varner); Albert Dekker (Brazos Hearn); Chill Wills (The Sniper)

Credits: Pandro S. Berman (producer); Jack Conway (director); Marguerite Roberts and John Sanford (screenplay); Harold Rosson (photography); Kalloch (gowns); Blanche Sewell (editor)

Run time: 104 minutes

Johnny Eager

A Metro-Goldwyn-Mayer Picture

Cast: Robert Taylor (Johnny Eager); Lana Turner (Lisbeth Bard); Edward Arnold (John Benson Farrell); Van Heflin (Jeff Harnett); Robert Sterling (Jimmy Courtney); Patricia Dane (Garnet); Glenda Farrell (Mae Blythe); Paul Stewart (Julio)

Credits: John W. Considine (producer); Mervyn LeRoy (director); John Lee Mahin and James Edward Grant (screenplay), from story by Grant; Harold Rosson (photography); Bronislau Kaper (musical score); Kalloch (gowns); Albert Akst (editor)

Run time: 107 minutes

Somewhere I'll Find You

A Metro-Goldwyn-Mayer Picture

Cast: Clark Gable (Jonny Davis); Lana Turner (Paula Lane); Robert Sterling (Kirk Davis); Patricia Dane (Crystal McRegan); Reginald Owen (Willie); Lee Patrick (Eve); Van Johnson (Lt. Wayne Halls); Keenan Wynn (Sgt. Tom Purdy)

Credits: Pandro S. Berman (producer); Wesley Ruggles (director); Marguerite Roberts (screenplay); Walter Reisch (adaptation); Charles Hoffman (story); Harold Rosson (photography); Frank E. Huli (editor)

Run time: 108 minutes

Du Barry Was a Lady

A Metro-Goldwyn-Mayer Picture

Cast: Red Skelton (Louis Blore/King Louis XV); Lucille Ball (May Daly/Madame Du Barry); Gene Kelly (Alec Howe/Black Arrow); Virginia O'Brien (Ginny); Rags Ragland (Charlie/Dauphin); Zero Mostel (Rami the Swami/Taliostra)

Credits: Arthur Freed (producer); Roy Del Ruth (director); Irving Brecher, Nancy Hamilton, and Wilkie Mahoney (screenplay), from play by Herbert Fields and B. G. DeSylva; Karl Freund (photography); Georgie Stoll (musical director); Charles Walters (dance director); Blanche Sewell (editor)

Run time: 101 minutes

The Youngest Profession

A Metro-Goldwyn-Mayer Picture

Cast: Virginia Weidler (Joan Lyons); Edward Arnold (Burton V. Lyons); John Carroll (Dr. Hercules); Agnes Moorehead (Miss Featherstone); Jean Porter (Patricia Drew); Lana Turner, Greer Garson, Walter Pidgeon, Robert Taylor, William Powell (themselves)

Credits: B. F. Zeidman (producer); Edward Buzzell (director); George Oppenheimer, Charles Lederer, and Leonard Spigelgass (screenplay), from novel by Lillian Day; Charles Lawton (photography); Ralph Winters (editor)

Run time: 81 minutes

Slightly Dangerous

A Metro-Goldwyn-Mayer Picture

Cast: Lana Turner (Peggy Evans); Robert Young (Bob Stuart); Walter Brennan (Cornelius Burden); Dame Mae Whitty (Baba); Eugene Pallette (Durstin); Alan Mowbray (English Gentleman); Florence Bates (Mrs. Roanoke-Brooke)

Credits: Pandro S. Berman (producer); Wesley Ruggles (director); Charles Lederer and George Oppenheimer (screenplay); Ian McLellan Hunter and Aileen Hamilton (story); Harold Rosson (photography); Bronislau Kaper (musical score); Irene (costumes); Frank E. Hull (editor)

Run time: 104 minutes

Marriage Is a Private Affair

A Metro-Goldwyn-Mayer Picture

Cast: Lana Turner (Theo Scofield West); James Craig (Miles Lancing); John Hodiak (Tom West); Frances Gifford (Sissy Mortimer); Hugh Marlowe (Joseph I. Murdock); Natalie Schafer (Mrs. Selworth); Keenan Wynn (Maj. Bob Wilton); Herbert Rudley (Ted Mortimer)

Credits: Pandro S. Berman (producer); Robert Z. Leonard (director); David Hertz and Lenore Coffee (screenplay), from novel by Judith Kelly; Ray June (photography); Irene (costumes), Marion Herwood Keyes (associate); George White (editor)

Run time: 116 minutes

Keep Your Powder Dry

A Metro-Goldwyn-Mayer Picture

Cast: Lana Turner (Valerie Parks); Laraine Day (Leigh Rand); Susan Peters (Ann Darrison); Agnes Moorehead (Lt. Col. Spottiswoode); Bill Johnson (Bill Barclay); Natalie Schafer (Harriet Corwin); Lee Patrick (Gladys Hopkins); Jess Barker (Junior Vanderheusen)

Week-End at the Waldorf

A Metro-Goldwyn-Mayer Picture

Cast: Ginger Rogers (Irene Malvern); Lana Turner (Bunny Smith); Walter Pidgeon (Chip Collyer); Van Johnson (James Hollis); Edward Arnold (Martin X. Edley); Keenan Wynn (Oliver Webson); Robert Benchley (Randy Morton)

Credits: Arthur Hornblow, Jr. (producer); Robert Z. Leonard (director); Sam and Bella Spewack (screenplay); Guy Bolton (adaptation), suggested by play by Vicki Baum; Robert Planck (photography); Irene (costumes), Marion Herwood Keyes (associate); Robert J. Kern (editor)

Run time: 130 minutes

The Postman Always Rings Twice

A Metro-Goldwyn-Mayer Picture

Cast: Lana Turner (Cora Smith); John Garfield (Frank Chambers); Cecil Kellaway (Nick Smith); Hume Cronyn (Arthur Keats); Leon Ames (Kyle Sackett); Audrey Totter (Madge Gorland); Alan Reed (Ezra Liam Kennedy)

Credits: Carey Wilson (producer); Tay Garnett (director); Harry Ruskin and Niven Busch (screenplay), from novel by James M. Cain; Sidney Wagner (photography); Irene (costumes), Marion Herwood Keyes (associate); George White (editor)

Run time: 113 minutes

Green Dolphin Street

A Metro-Goldwyn-Mayer Picture

Cast: Lana Turner (Marianne Patourel); Van Heflin (Timothy Haslam); Donna Reed (Marguerite Patourel); Richard Hart (William Ozanne); Frank Morgan (Edmond Ozanne); Edmund Gwenn (Octavius Patourel); Dame May Whitty (Mother Superior); Gladys Cooper (Sophie Patourel)

Credits: Carey Wilson (producer); Victor Saville (director); Samson Raphaelson (screenplay), from novel by Elizabeth Goudge; George Folsey (photography); Walter Plunkett (women's costumes); George White (editor)

Run time: 141 minutes

Cass Timberlane

A Metro-Goldwyn-Mayer Picture

Cast: Spencer Tracy (Cass Timberlane); Lana Turner (Virginia Marshland); Zachary Scott (Bradd Criley); Tom Drake (Jamie Wargate); Mary Astor (Queenie Havock); Albert Dekker (Boone Havock); Margaret Lindsay (Chris Grau); Rose Hobart (Diantha Marl)

Credits: Arthur Hornblow, Jr. (producer); George Sidney (director); Donald Ogden Stewart (screenplay); Stewart and Sonya Levien (adaptation), from novel by Sinclair Lewis; Robert Planck (photography); Irene (costumes); John Dunning (editor)

Run time: 119 minutes

Homecoming

A Metro-Goldwyn-Mayer Picture

Credits: George Haight (producer); Edward Buzzell (director); Mary C. McCall, Jr. and George Bruce (screenplay); Ray June (photography); Irene (costumes), Marion Herwood Keyes (associate); Frank E. Hull (editor)

Run time: 93 minutes

Cast: Clark Gable (Ulysses Johnson); Lana Turner (Jane "Snapshot" McCall); Anne Baxter (Penny Johnson); John Hodiak (Robert Sunday); Ray Collins (Lt. Colonel Silver); Gladys Cooper (Mrs. Kirby); Cameron Mitchell (Monkevickz)

Credits: Sidney Franklin and Gottfried Reinhardt (producers); Mervyn LeRoy (director); Paul Osborn (screenplay); Jan Lustig (adaptation); Sidney Kingsley (story); Harold Rosson (photography); John Dunning (editor)

Run time: 114 minutes

The Three Musketeers

A Metro-Goldwyn-Mayer Picture

Cast: Lana Turner (Lady de Winter); Gene Kelly (D'Artagnan); June Allyson (Constance); Van Heflin (Athos); Angela Lansbury (Queen Anne); Frank Morgan (King Louis XIII); Vincent Price (Richelieu); Keenan Wynn (Planchet)

Credits: Pandro S. Berman (producer); George Sidney (director); Robert Ardrey (screenplay), from novel by Alexandre Dumas; Robert Planck (photography); Walter Plunkett (costumes); Robert J. Kern and George Boemler (editors)

Run time: 126 minutes

A Life of Her Own

A Metro-Goldwyn-Mayer Picture

Cast: Lana Turner (Lily James); Ray Milland (Steve Harleigh); Tom Ewell (Tom Caraway); Louis Calhern (Jim Leversoe); Ann Dvorak (Mary Ashlon); Barry Sullivan (Lee Gorrance); Margaret Phillips (Nora Harleigh)

Credits: Voldemar Vetluguin (producer); George Cukor (director); Isobel Lennart (screenplay); George Folsey (photography); Helen Rose (gowns); George White (editor)

Run time: 108 minutes

Mr. Imperium

A Metro-Goldwyn-Mayer Picture

Cast: Lana Turner (Fredda Barlo); Ezio Pinza (Mr. Imperium); Marjorie Main (Mrs. Cabot); Barry Sullivan (Paul Hunter); Sir Cedric Hardwicke (Bernand); Debbie Reynolds (Gwen)

Credits: Edwin H. Knopf (producer); Don Hartman (director); Edwin H. Knopf and Don Hartman (screenplay), from play by Knopf; George Folsey (photography); Walter Plunkett (costumes); George White and William Gulick (editors)

Songs: "My Love and My Mule," "Andiamo," "Let Me Look at You" (Harold Arlen and Dorothy Green); "You Belong to My Heart" (Ray Gilbert and Augustin Lara)

Run time: 87 minutes

The Merry Widow

A Metro-Goldwyn-Mayer Picture

Cast: Lana Turner (Crystal Radek); Fernando Lamas (Count Danilo); Una Merkel (Kitty Riley); Richard Haydn (Baron Popoff); Thomas Gomez (King of Marshovia); John Abbott (Marshovian Ambassador); Marcel Dalio (Police Sergeant)

Credits: Joe Pasternak (producer); Curtis Bernhardt (director); Sonya Levien and William Ludwig (screenplay), from operetta by Franz Lehar (composer) and Victor Leon and Leo Stein (book); Robert Surtees (photography); Jay Blackton (musical director); Jack Cole (dance director); Helen Rose and Gile Steele (costumes); Conrad Nervig (editor)

Songs: "Vilia," "Night," "I'm Going to Maxim's," "Girls, Girls, Girls," "Can-Can," "The Merry Widow Waltz" (Franz Lehar and Paul Francis Webster)

Run time: 105 minutes

The Bad and the Beautiful

A Metro-Goldwyn-Mayer Picture

Cast: Lana Turner (Georgia Lorrison); Kirk Douglas (Jonathan Shields); Walter Pidgeon (Harry Pebbel); Dick Powell (James Lee Bartlow); Barry Sullivan (Fred Amiel); Gloria Grahame (Rosemary Bartlow); Gilbert Roland (Victor "Gaucho" Ribera); Elaine Stewart (Lila)

Credits: John Houseman (producer); Vincente Minnelli (director); Charles Schnee (screenplay); George Bradshaw (story); Robert Surtees (photography); David Raksin (music); Helen Rose (costumes); Conrad A. Nervig (editor)

Run time: 117 minutes

Latin Lovers

A Metro-Goldwyn-Mayer Picture

Cast: Lana Turner (Nora Taylor); Ricardo Montalban (Roberto Santos); John Lund (Paul Chevron); Louis Calhern (Grandfather Santos); Jean Hagen (Anne Kellwood); Rita Moreno (Christina)

Credits: Joe Pasternak (producer); Mervyn LeRoy (director); Isobel Lennart (screenplay); Joseph Ruttenberg (photography); George Stoll (musical director); Frank Veloz (dance director); Helen Rose and Herschel McCoy (costumes); John McSweeney, Jr. (editor)

Songs: "A Little More of Your Amor," "Come to My Arms," "Night and You," "I Had to Kiss You," "Carlotta, You Gotta Be Mine" (Nicholas Brodszky and Leo Robin)

Run time: 104 minutes

Flame and the Flesh

A Metro-Goldwyn-Mayer Picture

Cast: Lana Turner (Madeline); Pier Angeli (Lisa); Carlos Thompson (Nino); Bonar Colleano (Ciccio); Charles Goldner (Mondari); Peter Illing (Peppe); Rosalie Crutchley (Francesca)

Credits: Joe Pasternak (producer); Richard Brooks (director); Helen Deutsch (screenplay), from novel by Auguste Bailly; Christopher Challis (photography); Albert Akst and Ray Poulton (editors)

Run time: 104 minutes

Betrayed

A Metro-Goldwyn-Mayer Picture

Cast: Clark Gable (Peter Deventer); Lana Turner (Carla Van Oven); Victor Mature ("The Scarf"); Louis Calhern (Ten Eyck); O. E. Hasse (Helmuth Dietrich); Wilfrid Hyde White (Charles Larraby); Ian Carmichael (Jackie Lawson)

Credits: Gottfried Reinhardt (producer and director); Ronald Millar and George Froeschel (screenplay); F. A. Young (photography); Balmain-Paris (costumes); John Dunning and Raymond Poulton (editors)

Run time: 111 minutes

The Prodigal

A Metro-Goldwyn-Mayer Picture

Cast: Lana Turner (Samarra); Edmund Purdom (Micah); Louis Calhern (Nahreeb); Audrey Dalton (Ruth); James Mitchell (Asham); Neville Brand (Rhakim); Walter Hampden (Eli); Taina Elg (Elissa); Sandra Descher (Yasmin); Cecil Kellaway (Governor)

Credits: Charles Schnee (producer); Richard Thorpe (director); Maurice Zimm (screenplay); Joe Breen, Jr. and Samuel James Larsen (adaptation), from Bible story; Joseph Ruttenberg (photography); Herschel McCoy (costumes); Harold F. Kress (editor)

Run time: 115 minutes

The Sea Chase

A Warner Bros. Picture

Cast: John Wayne (Karl Ehrlich); Lana Turner (Elsa Keller); David Farrar (Commander Napier); Lyle Bettger (Kirchner); Tab Hunter (Cadet Wesser); James Arness (Schlieter); Richard Davalos (Walter Stemme); John Qualen (Chief Schmitt)

Credits: John Farrow (producer and director); James Warner Bellah and John Twist (screenplay), from novel by Andrew Geer; William Clothier (photography); Moss Mabry (wardrobe); William Ziegler (editor)

Run time: 117 minutes

Diane

A Metro-Goldwyn-Mayer Picture

Cast: Lana Turner (Diane de Poitiers); Pedro Armendáriz (King Francis I); Roger Moore (Prince Henri); Marisa Pavan (Catherine de Medici); Sir Cedric Hardwicke (Ruggieri); Torin Thatcher (Count de Breze); Taina Elg (Alys); John Lupton (Regnault); Henry Daniell (Gondi)

Credits: Edwin H. Knopf (producer); David Miller (director); Christopher Isherwood (screenplay); John Erskine (story); Robert Planck (photography); Walter Plunkett (costumes); John McSweeney, Jr. (editor)

Run time: 110 minutes

The Rains of Ranchipur

A Twentieth Century-Fox Picture

Cast: Lana Turner (Edwina Esketh); Richard Burton (Dr. Safti); Fred MacMurray (Tom Ransome); Joan Caulfield (Fern Simon); Michael Rennie (Lord Esketh); Eugenie Leontovich (Maharani); Gladys Hurlbut (Mrs. Simon)

Credits: Frank Ross (producer); Jean Negulesco (director); Merle Miller (screenplay), from novel by Louis Bromfield; Milton Krasner (photography); Helen Rose (gowns); Dorothy Spencer (editor)

Run time: 103 minutes

The Lady Takes a Flyer

A Universal International Picture

Cast: Lana Turner (Maggie Colby); Jeff Chandler (Mike Dandridge); Richard Denning (Al Reynolds); Andra Martin (Nikki Taylor); Chuck Connors (Phil Donahue); Alan Hale, Jr. (Frank Henshaw); Jerry Paris (Willie Ridgley)

Credits: William Alland (producer); Jack Arnold (director); Danny Arnold (screenplay); Edmund H. North (story); Irving Glassberg (photography); Bill Thomas (costumes); Sherman Todd (editor)

Run time: 93 minutes

Peyton Place

A Jerry Wald Picture

A Twentieth Century-Fox Release

Cast: Lana Turner (Constance MacKenzie); Hope Lange (Selena Cross); Lee Philips (Michael Rossi); Lloyd Nolan (Dr. Swain); Diane Varsi (Allison MacKenzie); Arthur Kennedy (Lucas Cross); Russ Tamblyn (Norman Page); Terry Moore (Betty Anderson); Barry Coe (Rodney Harrington); David Nelson (Ted Carter)

Credits: Jerry Wald (producer); Mark Robson (director); John Michael Hayes (screenplay), from novel by Grace Metalious; William Mellor (photography); Franz Waxman (musical score); Charles LeMaire (costume supervisor); Adele Palmer (costumes); David Bretherton (editor)

Run time: 157 minutes

Another Time, Another Place

A Lanturn Picture

A Paramount Release

Cast: Lana Turner (Sara Scott); Sean Connery (Mark Trevor); Barry Sullivan (Carter Reynolds); Glynis Johns (Kay Trevor); Sidney James (Jake Klein); Terence Longdon (Alan Thompson); Doris Hare (Mrs. Bunker)

Credits: Joseph Kaufman and Smedley Aston (producers); Lewis Allen (director); Stanley Mann (screenplay), from novel by Lenore Coffee; Jack Hildyard (photography); Geoffrey Foot (editor)

Run time: 91 minutes

Imitation of Life

A Universal International Picture

Cast: Lana Turner (Lora Meredith); Juanita Moore (Annie Johnson); Sandra Dee (Susie); Susan Kohner (Sarah Jane); John Gavin (Steve Archer); Robert Alda (Allen Loomis); Dan O'Herlihy (David Edwards); Mahalia Jackson (herself); Karin Dicker (Sarah Jane—age 8); Terry Burnham (Susie—age 6); Troy Donahue (Frankie)

Credits: Ross Hunter (producer); Douglas Sirk (director); Eleanore Griffin and Allan Scott (screenplay), from novel by Fannie Hurst; Russell Metty (photography); Frank Skinner (musical score); Jean Louis (gowns); Milton Carruth (editor)

Run time: 125 minutes

Portrait in Black

A Universal International Picture

Cast: Lana Turner (Sheila Cabot); Anthony Quinn (Dr. David Rivera); Richard Basehart (Howard Mason); Sandra Dee (Catherine Cabot); John Saxon (Blake Richards); Lloyd Nolan (Matthew Cabot); Ray Walston (Cob O'Brien); Virginia Grey (Miss Lee); Anna May Wong (Tani)

Credits: Ross Hunter (producer); Michael Gordon (director); Ivan Goff and Ben Roberts (screenplay), from play by Goff and Roberts; Russell Metty (photography); Jean Louis (gowns); Milton Carruth (editor)

Run time: 112 minutes

By Love Possessed

A Mirisch Picture, in association with Seven Arts Productions

A United Artists Release

Cast: Lana Turner (Marjorie Penrose); Efrem Zimbalist, Jr. (Arthur Winner); Jason Robards, Jr. (Julius Penrose); George Hamilton (Warren Winner); Susan Kohner (Helen Detweiler); Barbara Bel Geddes (Clarissa Winner); Thomas Mitchell Noah Tuttle); Everett Sloan (Reggie); Yvonne Craig (Veronica Kovacs)

Credits: Walter Mirisch (producer); John Sturges (director); John Dennis (screenplay), from novel by James Gould Cozzens; Russell Metty (photography); Bill Thomas (Lana Turner's wardrobe); Ferris Webster (editor)

Run time: 115 minutes

Bachelor in Paradise

A Ted Richmond Picture

A Metro-Goldwyn-Mayer Release

Cast: Bob Hope (Adam J. Niles); Lana Turner (Rosemary Howard); Janice Paige (Dolores Jynson); Jim Hutton (Larry Delavane); Paula Prentiss (Linda Delavane); Don Porter (Tom Jynson); Virginia Grey (Camille Quinlaw); Agnes Moorehead (Judge Peterson)

Credits: Ted Richmond (producer); Jack Arnold (director); Valentine Davies and Hal Kanter (screenplay), from novel by Vera Caspary; Joseph Ruttenberg (photography); Henry Mancini (musical score); Helen Rose (costumes); Richard W. Farrell (editor)

Run time: 108 minutes

Who's Got the Action?

An Amro-Claude Picture

A Paramount Release

Cast: Dean Martin (Steve Flood); Lana Turner (Melanie Flood); Eddie Albert (Clint Morgan); Nita Talbot (Saturday Knight); Walter Matthau (Tony Gagoots); Margo (Roza); Paul Ford (Judge Boatwright)

Credits: Jack Rose (producer); Daniel Mann (director); Jack Rose (screenplay), from novel by Alexander Rose; Joseph Ruttenberg (photography); Howard Smith (editor)

Run time: 93 minutes

Love Has Many Faces

A Jerry Bresler Picture

A Columbia Pictures Release

Cast: Lana Turner (Kit Jordan); Cliff Robertson (Pete Jordan); Hugh O'Brian (Hank Walker); Ruth Roman (Margo Eliot); Stefanie Powers (Carol Lambert); Virginia Grey (Irene Talbot); Carlos Montalban (Don Julian); Jaime Bravo (Manuel Perez)

Credits: Jerry Bresler (producer); Alexander Singer (director); Marguerite Roberts (screenplay); Joseph Ruttenberg (photography); David Raksin (musical score); Edith Head (wardrobe); Alma Macrorie (editor)

Run time: 105 minutes

Madame X

A Ross Hunter-Eltee-Universal Picture

Cast: Lana Turner (Holly Parker); John Forsythe (Clay Anderson); Ricardo Montalban (Phil Benton); Burgess Meredith (Dan Sullivan); Constance Bennett (Estelle Anderson); Keir Dullea (Clay Anderson, Jr.); John Van Dreelen (Christian Torben); Virginia Grey (Mimsy)

Credits: Ross Hunter (producer); David Lowell Rich (director); Jean Holloway (screenplay), from play by Alexandre Bisson; Russell Metty (photography); Frank Skinner (musical score); Jean Louis (gowns); Milton Carruth (editor)

Run time: 100 minutes

The Big Cube

A Francisco Diez Barroso Picture

A Warner Bros.-Seven Arts Release

Cast: Lana Turner (Adriana Roman); George Chakiris (Johnny Allen); Richard Egan (Frederick Lansdale); Daniel O'Herlihy (Charles); Karin Mossberg (Lisa Winthrop); Pamela Rodgers (Bibi); Carlos East (Lalo); Regina Torne (Queen Bee)

Credits: Lindsley Parsons (producer); Tito Davidson (director); William Douglas Lansford (screenplay); Tito Davison and Edmundo Baez (story); Gabriel Figueroa (photography); Travilla (gowns); Carlos Savage, Jr. (editor)

Run time: 98 minutes

Persecution

A Tyburn Picture

A Fanfare Release

Cast: Lana Turner (Carrie Masters); Trevor Howard (Paul Bellamy); Ralph Bates (David Masters); Olga Georges-Picot (Monique Kalfon); Suzan Farmer (Janie Masters); Patrick Allen (Robert Masters); Mark Weavers (Young David)

Credits: Kevin Francis (producer); Don Chaffey (director); Hugh Attwooll (associate producer); Robert Hutton and Rosemary Wootten (screenplay and story), Frederick Warner (additional dialogue); Kenneth Talbot (photography); Mike Campbell (editor)

Run time: 92 minutes (U.K.), 88 minutes (U.S.)

Bittersweet Love

An AVCO Embassy Picture

Cast: Lana Turner (Claire); Robert Lansing (Howard); Celeste Holm (Marian); Robert Alda (Ben); Scott Hylands (Michael); Meredith Baxter (Patricia); Gail Strickland (Roz); Richard Masur (Alex); Denise DeMirijian (Nurse Morrison); John Friedrich (Josh)

Credits: Joseph Zappala, Gene Slott, and Joel B. Michaels (producers); David Miller (director); Adrian Morrall and D. A. Kellogg (screenplay); Stephan Katz (photography); Bill Butler (editor)

Run time: 92 minutes

Witches' Brew

Cast: Teri Garr (Margaret Lightman); Richard Benjamin (Joshua Lightman); Lana Turner (Vivian Cross); James Winkler (Linus Cross); Kathryn Lee Scott (Susan Carey); Kelly Jean Peters (Linda Reynolds)

Credits: Jack Bean, Donna Ashbrook, and W. L. Zeltonoga (producers); Richard Schorr and Herbert Strock (directors); Syd Dutton and Richard Schorr (screenplay), from novel by Fritz Leiber, Jr.; Norman Gerard (photography); Herbert Strock (editor)

Run time: 98 minutes

Index

Acknowledgments

Lana came together in record time with the help of many people who generously gave of their time, knowledge, and experience, some on a deeply personal level, none more than my co-author, Cheryl. Opening your heart and your incredible memory bank allowed this to be a tribute to a mother, a film star, and a woman like none other. Josh: You ought to be billed as a third author because through difficult memories, tears, many, many, many laughs, and an equal number of delicious meals and "delovely" specialties, you were equally invested in this process. I do believe Mumsy is proud.

Dear Lou Valentino—we could *never* have done this without you. If ever a person deserved the title of a celebrity's Number One Fan, it is you. Besides that you are an extraordinary human being. I know this was a painful process for you at times. We hope that you are pleased with the results.

Both Cheryl and I are also enormously grateful to our many supportive friends and family members who enrich our lives. I am ever-appreciative of my mother and father. You make me strive to be as "exceptional" as you think me to be. Trish, my sister, friend, and counselor; Manny, Jess, Jenny, Geri, Kim, and, of course, TrisBaby—you may not think you have done anything, but thank you.

At Running Press: Jon Anderson, our publisher, thank you for the faith you have shown in me through three books with RP. Greg Jones, you trusted a twenty-one year old with a big binder she called a book, then put me where I am and made possible all my professional accomplishments. Jennifer Kasius, the gifted editor of our bestsellers, I was thrilled when this book was placed in your hands. Corinda, I am sure I'm maddeningly detail-oriented, but through two books we've worked well *together*. Thank you for another gorgeous one. DC—that is some fine-looking paper you got for us. Thank you.

Frank, Betsy, Melissa, Jordana, Jen C. You are dear friends of mine, far beyond being co-workers. Along with them, Greg, Joanne, Dan, Josh, Mark G., Seta, Kelli, Craig, Jen L., and the rest of the group at RP enhance each work day for me. I have spent time with many of you both in and out of the office. You are pros who encourage and inspire me besides being a great group of people.

This book also owes a debt of gratitude to the staffs of the following research facilities which housed a wealth of facts and files on the life and films of Lana Turner: the Academy of Motion Picture Arts and Sciences' Center for Motion Picture Study, UCLA's Cinema Arts Library, the American Film Institute, the New York Public Library for the Performing Arts, the Free Library of Philadelphia, USC's Cinema/Television Library (with special mention to Ned Comstock), Temple University's Urban Archives Library, and the Museum of Modern Art.

And to Lana, a beautiful soul who never lost that dreamy quality.

—Cindy De La Hoz, May 2008